BABY IN THE BATHWATER:
Memories of A Political Journalist

BABY IN THE BATHWATER:
Memories of A Political Journalist

Gordon Schaffer

The Book Guild Ltd
Sussex, England

The Book Guild Ltd
25 High Street,
Lewes, Sussex

First published 1996
© Gordon Schaffer, 1996
Set in Linotron Palatino by
Rowland Phototypesetting Ltd,
Bury St Edmunds, Suffolk

Printed in Great Britain by
Bookcraft (Bath) Ltd

A catalogue record for this book is
available from the British Library

ISBN 1 85776 078 6

CONTENTS

ACKNOWLEDGEMENTS

Among those who have assisted me, I owe a particular debt to Steve Lawton, who has worked and persevered with me over many years to ensure that this story would ultimately see the light of day.

I would also like to thank Una Sanglin, Helen Snow, Frank Allaun, Antoinette Ansaldo and Brian Bastin for their help at various stages of preparation.

And in keeping body and soul together, Jean Rose has been an indispensable friend.

FOREWORD: BY TONY BENN

This is a book that tells the story of a life lived by someone who has been at the heart of the progressive movement since the 1920s and is still active today.

Gordon Schaffer learned his socialism by experience and he has shown himself ready to learn from everything that has happened to him and to humanity during his lifetime.

Being a professional journalist – and one with complete integrity – his account is immensely readable, setting out the background to the major events that have occurred over the years and then filling it in, with personal anecdotes and assessments of the people whom he has met and with whom he has worked.

For the older generation whose memories go back to the 1930s, this is the history through which they have lived, and for younger readers, what Gordon has to say will come with a freshness and excitement that is not always to be found in the literature of the Left.

This book offers an alternative explanation of the politics of the last half-century and more meticulously documented, and with a commentary that throws quite a different light on what has happened than is available from the establishment media.

Gordon has always been an activist at many levels and this has protected him from the charge that he watched the world from the remote security of an editorial chair. But his work as a newspaperman did bring him close to those who have worked in the corridors of power and given him a very clear idea of what was going on in their minds.

In these pages, we are taken through the politics of the 1920s, the defection of the MacDonald government, the depression in the 1930s, the rise of fascism, Chamberlain's appeasement of Hitler, the war itself – won by an Anglo-Soviet alliance – and on to the Cold War which has paved the way for the hard Right to return.

We also share his excitement at the birth of the welfare state as Labour won its landslide victory in 1945, and watch the steady abandonment of those aspirations by Labour leaders who could not stand up to the assaults of the radical Right.

There are many ways in which this book can be read, and for those who have never really shared the popular hopes for social transformation through democracy, it may be wrongly dismissed as proof that naive idealism could never form the basis for political action.

But reading it, as it is really written, will have the very opposite effect for it chronicles the many lost chances that could have been seized and charts a new way forward for a generation that has experienced the hard Right back in power and knows how brutal it can be in imposing its will on society.

For, from the beginning of time, those who have had control of the wealth, created by working people, have been prepared to go to any lengths to hold on to their privileges. By their own media and military power, they have worked unceasingly to undermine and destroy all those who sought a fairer world, and the establishment of social justice.

From the Russian Revolution in 1917 until this very day, that objective – the destruction of socialism and the peace movement which attempted to liberate humanity from militarism and oppression – has been the overriding consideration of those in control of the capitalist world.

Gordon gives us a glimpse of how it could have been, if we had had the understanding of what was really happening and the courage to stand up against it.

He also looks forward to a future where the choice will always be between socialism and barbarism and recognises that the achievement of socialism itself is critically dependent upon democracy and cannot be imposed by force.

In setting out this perspective for young people today, he has done a great deal to restore hope to those who may be tempted to despair, with all that could mean in inviting a return to fascism.

It is a marvellous book and I hope that it is widely read by all those who share his vision and are determined to make it real by their own efforts.

INTRODUCTION

'When you shall these unlucky deeds relate,
speak of me as I am, nothing extenuate,
nor set down ought in malice.'

Othello

When I began to write these reminiscences I had a pretty clear picture of the world. The United States, leader of the capitalist countries, and the Soviet Union, leader of the countries building socialism, were finding their way to coexistence.

The developing countries, overburdened with debt, were beginning to demand not only political but economic freedom. I did not see it as a black and white picture. I was conscious of the failures of the socialist countries. But, like millions of my generation, I had witnessed the evils of fascism and lived through the Spanish Civil War. The immortal story of the International Brigade and the shameful story of the British and French acceptance of non-intervention was a bitter memory. I knew that in World War II the Soviet Union, at the cost of immeasurable sacrifice, saved us all.

When I headed two deputations to the Soviet embassy to protest at the Soviet intervention in Czechoslovakia in 1968, I was accused of 'Talking like the *Daily Telegraph*'. I told the GDR Peace Committee that for German troops, even from a socialist country, to return as interventionists to Czechoslovakia, was little short of a crime.

I wrote to the Rumanian ambassador protesting against the actions of his government and particularly the treatment of the Hungarian minority and the destruction of villages. I had written that I no longer regarded China as a genuinely socialist country after its backing for the infamous Pol Pot regime in Cambodia. But I felt, like Tom Paine, when he challenged Burke's denunciation of the excesses of the French Revolution, 'He pities the feathers and forgets the dying bird.' And to me the dying bird was monopoly capitalism.

My attitude to the Soviet Union, like that of millions of others, was conditioned by the memory of the alliance that saved my country from nazi occupation. Yet travelling in the Soviet Union in the later post-war years I felt that the devotion of the people to the building of their socialist country, which I had witnessed between the wars, was no longer there.

In the GDR the massive social achievements were being ignored, particularly by the youth, in favour of the meretricious appeal of the West, constantly displayed on television. I was nevertheless shattered by the swift collapse of the socialist camp. The capitalists had succeeded in the aim they had never abandoned since the war of intervention against the newly formed Soviet Republic.

Looking back, with the benefit of hindsight, I ask myself whether I should not have realised that the communist leadership had turned the conception of the 'dictatorship of the proletariat', which was meant to infer rule by the majority working class, into the dictatorship of an elite. I saw this happening in the British communist party, but I did not anticipate it happening in countries where the communists were in power. I should not have accepted the Soviet official version of the pre-war trials, or dismissed the reports of the slave camps. But my thinking was dominated by the rise of fascism, and rightly so, as events turned out. I regarded the Soviet Union as the only power able, or willing, to resist. After the war it was clear that the communists who had played the leading part in the anti-nazi resistance would play a prominent role in the liberated countries. I nevertheless protested to the Czechs against the trial and execution of half the party's central committee, some of whom I knew personally.

When, in 1947, I wrote a book called *The Soviet Zone of Germany*, I believe I gave a true picture describing how the united communist and Socialist parties were genuinely cooperating with other parties and organisations in trying to eliminate the active nazis, the economic basis of the nazi regime, and the implementation of the Potsdam agreement.

In the post-war years, the Soviet Union crippled itself because it had to arm with nuclear weapons against what it believed to be the threat of nuclear war. That threat is denied now, but the proof is there in official American documents, and the memoirs of James Forrestal, the American defence secretary, and others. The Western powers have achieved their objective without a war. As Pitt said after Napoleon's victories, 'You can roll up the map of Europe.'

Restoring capitalism in Eastern Europe and in the Soviet Union, will not solve the capitalist rivalries which have fostered crippling arms races and precipitated past wars.

Germany and Japan, now the most powerful world economies, will not indefinitely accept a lower status in the UN and will demand membership of the Security Council. The developing countries will not abandon the struggle for socialism, though hopefully they will have learned how to avoid the failures of the past.

As I write these memoirs I am certain of one thing. The work of the pioneers will remain. In Britain, the Chartists, the Rochdale pioneers, the Match girls and the dockers who waged the struggle against the exploitation of Victorian England, will remain an inspiration to future generations.

Socialism, in whatever form it reemerges, will still be the alternative to the crude inequalities of the market economy.

The baby has not been thrown out with the bath water.

1

Message of the Zeppelins

There is not a lot of value in staying on this planet longer than most, but it does give you an opportunity to set out some first-hand history. And my lifetime has covered a period when the development of the media has made possible a better knowledge of the world about us, but tragically, the power to lie and distort as never before.

Above all, it has been a period in which science has transformed all our lives. It has probed the secrets of the atom and reached out to the stars. It has shown the way to use the rich resources of nature for a better life for all, but it has also destroyed the balance of nature, threatening worldwide disaster.

Science prepares to usher in a new century, with humankind balanced on the knife-edge of annihilation, only sustained by tenuous hopes that sanity will prevail. A way needs to be found to remove the death-dealing weapons, and create a world in which all peoples and nations can live together in peace and enjoy the heritage that belongs to us all.

I have rejected most of the religious dogma on which I was brought up, but there's one Bible story which is surely a parable for the human race today: the story of how God commanded Adam, 'Of every tree in the garden thou mayest freely eat, but of the tree of knowledge thou shalt not eat, for on the day thou eatest thereof thou shalt surely die.' For

1

good or evil in this century we have eaten of the tree of knowledge, and the stark issue is life or death.

I was born in Clapham, South London, in 1905, and I dimly remember the surroundings before World War I. Marks and Spencer was a penny bazaar. Across the Balham branch was the notice, 'Don't ask the price, it's a penny.' Today, every road in Clapham is jam-packed with cars; then, there was hardly one to be seen. The streets were lit with gas, and the lamp-lighters went around at dusk and dawn operating the by-pass on each lamp with a long pole. Our baker came round with loaves in a basket on his bicycle, and the milkman came with a churn to deliver the milk into your jug.

One of my Saturday jobs was to cut the *Daily News* into squares to hang in the lavatory. I remember the last of the horse buses going along Clapham Park Road. Almost every winter there were pea-soup fogs, choking yellow fumes so dense you could not see more than a few feet ahead. Truly a long-past world.

With my parents and three brothers I was staying in the village of Nine Ashes, near Ongar, in August 1914 when war broke out. My uncle Sam, who lived next door, came in and said, 'The German Fleet is in the North Sea.' I dimly understood that he was talking about a war, but I thought it was something that happened in the Bible or in the 'olden days'. I said, 'They don't kill each other now?' 'Of course they do,' they told me.

I had accepted all the Bible stories and decided the only thing I could do was to ask God to stop the war. I prayed like mad, but God let me down. It must have been about the same time that I tried to solve another problem with a Bible story. It was about a fellow called Gideon, who was very close to God and one day God gave him a job to do. Gideon wasn't sure if this was God talking. He said, 'Look God, I want a sign. I'm going to put a fleece out, and tomorrow morning I want the fleece to be wet with dew and all around to be dry.' Sure enough, it happened. Gideon was not satisfied, and he asked God to do it the other way round. It happened again. I put a flannel out in the garden and asked God to do it, just as He had for Gideon. He let me down again.

As the war developed, I fell for the propaganda. I remember a poster with a picture of Scarborough which the Germans had shelled. It read, 'Men of England, will you stand this?' That was in the early period before conscription. Another recruiting poster had a poem which ran something like, 'What will you lack sonny, what will you lack when the girls come down the street, shouting their joy to the boys come back from the foe they rushed to beat.' Then it went on to address the boy who did not go, and finished with, 'What will you lack sonny, what will you lack when they tell you how you funked.'

I used to stand in front of this poster reading it aloud. I would say to the family, 'If only I was ten years older.' I got so upset about the men in the trenches. I asked, 'Why should I have a comfortable bed?' And one night I decided to sleep on the floor. My mother found me and lifted me still asleep into bed.

Most memories of that war are vague, but there is one episode still vivid in my memory of one of the Zeppelin raids. We watched the pencil of light moving across the sky. There was a burst of flames and, in minutes, the airship was ablaze. As those men died, the cheering rolled round London. Such a short time in terms of history, but today the danger is of a planet blazing. And there will be no one left to cheer.

I have a vivid memory of Armistice Day, 1918, and it was a description of that day which saw my first printed piece. One of the teachers picked out my essay for the school magazine. It read:

> The word 'Armistice' will call to the mind of practically everybody who has lived through the Great War, the day when hostilities finally ceased between the Entente and the Quadruple Alliance.
> At about 11 o'clock on the morning of November 11th, 1918, guns were heard and hooters screamed forth the

message of victory, gained after four and a quarter years of war.

The news is soon grasped by an enthusiastic populace, bells peal forth and cheer upon cheer is heard from every quarter. For a moment one is unable to realise the situation; the greatness of the news for the time-being paralyses one's power of thought and action.

Gradually, we begin to realise what it means; we think of our relatives who are freed from the obligation to kill their fellow-beings. We think of the political significance of the victory which has been gained by democracy over autocracy, of the last of the autocrats an exile, and a fugitive from justice.

We review the events of the Great War – of the Battle of Mons and the heroic stand of the 'Contemptible Little Army' and as we pursue this train of thought, we think of the offensive in March when the last effort of Germany was made.

Then from July onward, the gradual turning of the tide, and now – the victory. We realise how near defeat we have often been, and a great feeling of thankfulness and a desire that never again shall the world be plunged into bloodshed become uppermost in our mind.

H G Schaffer (IVB)

I must go back a few years. School meant first mixed infants (boys and girls from five to seven), then the 'big boys'. From then on, it was an entirely male world. With no sisters, I had no contact with girls. I used to wonder how God managed to make another sort of human being. Our syllabus did not include art or sculpture. Occasionally, we went to the Old Vic to see Shakespeare, but there were no visits to picture galleries or museums. At the local library a magazine on art was kept for adults only, lest we should be led into sin by a picture of a naked woman.

This boys' school, Bonneville Road, was ruled by the cane. The day started with one of two hymns, *Fight the good fight* or *New every morning*. On my first day, having sung the hymn, three boys were brought to the front and bent over to be caned by the headmaster. Each master had his own technique. The culprit would be sent to get the cane, and a punishment book from a drawer in the hall. If the drawer was empty, he had to go from class to class until he located it. Some masters made the boy touch his toes, others made him bend over a chair.

There was one teacher who made him bend over a table and wait while he rolled up his sleeves and entered the culprit's name in the book. On one occasion, having administered the punishment, he rushed out of the room. One of the boys said, 'He's gone to toss himself off.' I did not know what that meant then. I am now certain the teacher got a sexual kick out of it.

None of us boys protested. Parents did not. It was the English tradition. In public schools it was worse. At Emmanuel School in nearby Wandsworth, in those days, prefects had the right to cane. It was said that they chalked the cane, providing a chalk mark to aim at for subsequent strokes. Juvenile Courts also had the authority to order the cane. But despite it all, I still have pleasant memories of my years at Bonneville Road.

Our lives were governed by the eleven plus exam. At that age you took an examination to decide whether you were to be one of the lucky minority to go to a secondary school. My exam was on a Saturday morning, an essay and sums. If I had been ill that morning, my life would have been different. There was no second chance, no report from the school, just a remote examiner looking at those papers. I was lucky and took the scholarship at Sir Walter St Johns, Battersea, with a grant from the London County Council of £15 a year, and a free school cap.

Compared with lives of children today those early years must sound dull. But I wonder whether the present television-dominated generation is not missing something we had. By the time I reached my teens, I had read some of the works of Dickens, Thackeray, Scott, George Eliott, Henty, Ballantyne, as well as moderns like Rider Haggard and even Baroness Orczy.

During World War I, Wandsworth, my borough, being under Tory rule, closed the libraries. Battersea, Labour controlled, kept them open. I used to make up to any boy from Battersea to try to borrow his library ticket. I wonder whether I would have succeeded in journalism without the feeling for the English language provided by my early reading, which included the Bible. Every morning after breakfast the family had a reading from the Bible, and the poetic language of the authorised version remains with me.

My story is typical of the working class children in the early years of the century. My mother would light the copper fire on Monday morning, having given us four children breakfast and sent us to school. Then dirty clothes had to be boiled in the copper; she would take them to a big pot on the scullery table filled with warm water. The clothes would be rubbed with soap on a scrubbing board. They would be rinsed and run through the mangle, an enormous contraption with two wooden rollers turned by hand. They would be hung out in the garden and brought in if it rained.

In between, she would get the midday meal for us children, give us our tea and prepare my father's evening meal. Compare that with the washing machine, the hoover, the drip-dry fabrics of today. That did not finish my mother's programme. Tuesday was ironing day, a flat iron heated on the gas ring. We did not have electricity until many years later.

2

Learning The Hard Way

My father was a gold blocker. He worked with gold leaf and made some exquisite articles for Queen Victoria's jubilee and for the coronations of Edward VII and George V. It is now a dying craft. He had to come out of retirement because he alone knew how to carry out some special process. His firm was in the Clapham Road, near Stockwell, and he used to go to and fro on his ancient fixed-wheel bike. The first lesson I had in economics was when he told me, 'You see my boy, we need the rich people, otherwise we could not sell the goods we make.'

Later, I learned a different lesson. My father worked for a family firm. He was on good terms with the 'governor' and the son, master Tom. They always gave us a turkey for Christmas. Then the firm sold out to a company. The new boss's first step was to announce that they would get rid of the old ones. My father was in his fifties, and was to be one of the victims.

He went to master Tom. 'You can't do this to me,' he said. 'I've been here since I was a boy. How are we going to live?' 'It is nothing to do with me now,' said master Tom, 'but I'll see what I can do.' They let him stay, but at a reduced wage. He had no trade union.

I did not learn to be a rebel from books. My father voted Liberal and the *Daily News* gave some progressive ideas, but it was this treatment of my father which made me ask, 'What sort of society is willing to throw a man on the scrap heap, and threaten his family with starvation?'

Then there was the treatment of my uncle Jim. He came from farming stock and married my mother's sister. He rented a small farm at Norton Heath, near Ongar. He put everything into it, bringing the land into good heart, improving the yields, and investing in improvements.

One day the landlord told him, 'I'm selling the farm but I'll give you first chance.' My uncle protested, 'I've worked day and night on this farm, you are selling my work.' 'Sorry,' said the landlord, 'that's how it is.'

Uncle Jim managed to rent a house at nearby Blackmore. He kept his horses and machinery and hired himself out to neighbouring farmers using a horse-drawn binder to cut the corn, and a horse-drawn plough, and so on.

Just before World War I, a 50-acre farm was for sale at nearby Hook End. This time he managed to borrow the money. He started again with a few cows and a mixture of crops. I spent my holidays there. I learned to milk, to set up the sheaves of corn left by the binder, to collect the eggs from the free range hens, and so on. But come the war and his land was requisitioned by the army.

They dug trenches across his land and used the outhouse to accommodate the soldiers. The house had always had an outdoor closet, but now it was horrifying to find that the soldiers dug a trench and lay wooden boards over it for the same purpose. I asked myself, is this the way they treat the men ready to die for their country?

The land was virtually ruined when it was returned. Compensation was negligible. I remember how my uncle, my brother Ed, and I picked the ears of corn by hand out of the weeds from that first, post-war crop.

My uncle had had enough. The men were being demobilised and a neighbouring farmer was carving up his land and selling it for smallholders. Uncle Jim decided to do the same. There were no restrictions on building. He had a surveyor divide the plots and a solicitor draw up the contracts. The occupants could build their own houses or bungalows, sink their wells, use oil or calor gas and organise their own sanitation – using the usual chemical methods. Some of the structures remained until after World War II. Uncle Jim then sold the farmhouse and an adjoining meadow and bought another farm at Doddinghurst, part of which he broke up and sold in the same way. This land is now in the commuter belt and worth millions.

My uncle had a car and chauffeur and used to ride round collecting the purchase price in instalments. But most of the money went to the surveyors and the solicitors and various hangers on. My aunt had just enough to live on. Uncle Jim was not cut out to be a businessman. He was a good farmer and would have liked to remain a farmer.

It was a long time before I freed myself from the Victorian religious fanaticism which made sex a taboo. My mother and father were lovely people. They lived their Christianity. They were always ready to help people poorer than themselves. But they caused me some agonising years.

Like every boy I discovered masturbation. My parents must have realised it, but I had no sex education. They left out a book by a Victorian parson about the 'hidden sin'. I knew what that was. I went on to read that half the diseases were caused by masturbation, and that many who indulged in it ended up in lunatic asylums.

This parson did not say so explicitly, but he also hinted that venereal diseases, which I did not know about then, were due to it. He described an incident when a young man probably suffering from acne was told by his doctor that he needed a woman. 'This doctor should be prosecuted,' he thundered.

I thought of ways to commit suicide. I had committed this terrible sin. This was God's judgement and I was doomed to die anyway. I stopped sinning but nature has its way and I had wet dreams instead. This was the proof that I was beyond redemption. I tried praying. I did not dare say to God, 'Don't let this happen,' so I said, 'Please God don't let me lose my strength during the night.' I was convinced my strength was ebbing away. But God let me down.

I would a hundred times rather have the permissiveness which the Mrs Whitehouses fulminate against today. I could not talk to anybody, least of all my parents or the teacher at the Sunday School I had to attend every week. Sex education at school was taboo. I had not the courage to talk to the other boys or I would have found they all did it. I thought I was unique in yielding to this hidden sin.

My parents belonged to the generation which was compelled to face the challenge to the old, established, religious beliefs. Or, as was the case of the non-conformist sects, to which my parents belonged, and some of the other denominations, to evade it.

How to reconcile Darwin's proof of evolution with a Bible, which in marginal notes put the creation of the world at around 4000 BC? My dear mother believed it all. God created everything in six days. He did not work the seventh and neither must we.

It took me a long time to escape from the fetters this dogma imposed. When I was about 16 the school debating society had a motion, Men are descended from monkeys – a crude way of supporting Darwin. I opposed it arguing if you accept this, you must accept the challenge to all religious beliefs. I was right and wrong.

When I was 17, I was run over by a lorry on my way to school. I was riding my father's old fixed-wheel bike. It may have been because of the old-fashioned, inadequate brakes, I do not know. The wheel went over my arm, and my left leg was broken in two places. A passing greengrocer who had been in the war stopped the bleeding until the ambulance came. I was conscious up to the time they got me into the operating theatre.

In those days there was no blood transfusion, no antibiotics. They tried to save my arm, but after ten days a specialist came to the bed to tell me it must be amputated. They needed my consent. I said, 'No, I'm not going through life with one arm. 'I shouldn't give up,' he said, 'you will be able to play hockey.' It sounds silly but I thought I do not *want* to play hockey. I want to be able to play fives, at which

I had been rather good, and that needs two hands. 'I must tell you,' said the specialist, 'if you don't have it done, you'll die.' 'I know,' I said.

That night my mother and my brother were sitting by my bed. Neither mentioned the decision I had taken. I thought I can't do this to them. I called the nurse and said, 'I'll have it done.' They amputated that morning. Four weeks later septicaemia had set in. When the night sister took over, the day sister said, 'You won't have Bertie Schaffer here in the morning.' The night nurse (she was acting sister) determined I was not going to die in her care. I survived that night and from then on recovered. I was released after five months. I kept in touch with that night sister and five years later we married.

My brother Ed – two years my senior – and I were as close as any people could be. He secured a scholarship to Sloane School. His school reports, which I still have, show he was top in almost every subject. The school wanted him to go on to university and he could have got a place. My brother Rob had left the army in 1918 after three months as a conscript and went back to school. As a result of being an exserviceman he got a very generous scholarship to Merton College, Oxford, where he got a first-class degree. But my father could not quite see the value of further education, and when Ed's turn came my father said he must earn his living like any other working class boy. So Ed left school and got a job in a bank in Westminster. He absolutely hated it.

We spent our holidays on Uncle Jim's farm and Ed pined for that life. He was told to work Sundays at the bank, and my mother caused him terrible embarrassment by going to see the manager saying her boy would not work on the Sabbath! My Uncle Jim said Ed could work for him, but all he got was his pocket money.

Ed was delivering milk one day to neighbouring villages when he was taken ill with pains. He went to the doctor who told him to go to bed for a day or two and 'I will come round and see you.' He went home, went to bed and the pains got worse. But my aunt, in the way of village people

11

of the time, did not dare worry the doctor. And when he did come (there were no telephones), my brother was dying. He had appendicitis which developed into peritonitis, and by then it was too late. (Ed had applied for a place at the Agricultural College in Essex. If he had secured that a little earlier he might be alive today.) That was the most tragic event of my early youth. I will never forgive the doctor who, incidentally, was later struck off the register, not for neglecting his patients, but because he swindled an old lady out of money.

I lost a school year through my accident and took the higher school exam a year later. That meant I had three months, instead of 15, to prepare to compete for a university place.

In those days the universities offered places and organised their own examinations. I could not apply for some of them because they insisted on Latin. I had chosen to take German instead of Latin at school, mainly because a lot of the boys said they would not learn the 'Huns' language'. I said it was the language of Goethe.

There was one group of colleges at Cambridge which allowed a second language other than Latin, so I took the exam in Cambridge. The competitors came from all over England, some from famous public schools. I had an interview at St John's college. One of the set essays read 'biography is history out of perspective'. I began by saying history is the record of human progress. The tutor said, 'You're a very bold young man. Don't you think there is retrogression too?' I cannot remember much more, but I know I told him I would like to be a journalist working at the League of Nations.

I got a card from St John's saying I had come eleventh and top of the exhibition group. But the available money had gone to the ten in the scholarship group. They could offer me a free place. I had no one to advise me. There were organisations with funds which would answer an appeal, but my father belonged to none of them. The headmaster could have applied for help from various foundations but he did nothing. He told one of the other boys he was not going to help a young bolshevik like Schaffer. He did not even return my letter from St John's offering me a free place. That would, after all, have been a valuable reference. It is hard to credit this hostility because of what he called my left-wing views.

How had I got that reputation? The headmaster was a 100 per cent true blue Tory. He used to read prayers at morning assembly as if he were in church. He took us for divinity and empire history. When I was at elementary school we used to line up on May 24th, Empire Day, with our union jacks, and a huge map behind with great areas coloured red – India, Australia, Canada, chunks of Africa, Asia and the rest.

They said it all belonged to us. I was puzzled. If we owned all that, why could not my parents afford to buy me a pair of skates? That is what I was thinking when the headmaster told us about our imperial heritage. I asked him what use was the empire to me and my dad? He did not answer. I am sure he thought it was deliberate provocation. In fact, I just wanted to know.

In 1923, when the first Labour government took office, it was a foggy morning. 'Symbolic' he told us sixth formers. Later a visitor came to talk to us. He was introduced as the President of Azerbaijan. I did not know that he was an emigré. All I knew about the Russian revolution was from the *Daily News* and from an occasional copy of the *Daily Herald*. I had taken the side of the Labour government in the debating society. That probably finished me with the headmaster. When I was a reporter on the *Clapham Observer*, he wrote a book about the parish church and got his Ph.D for it. I did a story about him and the school. I even got him a reference on the local radio. He positively fawned on me. You learn a lot working on a local paper.

I bought the *Daily Herald* surreptitiously when I saw a street seller (it was not on sale at newsagents). That probably had more influence on my thinking than I realised. In those days it embodied the enthusiasm and the hopes of the

13

Labour party. It was supported by groups of readers all over the country.

In 1929 Odham's Press persuaded some of the union leaders that if they took over the *Herald* they could get a million circulation. There was a bitter fight. The decision had to be taken by a conference vote. Union leaders with a decisive vote were invited to write articles for some of the Odham's publications for a reasonable fee. Perfectly above board, of course!

The agreement was that the new *Herald* would follow the policy of the Labour party, but it was a pale shadow of its former self. *The People*, with a similar make-up, another Odham's publication, would contradict on Sunday what the *Herald* had said during the week.

It is a sad thought that after World War II, to try to keep and attract readers, the *Herald* was changed to the *Sun*. To save jobs it was sold to Rupert Murdoch and was transformed into the most reactionary, sex-ridden paper on the news stands.

3

Start In Journalism

I stayed on at school until the end of the summer term, teaching myself shorthand and choosing my own reading, and at the age of 20 got my first job on the *Clapham Observer*. No salary, just expenses. A 2d bus fare to Balham, and so on. In later years there were training courses for young journalists. When I was on the executive of the union I helped set them up, but I was thrown in at the deep end. Looking back, I shudder to think how ignorant I was, but I learned quickly with the help of the available books: about contempt of court, the need to balance reports, the danger of libel, and so on.

You learn a lot about people on local papers. One of my first jobs was reporting the funeral of a boy who was killed in a street accident. As I left the office the editor called out, 'Get a list of the wreaths.' I said to myself I cannot visit the bereaved family. I went to the undertaker and the parson. 'It was a lovely funeral,' they said, but they could not help with wreaths.

The cemetery was too far away for me to copy the inscriptions. I went to the boy's home, timidly knocked at the door. 'I'm from the *Clapham Observer*,' I said. 'Come in,' said the woman who opened the door, presumably the mother, 'I've got the list of wreaths ready!'

Another time, I was covering a story of a man who had disappeared and for whom there was a nationwide search. They found him hanging in his own loft. I called on the widow. 'There he was,' she said, 'hanging up there all the time, the old devil.' That comment did not go in the paper.

Abortion at the time was illegal. I have always hated the idea of destroying a potential life, but my experience reporting the coroner's court was too terrifying to be ignored. Case after case of girls dying after backstreet operations. In one case the lover used an unsterilised hat pin. On the other side there were the prosecutions of doctors who carried out these illegal operations. I reported one trial of a doctor who did not do it for money but out of sympathy, and to avoid the women falling into the hands of the back-street abortionists. He got five years.

One incident during my *Clapham Observer* days had an unexpected result. A story broke in the morning papers that the body of Lord Kitchener, who had drowned off Murmansk during the war, had been brought back to England, and the coffin had been seized by the police and taken to Lambeth Coroner's Court.

I arrived at the court to find it surrounded by reporters from Fleet Street. I went to the door and, as the regular local reporter, was let in. I knocked at the door of the coroner's room. He was Ingleby Oddie, a very well known character. I asked if he would be holding the inquest on Lord Kitchener. He chuckled. 'There won't be an inquest,' he said, 'the coffin was full of bricks.' I walked past the Fleet Street reporters and phoned the *Evening Standard*.

I never heard the reason for that hoax, but it boosted my position as local correspondent of the *Standard*, and when the news editor, Henry Martin, went to the Press Association as editor, he offered me a job. That is how I got in to Fleet Street in 1928.

Those years on the *Clapham Observer* taught me a lot. For the first two years I was paid a few shillings because I was supposed to be learning. In fact I was soon doing the same work as the other two reporters who started at 16, and were getting the union minimum.

It was a non-union office and in the General Strike of 1926, although I was on the side of the strikers, I saw nothing contradictory in taking down in shorthand the radio speech of Prime Minister Stanley Baldwin and using it for a strike bulletin.

I was thrilled by the demonstration in Hyde Park on the eve of the strike, and walked to Bow Street (all transport was on strike) to hear the case against Shapurji Saklatvala, the communist MP for Battersea. I realised the power of the working class, and wrote a story for the next bulletin backing an appeal by church leaders supporting negotiations. However, the strike was called off by the TUC, some would say betrayed, before that bulletin was printed. It might have cost me my job. Earlier I had put in a few inches summarising the Labour party's policy in a local election. The owner called me to his office to tell me, 'You're not turning my paper into a Bolshevik rag.'

Two reporters on another local paper which had printed pro-government material during the strike refused to blackleg. They were helped by the union to set up a freelance agency. They invited me to join them at a wage that enabled me to join the union. It was valuable experience but one of the two, Stuart Emeny, got a job on the *Daily Chronicle*. He was killed reporting in Burma during the war. The other, Hugh Chevins, who lay down in front of blackleg buses during the strike, finished as the respected industrial correspondent of the *Daily Telegraph*. I was invited back to the *Clapham Observer*, this time at the union minimum of £4 13s a week; double that of a railwayman. It took me a long time to repudiate the humility which so many of the working class accepted. I was puzzled as a boy at the deference with which my parents treated the doctor. They called him 'Sir' and, to avoid embarrassing him, put his 3s 6d on the hall stand which he picked up as he left.

In our hymn book at Sunday school there were the lines, 'the rich man in his castle, the poor man at his gate, God made them high or lowly and gave them their estate.' When I first met local celebrities like the Mayor, the Chairman of the Chamber of Commerce, Vicars, and so on, I was humble. I assumed they must be specially intelligent. I soon found it wasn't true. With the PA and later *Reynolds News*, I met MPs, trade union leaders, cabinet ministers, and realised it was not true of them either.

Those were the years when the anti-war play, *Journey's End*, and the German novel, *All Quiet on the Western Front*, created a movement against war in both countries. One story told me by Ted Dixon of Coventry, who was active in the peace movement, summed up the horror. He was on one of the fronts. The brass hats had decided to break the trench-war stalemate by bombarding the enemy line for days on end. They convinced themselves that none of the enemy could survive. They even proposed to head the advance after the bombardment with a band. We now know they were advised that the German dug-outs would survive.

Ted Dixon described how he and his comrades watched the opening of the attack, how contingents went over at intervals throughout that terrible day, mowed down as they attempted to cross no-man's land, impaled on barbed wire, or marooned in bomb holes. Dixon and his companions were due to go over at 4 p.m. They were waiting to die. The officer in charge cancelled the order. They lived. The officer was court-martialled. If there had then been television coverage of those horrors, I think public opinion would have forced a change of policy.

My own early revulsion to the whole idea of war was reinforced by these first-hand witnesses. I signed the peace pledge refusing to support any future war. The appeal was organised by the Rev. Dick Shepherd of St Martin's-in-the-Fields, Trafalgar Square.

On the north side of Clapham Common lived John Burns, one of the leaders of the new unionism which had emerged from the strikes of the Match girls and the dockers at the end of the century. He later became a member of the Asquith cabinet but resigned in protest against the war. He had retired to Clapham Common and, in my *Clapham Observer* days, I passed him sweeping up leaves in his front garden. I greeted him. One of his remarks stands out in my memory. He said, 'I am a happy man, and do you know why? Because

18

I haven't the deaths of millions of young men like you on my conscience.'

As the *Clapham Observer* reporter, I was invited to a local private showing of a film of a dialogue between Bernard Shaw, Sybil Thorndyke and her husband, Lewis Casson. It was when the 'talkies' were in the experimental stage.

I can't remember much about the film, but I recall Shaw's conversation. He referred to the then Prince of Wales, who had been getting a lot of adverse publicity for dancing with typists, visiting pubs, and sometimes appearing obviously under the influence. 'It's no good,' I remember Shaw saying. 'We pay royalty to walk over us.'

He went on – fascinating satire – describing the contradiction of so-called democratic governments and the reality, and how the Americans were taking us over. Years later, these ideas reappeared in *The Apple Cart*. But one reference Shaw made I have never been able to check. He said Rodin had sculptured him, or maybe *wanted* to sculpture him. I do remember him saying, 'Without clothes, people would want to see what the real Shaw looks like.'

Years later, Louis Casson recalled the incident. He told me that they had searched everywhere for the film including the conversation in which Sybil certainly held her own, but it had been lost.

4

Inside Story Of An Election Trick

The old established *Clapham Observer* was challenged by a give-away local paper. The owner, after a short spell of competition, sold out to the newcomer. I lost my job early in 1928.

That was where my contact with Henry Martin, whom I mentioned earlier, came in. He had left the *Standard* to become editor of the PA. Martin asked me to call in. I was interviewed by A C Gray, the news editor. He did not show any concern at my missing arm. I was offered a job at 7 guineas a week.

Those years on the *Clapham Observer* cured me of the deference, almost humility, which my parents and most of our friends and neighbours showed to the so-called better class people.

I started at the PA as assistant to Hughie Stalker, the night news editor. Hughie had served at the front right through the war and came back unscathed. He often said he never expected to survive; few of his comrades did. In those years after World War I the survivors had a considerable influence. Strangely, some of them talked nostalgically about their mob and the comradeship which they could not find again in civvy street. Mainly, however, when they did talk, it was to describe horrors, which we who had read only the doctored newspaper reports and the casualty lists could not fully comprehend.

The newsroom of the PA was an ideal vantage point for

a bird's eye view of the national and international scene. The PA collected the home news and handled foreign news from Reuters for distribution to the home press. The picture was one of mounting economic crises at home and abroad. The Tory government had used its victory in the General Strike to pass an act curtailing the powers of the trade unions (though nothing like the measures of the Thatcher government nearly 60 years later).

The Tories were clearly losing ground and there was no surprise at their defeat in 1929. The second Labour government took power, again under the leadership of Ramsay MacDonald. As in 1924, it was a minority government depending on Liberal support. One of their conditions of support was an Electoral Reform Act based on proportional representation. That measure was almost through when it was killed by the economic crisis, which ironically was precipitated by the Liberals.

In the 1929 election campaign I was at a wildly enthusiastic Labour demonstration at the Albert Hall. MacDonald passed the cheering crowd outside with his nose in the air. I said to a companion, 'That man cannot lead the workers or he would never treat them like that.' Some time earlier I was at a meeting with his daughter, Ishbel. In an aside, she said, 'The trouble with daddie is that he is so vain.' After he went over to the Tories he was quoted as saying, 'Every duchess will want to kiss me.'

On the eve of the election Herbert Morrison, one of the Labour leaders, had confidently prophesied that the economic crisis was passing and we were on the road to recovery! The Labour party took power and was hit by the crisis. Unemployment mounted and the press launched a continuous attack. 'The spongers on the dole' was their theme song. It was possible to find a few cases of abuse, but it was utterly unfair to label the unemployed as 'work shy'. The word dole was invented as a way of disguising the fact that unemployment pay came out of an insurance fund to which every worker contributed. Then they introduced the family means test. If the father was unemployed, grown up sons and daughters, if they were in work, had to contribute to their upkeep. The inevitable result was that families split up.

In this atmosphere of panic the Liberals demanded action to deal with the economic crisis. The government set up a commission to consider economies, and to back it up, passed an Anomaly Act depriving sections of the unemployed of benefit. The way the committee was expected to work was clear when Sir Ernest May, head of the Prudential Insurance Company, was appointed chairman.

At the beginning of the summer recess, while the commission was still sitting, J. H. Thomas, railwaymen's leader and a member of the government, talking to correspondents in the House of Commons lobby said, 'We'll be back soon and we'll have a national government.' The commission recommended all-round cuts.

The cabinet fought over the proposals for a long time and finally agreed on all the cuts, except the reduction in unemployment pay. MacDonald was told on the newly developed transatlantic telephone line that there would be no loan to save the economy if the cut was not made. The Bank of France said the same. MacDonald set off for the palace to resign. Jimmie Thomas told waiting reporters, 'There'll be a new government and I'm in it.'

Philip Snowden, who had come from the left wing Independent Labour party, went over with MacDonald to the Tories. Lord Sankey joined too, only he said, 'to save some hope for a liberal policy on India'. Thomas was made secretary for the colonies. MacDonald was prime minister but Baldwin, the Conservative leader, held the strings of power.

After the new government had taken office, MacDonald, at his Scottish home in Lossiemouth, told a reporter, 'The King told me the previous Spring I shall want you for a national government.'

The new government called a general election. It resulted in a huge Tory majority. Most of the Labour ministers were defeated. The most potent weapon in Tory hands was the fear of millions that their savings in the Post Office Bank were in danger. After the election I analysed the figures, comparing the Labour vote with the number of the unemployed and the likely number of wives in the constituencies where the Labour vote had collapsed. The conclusion was inescapable; even the unemployed voted Tory.

What is worse, I was the unwilling instrument of the Post Office scare. This is the story: I was in charge of the PA news room on the Sunday before polling day. At about 10.30 am the phone rang and the voice said, 'This is the Chancellor of the Exchequer speaking.'

The dialogue continued:

GS: Good morning, Mr Snowden, what can we do for you?

Snowden: Did Mr Runciman make a speech last night, and have you a report?

GS: (after looking up the file) Yes, we did have a short report.

Snowden: Did he say anything about Post Office savings?

GS: There is a brief reference saying, 'the Post Office funds had been used for the unemployment fund.'

Snowden: I'm rather sorry he mentioned that. But, as he has, would you care for a statement from me? [Snowdon then dictated the statement putting flesh and bones on Runciman's statement – he was the postmaster general. This was the front page news on the Monday morning.]

The dialogue continued:

GS: I am puzzled. Miss Bondfield always came to the House of Commons for authorisation to borrow for the unemployment fund [Margaret Bondfield was Minister of Labour in the Labour government].

Snowden: Yes, yes, that is true.

GS: Does it matter if borrowing is sanctioned by parliament, from what source it is taken?

Snowden: Yes, you have a point. But I think I'll stick to my statement.

The plot was transparent. Runciman had been set up to make the statement, but the Sunday papers had not picked it up. There must have been a consultation at No 10 or 11 Downing Street. I can imagine the conclusion, 'Philip, you get on to the PA.'

23

The PA rule is, you never hold a story. I broke the rule. I got on to Arthur Henderson, leader of the Labour party, who was in Burnley. 'Mr Henderson,' they told me, 'likes to rest on Sunday.' I told whoever answered the gist of the statement. 'This is terribly important,' I said. 'Ask Mr Henderson to phone the PA with a reply at once.' The reply did not come until late that day. Even then it only spoke of a last-minute scare, not even giving the explanation I had put to Snowden.

I dictated the Snowden statement and told the subs this is the red letter – and it was. I spoke to Snowden once after that. He had been given one promise by the Tories that a modest act to tax unearned income from land development by the community would remain on the statute book. The pledge was broken.

The machinery for valuing the land which this act had set up was scrapped. When the repeal clause came before the House of Lords in July 1934 (Snowden had been rewarded with a viscountcy) he made a bitter attack. 'The purpose of this clause,' he said, 'was the beginning of a system by which taxes would be levied on socially created values. This land system, all this exploitation of public necessities is responsible for the evil of the slums and very largely for the unemployment problem. This is deliberate sharp practice, the latest of many acts which show the true character of this government and expose the hypocrisy of its claim to be a national government.'

I cannot remember the reason I contacted Snowden in his last years. He was a pathetic figure, ignored by the Tories and ostracised by most, but not all his former Labour colleagues.

MacDonald was a different story. He became a figure of fun making long, often incoherent speeches. One day, Dick Ecclestone, PA chief reporter, came in to the news room and read from his notes of a Ramsay MacDonald speech. One phrase was 'We must go on and on and on and up and up and up.' I said, 'Dick, report him just like that.' And he did.

Jimmy Thomas was an even sadder case. He was a great

trade union leader. Members of his union, the National Union of Railwaymen, continued to stand by him (I got some angry letters when I wrote a critical obituary). Jim loved luxury. He was much more at home with his pals on the racecourse or in the city than with the workers who made his rise to power possible. He was involved in a financial scandal and disappeared from public life.

A C Gray, the PA news editor and I had a great deal in common. In quiet intervals we had discussions on the political situation, with the benefit of his long experience at the centre of events.

I worked from 2 pm to 10 pm, so overlapped with ACG, as we knew him, on part of his day turn. Those late hours meant I had no time for political activity.

Reuters covered foreign news which the PA circulated. On one occasion the evening papers carried a story about some scandalous event in the Soviet Union. I rang Reuter's news desk to ask about the story. 'We are not touching it,' was the reply. 'We checked it, it came from the Riga factory.' 'That's a new one,' I said. 'Didn't you know?' he said. 'It's an office where they invent anti-Soviet stories. It's in Riga.' (Then, as now, outside the Soviet Union.) 'They work out their stories and it comes back from so many places that even the inventors begin to believe it.'

One Sunday morning I rang Bernard Shaw, who had just come back from the Soviet Union. He talked about the visit. Then he said, 'You sound like a young man.' I admitted it. 'The future is over there,' said Shaw.

In the 1930s, public relations was still a young industry. There were hardly any government press officers. Today there are hundreds. One minister, who realised the value of publicity, was Hore-Belisha. It was after he had called a press conference as Minister of Transport to introduce his pedestrian crossings that Dick Eccleston decided to call them Belisha beacons, and the name has stuck to this day.

George Griffiths, the PA lobby correspondent, was asked by Hore-Belisha to recommend a press officer and he put me forward. I kept the appointment at the ministry. Hore-

Belisha was sitting on his desk eating an apple. 'I want somebody,' he said, 'who can put my work across and cut out all this civil service red tape. I'll give you an example. A civil servant handed me a list of rules and regulations for the River Thames. "A formality," he said, "but they need your signature." I insisted on reading them. One clause said, "No one shall pass through a lock unless clad from the knees to the neck." So I wrote in the margin that I refused to sanction such an archaic Victorian bye-law. The civil servant said, "Minister, this is a pure formality." I asked if that required my signature? He had to agree that it did. Now that is a good story but I can't release it myself, it would look as if I am seeking publicity. How would you handle it?'

I said, 'I would send a letter to the Thames Conservancy explaining why I couldn't sanction such a ridiculous bye-law and my press officer would find a way to get it to the press.' 'That's it,' he said, 'when are you coming?'

I was tempted, but that evening a big story broke. That is the joy of journalism. I realised I could not settle down as a civil servant. At that stage I thought only of my career as a journalist. Had I taken the job, I doubt whether I would have survived. Anyway, Henry Martin seized the opportunity to meet Belisha at his home and said he did not want him to take one of his best men.

This episode reminds me of a meeting I had with George Lansbury, when he was Minister of Works in the 1929 Labour government. I found him on top of one of the double decker trams. We had met before. He said, 'I got the idea that people should be able to bathe in the Serpentine. I mentioned it to the civil servants. "Oh Minister, you can't do that," they told me. "It's a Royal Park." I said, "If I put my signature to an order enabling the Serpentine to be open for bathing would that be an order?" They said, "Well, yes minister." So I did.'

That was quite a revolution. Not just the rich riding their horses in Hyde Park, but the common people bathing in the Serpentine. I had a swim there and was sunbathing. The shoulder strap of my costume was undone, revealing a nipple. An attendant commanded, 'Cover yourself up.'

Sadly, the Serpentine lido, which became a happy part of the London scene, was closed down by the economy-mad Thatcher government, because it would not spend the money to free if from pollution.

George Lansbury was not afraid to stand up to the establishment. When he was head of Poplar Guardians, the body responsible for giving poor law relief in that poverty stricken area of east London, they distributed more than the government allowed. They were prosecuted and in a body they went to prison.

After World War II, Harold Wilson was for a time in the same job as George Lansbury when he sanctioned Serpentine bathing. The iron railings surrounding gardens open to the nearby residents had been taken down to be used for the war effort. Wilson suggested they should not be replaced. He was over-ruled.

When the area surrounding St Paul's cathedral was demolished by the nazi bombers, I wrote an article in *Reynolds* saying that, after the Great Fire of London, an opportunity was lost to rebuild the area as a centre for the people's enjoyment. Now there was another opportunity, but it was a vain hope.

During the 1930s, Churchill was in the wilderness. He would ring up the PA and his voice was unmistakable. 'I'm speaking at so and so tonight. How much are you going to give me?' 'Half a column, Mr Churchill.' 'You gave that fellow Herbert Samuel half a column, I want a column.'

Churchill used to learn his speeches. He was not good when he had to speak spontaneously, although he excelled in biting comments as in his reported description of a speech by Anthony Eden. 'Used every cliché, except "please adjust your dress before leaving."'

He was speaking on one occasion in Manchester as part of his campaign against the moves for the liberation of India. Morley Richards, the PA reporter, called at his hotel to see if he had a manuscript of his speech. Churchill said he had not written anything. 'I tell you what, I'll recite to you in my bath.' So there was Morley taking it down in shorthand while Churchill, busy tubbing himself, was coming out with his rolling sentences.

There were humorous interludes at the PA. Once we rang up some noble lord about a story. An obsequious man-servant answered. 'I'm sorry, his lordship is sleeping with her ladyship tonight. I cannot disturb them.'

Justice McCarthy, who was not very popular with his colleagues, because of his outspoken comments, was found shot; obviously suicide. We followed the usual practice of asking for tributes. One fellow judge answered, 'Why have you rung me, you don't think I did it?'

In the 1930s there were a number of progressive papers. Gradually they disappeared. The *Westminster Gazette* went, a good Liberal paper. Then the *Chronicle* was swallowed by the *Daily News*. I was on the desk of the PA that day. The rumours were going round that the *Chronicle* was to die. In the late afternoon I rang the *Chronicle*. The news editor said, 'We are preparing tomorrow's edition as usual.' Soon after-wards the staff were told that the paper had been merged into the *News Chronicle*.

One of the fascinating stories during my time at the PA was the abdication of Edward VIII. The story of his affair with Mrs Simpson was known all over the world, but dutifully suppressed by the British press, including the PA. References to the affair in the American magazines were removed before they were sent to our shops. One of the PA staff, who handled the duplicating machines, got copies from America and reproduced the banned material. He had a ready sale.

Any references that came in were put on the spike. One afternoon a report came in of a speech by Bishop Blunt of Yorkshire, who said the King should be more attentive to his duties, or words to that effect. The sub-editor, according to instructions, put it on the spike. Some hours later the *Yorkshire Post* asked what we were doing with Bishop Blunt's speech. There was a hurried search, and with much trepidation the speech was released. Next morning, all the papers splashed the constitutional crisis. The amusing thing was that Bishop Blunt appeared not to be referring to or maybe he did not know about the love story. He was worried because the king had not been taking his duties as head of the church seriously.

Exciting days followed. Late in the evening while the story was running, I wrote what we called a 'new lead', pulling together the events of the day. Details poured in about the couple. The significance of an item about Mrs Simpson being divorced in a provincial town, which the papers had published without comment, was explained. How quickly the establishment were willing to repudiate their former darling.

There was a ceremonial dinner in London, where many of the guests sat down when the loyal toast was moved. The anger of the royal family was made clear very early. The reporter covering the palace reported, although it was not published, that if the King abdicated, he would become Mr Edward Windsor and no more.

The verse went the rounds reflecting the role of Archbishop Lang in the affair, who was said to have been told by the King at one point, 'You forget your Grace that I am the head of your organisation.' The verse was:

My Lord Archbishop what a scold you are,
In Christian charity how scant you are,
When a man is down how bold you are,
My Lord Archbishop, what a Cantuar.

(NB: Cantuar is the official title of the Archbishop of Canterbury.)

In London there was a lot of sympathy for the King, but in the shires there was a strong puritan tradition. Had he picked a woman, however humble, who had not been divorced, he might have got away with it. In the end, he got his dukedom but none of the royal family acknowledged his wife. None attended or sent greetings to his wedding.

To look ahead of my story. The couple lost support when they visited nazi Germany. They did not conceal their sympathy for the regime. After the war broke out, the Duke of Windsor liaised between the British and French armies. After France collapsed there was anxiety at the possibility that he might fall into the hands of the nazis. Arthur Greenwood, who was a member of the war cabinet, told me how Churchill ended the discussion by saying, 'I know, we'll make him King of the Bahamas.'

The captured German archives make clear that the nazi leaders, in collaboration with Franco Spain, planned to hold the Duke and use him. Ribbentrop, Germany's Foreign Minister (later tried at Nuremberg and hanged) is quoted in the archives as advising, 'The duke must be informed that Germany wants peace with the English people, that the Churchill clique stands in the way of it, and that it would be a good thing if the Duke would hold himself in readiness for further developments.

'Germany is determined to force England to peace, and upon this happening would be prepared to accommodate a desire expressed by the Duke, especially with a view to the assumption of the English throne by the Duke and Duchess.'

The archives carried a report confirming my story that Churchill had designated the Duke as Governor of the Bahamas, and ordered him to proceed to his post at once. Should he fail to do so, Churchill had threatened him with court martial. The couple sailed for the Bahamas on the American liner *Excalibur* on August 1st, 1940.

The Duke subsequently condemned the nazi papers as 'complete fabrication' and the Foreign Office stated officially that the Duke had never wavered in his loyalty to Britain. (See William L Shirer's *The Rise and Fall of the Third Reich*.)

During my period at the PA I used to report in the mornings inquests at Camberwell and Lambeth, and other places, before doing my stint in the news room. One of the tragic features, as I have already mentioned, were the number of deaths from illegal abortions.

Rosie, my wife, had qualified as a state registered nurse, midwife and health visitor. She secured a job as health visitor in Islington. After she was appointed for the job in 1938, the medical officer called her in and said, 'I want to give you one warning. If you are found teaching birth control you will be instantly dismissed.'

At that time the pioneers of birth control were the Marie Stopes clinic. They were giving information on birth control and contraceptives, virtually illegally. Rosie was horrified by the picture she found in her work as a health visitor – women dreading child birth but not able to do anything about it. She would hand a slip of paper to them giving the address of the Marie Stopes Clinic. Often the women would come up to her in the street and thank her.

5

I Qualify for an MI5 File

In 1936, while I was at the PA, I paid my first visit to the Soviet Union. I had read a good deal about this country which had destroyed the Tsarist regime, defeated the war of intervention, and was beginning to build a socialist society.

A publication from Moscow told of the gigantic schemes for reconstructing their shattered economy. I started reading Marxist material in the *Little Lenin* series, beginning with Lenin's letters from Switzerland in which he analysed the prospects of the revolution.

I booked an Intourist visit with Arthur Austin, a friend from school days – 26 days for £26, including the fare by boat. A few days before the start, everyone had received their visa except me. The Russians were very suspicious of journalists. Anyone reading the lies that were published about them during the revolution and in the following years will understand why.

Anyway, my visa came through at the last minute. That trip convinced me that the American journalist who said, 'I have seen the future, and it works' was right. The people remembered then the suffering under the Tsar, and they felt themselves part of the work of reconstruction that was evident everywhere.

I met a young student in Moscow. He spoke English. He told me that he was studying engineering. His sister was studying astronomy. They had come from a remote village where they had endured terrible hardships during the civil war and the war of intervention. They were near starvation.

I said, 'In those bad times, you must have felt that even the Tsarist times were better.' His eyes were blazing as he answered, 'Don't you understand, it's *our* country now.' That was the spirit that created the Stakhanovite movement and sustained the Soviet people during the war, despite the crimes of the Stalin period.

There was a significant episode when we returned. At Tilbury, we were handed immigration cards. As the passengers were dutifully filling them up I said to the immigration officer, 'I don't need this, I'm a British subject.' 'Only a formality,' he replied, 'but we need it.'

That was, I suppose, my first entry on the MI5 files. It was amusing because on the trip was a group of Tories who no doubt were also put on the list. It illustrated the attitude of the British government to any citizens who dared to visit the Bolsheviks.

One Sunday Oswald Mosley and his blackshirts were stopped at Cable Street in the East End, as they tried to march through to the centre of London. I was in charge of the PA news room. It was like being at an army headquarters watching and recording the progress of a battle. The people of the East End understood the evil nature of fascism. Mosley had been a minister in the 1929–31 Labour government and together with George Lansbury and Jimmy Thomas had formed a committee to study the problems of unemployment. It collapsed in the 1931 crisis.

Mosley, who had put forward some good ideas, was disillusioned, and tried to form The New Party. Some Labour ex-MPs were tempted. But the idea collapsed and Mosley soon showed his true colours. He fancied himself as a British Mussolini and organised his blackshirt followers on the Italian style. It was frightening, for those of us who had had the opportunity to study the true nature of fascism, to see how many responded to his demagoguery. He had plenty of press support, notably from the *Daily Mail*, but the advertisers put their foot down when Mosley embraced Hitler's anti-semitism, while the brutality of his blackshirts alienated

33

even those who, faced with unemployment and poverty, were willing to look for any alternative. There were plenty of Mosley supporters particularly in the upper classes.

Mosley and his wife were interned early in the war. When Herbert Morrison ordered their release, there was an outcry led by of all people the right-wing trade union leader, Arthur Deakin. I was invited to give a talk on the Canadian broadcast service about the protests and I told, across the Atlantic, the story of the Battle of Cable Street.

I was alerted to the crimes of the nazis when D N Pritt, and other well-known lawyers, organised a replica of the trial of Dimitrov who was accused of burning down the Reichstag. It exposed the deliberate burning of the Reichstag by the nazis and the frame-up of the fall guy, Van der Lubbe.

It quoted the immortal speech of Dimitrov when, from the dock, he denounced the nazis, and provoked Goering to shout 'Wait till I get you out of the power of this Court.' It had a big effect on public opinion. The action of the Soviet Union in demanding and securing Dimitrov's release showed the Soviet Union as the enemy of the nazis, also evidenced at the time by the Soviet film, *Prof Mamlock*, which exposed the mass persecution of Jews by the nazis.

In the 1935 election, I had not a lot of faith in the Labour leadership and, remembering the Reichstag trial, decided to work for D N Pritt in north Hammersmith. Ivor Montagu and his wife Hel were running the campaign which was successful. That began a life-long friendship with all three. D N Pritt was recognised as having one of the finest brains in the legal profession. He was unequalled in complicated financial cases. On one occasion, a case involving millions was in preparation. Solicitors on both sides were advised that the best man was Pritt, but both sides initially turned him down as being too left wing. In the end, he was approached by both sides.

He gave his services to victims of the anti-colonial struggle in Kenya, Ceylon (Sri Lanka) and other countries where the British were hanging on to power. I saw him in action defending a Malayan appealing to the Privy Council. The case against the prisoner was that he was found in possession of a weapon, which could mean the death penalty. Pritt argued that the weapon could have been planted. I think the man was acquitted.

Perhaps I might include here an episode which occurred much later. Pritt and Marie, his wife, befriended Gilbert Harding and helped him get a post with the BBC. He became a well-known personality, attracting attention by his rudeness.

A brains trust was organised in Pritt's constituency, north Hammersmith. Gilbert and I were on the platform. Later, during dinner at Pritt's flat, talk turned to a report that the then Pope had seen a vision of the Virgin Mary ascending to heaven. Gilbert was a convert to the Roman Catholic faith. I said to him, 'I don't want to offend your religious convictions, but do you seriously believe that?' 'No,' he replied, 'but it's awfully good for the peasants.' I was bewildered.

The development of civil aviation is one of the amazing developments in my lifetime. On our honeymoon in 1929, Rosie and I went by boat, train and Rhine steamers to Constanz on the Swiss border. We returned to Cologne by air.

The Weimar Republic was forbidden by the Treaty of Versailles to build military aircraft, but there was nothing to prevent construction of civil planes. By 1929 they had air connections between the principal cities. Our plane from Constanz to Frankfurt had just three seats, for us and the pilot. The manager of the airport came to see us off. The second plane from Frankfurt to Cologne seated, I think, ten. When I fly today in jumbo jets, and on occasions have watched Concorde take off, I marvel at what human genius can achieve in the service of peace.

My interest was aroused by these first flights and, when an invitation to the PA for a publicity flight came in, I volunteered. It is strange today, but in those early days many were frightened of flying. The result was I had a number of pioneering flights. One was on Hannibal, the first of a class of giant bi-planes which flew from London (Croydon) to Paris in an hour and twenty minutes, and served a meal on the way. Amy Johnson, the first airwoman to fly from England to Australia, was on the flight.

On an Imperial Airways flight to Budapest, our press party made a stop at Cologne. The nazis were in power and a brown shirt came round the restaurant where we were having dinner, with a collecting box. The diners meekly contributed. When he came to our table one of our party asked, 'What's it for?' Our guide interpreted, 'It's for the poor.' Our spokesman waved him away, 'We are poor too,' he said. The consternation on the face of our guide made me realise the atmosphere of fear created by that regime.

When the R101, the airship which was to carry the flag of the Empire to India was being prepared, there were discussions on whether the press would be given seats. I do not know whether I would have been chosen, but I was certainly in the running. In the end, there were so many VIPs demanding seats that the press were excluded. The R101 crashed before it reached Paris.

The German Tourist Agency organised boat trips from London to Hamburg. Germans boarded at Hamburg, and the British at Tilbury. When one national group disembarked on the return trip, a new group boarded. The British could pay with tourist marks at a much more favourable rate of exchange.

A group of us from the PA went on the trip. I walked through a Hamburg street. There were brownshirts at various points. A middle-aged German walked beside me and, somewhat to my surprise, began talking. He said, 'You see that block of flats, there used to be red flags at nearly all the windows. Do you think they've all changed?' I said warily, 'I hope not,' for he could have been an agent provocateur. He went on to tell me that he was on a German merchant ship, he did not say what rank, and had brought in illegal literature. I said, 'Why are you talking to me? If I were to report you to one of those brownshirts, and as far as you know I could be on their side, you would face imprisonment and even death.' He replied, 'I know the risk, but I hope that you will tell your countrymen that there are Germans fighting this evil regime.' I am sure he was genuine.

On the quayside, waiting to embark for home, we had drinks with some of the wives of the German crew. John Prince, of the *Daily Telegraph*, suggested we call Hitler 'Jimmy', in case our conversation was overheard. One of the women twigged who we meant. She leaned over and said, 'Jimmy, we call him what you say in English, a shit.' Small incidents, but it confirmed my belief that the best elements among the German people would eventually turn against their oppressors.

Henry Martin, as editor of the PA, improved efficiency and introduced what were then modern techniques, for example tape machines instead of messenger boys taking typed copies of the news round the Fleet Street offices. But he was an example, even in his modest field, that power corrupts. Journalists were frightened for their jobs. Every morning the papers were scrutinised, and if they carried reports judged better than that of the PA the reporter was on the carpet. The result was that reporters wrote too long reports to avoid missing anything which might appear in the papers. The sub-editors complained that they were having to cut these too-long reports. Martin sent round a letter with the threat, 'Reporters must do their job or get out.'

We would have protested through the union, but it was a row between reporters and subs and it was decided to send a letter to Martin saying his letter was disgraceful, an insult to reporters whose loyalty had never been challenged, and so on.

I signed, although I was assistant night news editor. I was the only one to be called to account. He shouted, 'I have no use for an executive who runs with the hares and hunts with the hounds. I expect executives to back me.' I said, 'I'm sorry, but my idea of an executive is one who has the confidence of his colleagues and you don't get that when you insult them.' He said, 'You are a big man in the NUJ, what are you going to do?' In fact, being on night work, I had taken little part in the union. He said something to the effect that he may have over-reacted. I realised later that he was frightened. If we had sent the correspondence to the directors, who came from the provincial papers, they would have taken our side.

A few months later as I was crossing the road near my home at Kingston, a car hit me and badly fractured my left leg. I was in hospital for three months. I had letters and visits from many of the staff but not a word from Martin. A year later I had a small rise. He said to me, 'You would have had this earlier if we hadn't had a disagreement on principle.'

Around that time, one Saturday evening, I met Ramage Jarvie, a former editor of *John Bull*, who had joined *Reynolds*, the Sunday paper which had been bought by the Cooperative movement, and was publishing in a ramshackle building off Fleet Street. Ramage suggested I 'come and see Sydney Elliot, my editor'.

I went with him. Elliot said, 'You want to join my paper?' I said, 'No, I've got a very good job.' He seemed to take this as a challenge. 'We are going to have the best staff in Fleet Street. But mind you, the first consideration is that they must be able to write.'

After the tussle with Martin I kept thinking to myself. Do you want to risk this sort of situation reoccurring, perhaps later on when you will be far more vulnerable. I remembered Sydney Elliot's statement that his staff must be able to write.

I wrote three model pieces, a leader for Armistice Day – the workers in the arms factories observing the two minutes silence, then returning to the machines turning out weapons of death – a news story and a feature. I had them profession-ally typed and sent them off. Some months later Sydney offered me a job as industrial correspondent.

I took the precaution of accepting before handing in my notice to the PA. Martin was furious. I realised I was very useful. When we thought Lloyd George might die (he lived for many more years after), I did the rush obituary. When George V died, all the executives went home and left me to turn out five columns for the evening papers. Martin said, 'You're a fool. If you stay, you will be in line for promotion as news editor or night editor.'

Walton Cole, who took my job and secured the promised promotion, finished as managing editor of Reuters at a salary many times what I could ever hope for. I had no regrets.

6

I Join Reynolds News

I took up the post on *Reynolds* in February 1937. It was a thrilling moment, an opportunity to work for a paper devoted to the ideals and convictions I had learned, not only from books but from life. I was already a trade unionist and a cooperator, and I at once joined Richmond Labour party. Up to that time, continuous night work had made activity impossible.

Reynolds, owned by the cooperative movement, was a unique and successful experiment in left-wing journalism. Previous efforts had been based on contributions from devoted, active supporters. The *Daily Herald*, before it was handed to Odhams Press, the *Daily Worker* (later the *Morning Star*) were examples.

Alf Barnes, who was the main architect of many cooperative developments, and created the London Co-operative Society from the cluster of societies in greater London, had the idea that the cooperative movement should be able to finance its own newspaper.

He began from the fact that the cooperative movement was an important section of the economy. In retail and foreign trade, banking and insurance, it controlled considerable resources. How could these be mobilised to create a newspaper capable of competing with the capitalist-controlled press?

He conceived the idea of a collective advertising fund to which all cooperative organisations would be invited to sub-

40

scribe, paying a farthing or a halfpenny in the pound on their sales. The subscribing societies would be members of the Cooperative Press, which would be, like any other cooperative, run by the members and their elected officials. That was how the cooperative movement acquired the means to buy and to run *Reynolds*.

It was founded by George Reynolds in the middle of the nineteenth century. He was diplomatic correspondent of the *Sunday Despatch*, but often his contributions were suppressed. So he started his own paper. It reflected the emerging revolt against the poverty and inequalities of Victorian England. It was banned in the army and navy. Its criticism of Queen Victoria and the monarchy was as sharp as any in the reign of Elizabeth II. It fell on bad times in the early years of the next century, but its progressive reputation remained.

As a cooperative Sunday it began life in the ramshackle building off Fleet Street where I first met Sydney Elliot. But soon, the Cooperative Press transferred the paper to a new building, with new machinery, in Grays Inn Road. Sydney was a brilliant editor. He had worked as secretary to John Wheatley, a Clydesider, who gave his name to the houses built by the Labour government after World War I. Sydney told how, when he reported on the comments of the morning newspapers, Wheatley used to say, 'If there are no attacks, we can't be doing our job.'

One of the first articles to appear under my by-line described a visit to Harworth colliery in Nottinghamshire, where the battle between the Miners Federation and the breakaway Spencer Union was coming to a head. The Nottingham miners had broken from the federation after their defeat in the General Strike, and set up their own association under Spencer, a former Labour MP.

Initial finance came from the National Union of Seamen, which was then under extreme right-wing leadership. The breakaway was a company union. Houses, shops and much else were owned and controlled by the coal owners. Despite persecution and victimisation the miners at Harworth pit, a

41

small group led by Mick Kane, formed a branch of the genuine union until it was strong enough to call a strike.

At the time of my visit, after 20 weeks strike, I wrote, 'There was to be a ballot on whether to call a national strike in their support. I found a miniature police state. The children were stopped on the way to the shops. The police would ask, "What's your father doing?" If the child said, "On strike," he was turned back. Their struggle sparked the revolt against the company's dictatorship and the demand for a return to the genuine union.'

Reading that article after 50 years, I was pleasantly surprised to see how it summed up basic trade union principles, for I was a newcomer to the field. I wrote, 'Those who support the Spencer Union spoke to me of high wages, contentment in the coalfield, absence of friction with the employers which reminded me irresistibly of the talk I had heard in Germany in praise of nazism.

'It may be an achievement to live for a decade without a strike, but there can be no free trade unionism if occasions never arise in which the interests of employer and worker are in conflict. The menace in Nottingham is the existence of a system which allows an industry to operate without effective trade union checks, gives dictatorial powers to the employer, and denies the right of free association in defence of elementary human rights.'

I described the spy organisation throughout the coalfield. 'Men know that every word in the welfare row, the public house or the street may be overheard and if hostile to the union or the company, is reported. The informer and the agent provocateur are part of the colliery machine. So there hangs everywhere a cloud of suspicion and hatred.'

I reported how the wife of a miner spoke at a meeting of the Labour Women's Guild at the village hall. Next morning her husband was called to the office and warned if he did not keep his wife quiet 'strong action' would be taken. A miner said on a bus that the Spencer Union was 'no good'. Within a few hours he was sent for and reprimanded.

I added, 'Behind the dictatorship is not only the threat of

unemployment but the power to deprive victims of their homes. To leave a job means to leave the village, so strong is the stranglehold on housing which the company possess.

'A man will be sacked on Friday, an eviction order obtained on the following Monday and the bailiffs sent in a week later. His relatives and friends, by the terms of their agreement, are forbidden to give him shelter. If he is a "federation" man, known to the employers as a "trouble maker" he can tramp the county without finding work.'

I finished by saying that the struggle of the men of Harworth for the right of free association must be the concern of the whole trade union movement. Eventually, Nottingham rejoined the rest of the coalfield. The Seamen's Union, which had been expelled from the TUC also returned to the fold.

I learned then that the unity of the working class movement is its strength; there is no future in breakaways. Fifty years later, after the strike of the miners against the decimation of their industry by the wholesale closure of pits, Nottinghamshire again broke away.

The by-line on my Harworth story was H G Schaffer. The feature editor (some time later) was laying out a page. He said, 'I want a longer by-line. What's your first name?' I said, 'Herbert.' 'I don't like that, haven't you got another one?' he said. 'Yes, Gordon,' I replied. Up to that time, I had been 'Bert' at home, and from school onwards 'Schaff'. Now I was Gordon and have been ever since.

It was a thrilling experience to be able to play a part in a struggle in which I passionately believed. I understood how George Reynolds must have felt when he started his own paper.

I attended my first TUC at Norwich in 1937. Ernest Bevin was president and he proudly proclaimed that the trade union movement 'was an integral part of the State'. That conception was broadly adhered to, until it was shattered by Margaret Thatcher 50 years later.

They were crowded years. The struggle of Republican Spain against Franco, the rebel general backed by Hitler and Mussolini, was in the forefront. The Spanish trade union leaders came to Britain to plead with the TUC for help. They got a dusty answer. Britain was a party to a non-intervention agreement which meant giving the fascist powers, who blithely ignored it, a free hand. I interviewed the Spaniards, but they were precluded from making propaganda as a condition of entry to the country. I date-lined my story 'Paris'.

The struggle to repudiate non-intervention was bitter. At one Labour party conference, Ellen Wilkinson (Labour MP for Jarrow who wrote *The Town That Was Murdered* by unemployment) promised to sit on the steps of Downing Street until government policy changed.

Isabel Brown, a leading member of the communist party and a powerful orator, raised hundreds of thousands of pounds for Spanish relief. The support for the Spanish government, legally elected, and by no means communist, was tremendous. I recall one meeting at the Albert Hall, which was packed. Touts were offering tickets at black market prices. Isabel warned, 'If the lights of freedom go out over Madrid; they will go out all over Europe.' I knew in my heart she was right.

One story I must tell about Isabel. When the miners were fighting alone after their defeat in the collapse of the General Strike in 1926, she made a speech comparing the baby just born to the royal family (later Queen Elizabeth) with miners' wives short of food or shelter for their babies. She was charged with sedition and given a short prison sentence.

I helped to set up the Spanish news service. The aim was to supply the media with news from the Republican side. We were objective, whether the news was good or bad. We were treated with respect and much of our material was used. As a result of this connection I was invited to visit the republic.

The foreign editor, Bill Biss, was not happy about the idea and tried to stop me. He said I would not get any more information than the correspondents already out there. But Sydney Elliot backed me. We got held up at Perpignan at the French frontier, but finally reached Barcelona. There I realised the hardship, the only food we had was bread and tomatoes. One night we were bombed, so I always told people I was bombed by Hitler in Barcelona before I was bombed by Hitler in London.

I was determined to get my story to prove that it was a worthwhile journey. I waylaid the foreign secretary, Alvarez del Vayo. He gave me an appointment for the following day but could not keep it saying, 'I am sorry I have to go to the front, I will have to see you some other time.'

I doubted whether I could wait for him to come back from the front and I was determined to get my story. I took hold of his shoulder and said, 'The people in Britain think you are defeated.' He took me by the arm and said come along, and gave me the interview.

I realised that I was talking to a man in agony. He knew he was fighting a just cause, he was fighting an evil and his country was striving for many of the things we in Britain and other democratic countries take for granted. I realised then, and still believe, that fascism is not a matter of a brown shirt or a black shirt – a Mussolini, a Hitler or a Franco – it is the system which uses democracy to destroy democracy in order to preserve power and privilege.

I got my story and had to get back to London. I divided my soap, which was like gold, between my two women interpreters and managed to secure a lift on a government lorry going to Perpignan. On the way we were followed but not bombed by a nazi plane. On this journey with me was a Spanish government official who eased my way through the controls. I got to Perpignan. The picture of the restaurants and markets flooded with goods after the poverty of Spain made me realise what sacrifices the Spanish people were making in their brave effort to preserve their freedom. I got on the train, very tired, needing a sleep. I sought out the stewardess. I must have looked a wreck. She looked at me and said, *'Gardez votre argent, mon pauvre petit'* (Look after your money, you poor little one). Her sympathy was practical because she put me in a bunk and didn't charge me. So I got to Paris, and from Paris to home.

Millions throughout the world understood the danger of

fascism as I am afraid they do not today. The International Brigade was symbolic, it was composed of volunteers from all over the world, from German anti-fascists, from France, from America and from Britain. The British force was visited by Clement Attlee, who later became prime minister. He gave his name to the Attlee Brigade.

Everyone expected Madrid to fall. Willy Forest, the *Daily Express* correspondent, sent a message to his paper saying that Madrid would not fall. They spiked his message because they did not believe it. But Madrid did not fall. There was a marvellous moment when marching through the streets of the city came the International Brigade. Franco had said that he had four columns advancing on Madrid and a fifth column inside. That is where the phrase originated. But Madrid stood firm.

Many of our best young men paid with their lives for Spain. There was novelist Ralph Fox, David Guest, one of the best theoreticians of the movement, and John Cornford. And all the time the role of the British was perfidious; they succeeded in getting Leon Blum, the Socialist Prime Minister of France, to agree to non-intervention and some of the hypocrisy was unbelievable.

Duff Cooper, who was in charge of the admiralty, actually admitted in the House of Commons that the British naval vessels allowed men to drown because, he said, 'If they went into coastal waters to rescue them there would be a breach of non-intervention.' Then there was an epic story of Potato Jones, the owner of a merchant ship, who ran the blockade in order to take supplies to the beleaguered Republic.

It was in the campaign for Spain that I started public speaking. I realised that I had some gift in that direction but it took me a long while to get used to it. I used to think that if I stopped everyone would walk out, but I found that you could stop, have a sip of water, and they still stayed. I realised too that if you finished on a good note, a good peroration, it did not matter whether there had been bad moments in your speech, you won an applause. Very soon I was speaking at a number of organisations.

In those days the cooperative movement was far more active than it is today. Many of the cooperative societies had education and political committees. They held public meetings, symposiums, weekend schools, and so on. And I was invited all the time. *Reynolds* had given me the opportunity to secure this platform.

In my first year with *Reynolds* I was elected delegate to the NUJ annual delegate meeting. There I moved the resolution condemning the Official Secrets Act. This was the one which had a catch-all so that anything you said about a public department was deemed to be an official secret. In the resolution which was passed we put on record that 'the tradition of honour of the profession was not to reveal sources of information.' That is still the policy of my union.

Spain was the international backcloth but there were many events going on at home. The 1930s was a time of distressed areas, poverty and unemployment. The industrial correspondents group did a lot of investigation at the time. On one occasion, we went for a tour of the derelict areas of the north.

There were very few press officers in those days but Sam Challoner, the press officer who was with us, took the view that his job was to show us the truth and leave us to do the reporting. We went to some of the derelict villages in the north and they treated us guests very well.

At lunch a pompous person sat next to me and said, 'Don't you weep any tears about those villages. I tell you every week, bags full of football coupons come out from their homes. I tell you this,' he went on, 'they are so lazy that when they go to the lavatory they are too lazy to pull the chain.' I said, 'Judging by some of the hovels I've seen they haven't any chains to pull.'

I went to a training centre and there was a man laying bricks. He was training to be a bricklayer and he stood back, looked at his work and said, 'Not much of a job, this is skilled work.' I said, 'What were you before you came here?' He said, 'I was a miner.' I said, 'Good God man, you hew coal out of the bowels of the earth and you don't realise your skill?' It was frightening.

I found other cases. Even the correspondents of the right-wing papers wrote the most devastating reports. I finished my report by saying, 'The clever people tell me that these things are inevitable. All I can say is, if they are inevitable the sooner we pull down the system which permits it and rebuild the better.'

Sam Challoner got into trouble because the powers-that-be thought a press officer should publicise his department, and Sam said his job was to give the press the opportunity to tell the truth.

We made similar visits to south Wales. It was the same story. I found villages where no one was at work, and the only money coming in was from the girls who were employed in what they called in those days 'good service'.

I wrote a pamphlet about these experiences. The theme was 'Never again'. It was called, *Who Owns Britain*. It showed the background to the creation of the distressed areas and the unemployment of the day. It sold 120,000 copies, made possible by *Reynolds* circulation system, and the fact that we could sell them for 2d. If you sell 5,000 of a pamphlet today it is very good indeed.

I made many friends during this time, among them was Bert Papworth. I first met him when he was leading a London busmen's strike. This was the time of the coronation of George VI. Some cynics said that it was to get the buses off the streets because of the crowds who were celebrating the coronation. But the busmen had a real grievance, they were forced to work split turns which meant they had a period in the morning, then a few hours off, and then back again at work. There was evidence that their health was suffering because of the fumes from the buses.

So the bus section of the T&GWU called a strike. Under the rules of the union the executive gave the busmen's section plenary powers to run the strike. Ernest Bevin was secretary of the union and he made a powerful case before an enquiry about the justice of the busmen's demands, but later he did a deal over the heads of the bus section and withdrew the plenary powers.

The busmen's leaders were furious. Some of them secured the support of Bill Brown, secretary of the Civil Service Clerical Association, in assisting them in setting up a separate busmens' union. Bert Papworth remained with the T&GWU.

The separate section did not last. Once again it reinforced the lesson I learned that disunity never achieves anything. Bevin was furious because I recorded the anger of the busmen's leaders and he attacked me publicly at a union dinner. Sydney Elliot stood by me. Later on I got on quite friendly terms with Bevin, but more of that later.

The 1995 Tory government, with its insensate hatred of all forms of public ownership, is intent on splitting London Transport into separate parts. No one in the Tory government apparently remembers that the 1931 Tory government adopted the Labour government's bill setting up London Transport because of the chaos that reigned previously. Different bus owners (pirates as we called them) competed with others picking up passengers on the best routes, leaving the unprofitable ones to the original bus company or letting them die. The Tories' present policy will have the same result and deterioration in the standards of the staff.

7

Riches and Poverty

A unique development in those years, dominated by the Spanish war and the shadow of world war, was the mushroom growth of the Left Book Club. Gollancz, the publishers, introduced a scheme under which subscribers guaranteed to buy a book a month at 2s 6d a time. The selection of authors, labour, communist, liberal and experts in various fields, represented the broad popular front that was taking shape. Membership grew at a phenomenal rate and Left Book Club groups sprang up all over the country. The club called a meeting at the Albert Hall. Every seat was filled.

The club also published an educational series, covering a wide range of subjects. Victor Gollancz, who apparently had been impressed by my articles in *Reynolds*, invited me to contribute to the series discussing *Riches and Poverty*. The brief was to take a book with the same title written by Leo Chiozza Money, a well-known economist at the beginning of the century, and to see how conditions had changed. It meant a lot of work, but it added to my knowledge and reinforced my socialist convictions.

I began the book saying 'Britain through the rose-coloured glasses of Capitalism is a land in which 47 million people share in any upward trend in trade and industry. It is a land of "small capitalists", of working men who buy their own houses, pour their surplus wealth into various saving schemes and thereby, in the words of Mr J L Garvin, in the

50

Encyclopaedia Britannica, "immensely increase the number of participating investors".'

Some 50 years later, it reads like a definition of Thatcherism. And the conclusions I drew then are little different today. I wrote, 'The real conclusions are inescapable. The great mass of the people of Britain are desperately poor. A vast number earn insufficient to provide the lowest minimum of food necessary for the maintenance of health. Insecurity and privation stalk most of the homes of Britain. Whether it be a time of "prosperity" or one of slump, an overwhelming proportion of the nation's wealth is poured into the lap of a tiny minority of its people.'

As for Chiozza's conclusions in *Progress and Poverty* 30 years earlier, I said, 'He did not have the detailed statistics which have become available, but he found that more than one third of the national income was enjoyed by less than one thirtieth of the population. In these 30 years science has placed untold resources at the disposal of mankind. The capacity to produce wealth has increased a hundred fold. For those who possess the nation's wealth, great liners speed across the seven seas, aeroplanes annihilate distance, a million comforts hitherto undreamed of are at their service. For those who have not, there is but a slight improvement in their conditions since the beginning of the century.'

I pointed out that the improvements in the 'nation of the poor' had been brought about by the trade unions, the cooperative movement and such measures as old age and widows' pensions, health and unemployment insurance, and factory legislation. But that these only ameliorated the situation, and that 'boom or slump, capitalism inexorably insists on luxury for the nation of the rich and insecurity for the vast proportion which makes up the nation of the poor.'

I analysed the evidence that some 300 families were the virtual rulers of Britain. I explained, 'They control private banks, clearing houses, discount companies, finance and investment trusts, oil, food, transport, power, mining and hundreds of industrial concerns. Through their control of credit, they dictate to thousands of smaller enterprises.

'They owe no responsibility to the community. Even their shareholders have no part in determining policy. Their sole duty is the quest of dividends and for these dividends men toil not only in England, but in the remotest parts of the earth.'

I told how the land of Britain had been taken over by the nation of the rich, how the efforts of Lloyd George and Snowden to take back a fraction of the unearned wealth acquired by community developments, had been sabotaged.

I quoted statistics provided by Sir John Boyd-Orr and Seebohm Rowntree showing that millions did not earn enough to maintain adequate nutrition for an average family. I quoted a report by the International Labour Office that 'Large numbers of the working population not only in impoverished or depressed areas but even in the most advanced industrial countries are inadequately nourished' and its conclusion that this was because of 'insufficiency of the means for acquiring the necessary foodstuffs.'

Seebohm Rowntree put forward 'as the only means of solving the problem a minimum wage sufficient for a couple and three children, and no surplus profits to be retained or distributed to shareholders until the adequate minimum wage had been paid to all workers.'

I added a typical comment by Dr Robert Hutchinson, President of the Royal Society of Medicine, that 'diseases due to over-nutrition are increasing while those due to under-nutrition were decreasing!'

I dealt with the inequalities in education, the plight of the unemployed highlighted by Prime Minister Neville Chamberlain's admission that old age pensioners were compelled to live on a sum fixed in 1914, when money was worth almost double, but refusing an investigation into the possibility of raising it.

I concluded, 'Fascism is possible in Britain, not because the men who control the economic system hate democracy, not because in the main, they are not honestly anxious to improve the lot of their fellow countrymen, but because they have to choose between sweeping changes in their system

52

and a pitiless drive to preserve the privileges which they enjoy.'

I quoted from Tolstoy's pamphlet *To the Working Class of all Nations*. It so beautifully sums up the story I had tried to tell that I cannot resist the temptation to reproduce it here:

> I see mankind as a herd of cattle inside a fenced enclosure. Outside the fence are green pastures and plenty for the cattle to eat. While inside the fence there is not quite grass enough for the cattle. Consequently, the cattle are trampling underfoot what little grass there is and goring each other to death in their struggle for existence.
>
> I saw the owner of the herd come to them and when he saw their pitiable condition, he was filled with compassion for them and thought of all he could do to improve their condition. So he called his friends together and asked them to assist him in cutting grass from outside the fence and throwing it over the fence to the cattle. And that they called Charity.
>
> Then, because the calves were dying off and not growing up into serviceable cattle, he arranged that they should each have a pint of milk every morning for breakfast. Because they were dying off in the cold nights, he put up beautiful, well-drained and well-ventilated cowsheds for the cattle.
>
> Because they were goring each other in the struggle for existence, he put corks on the horns of the cattle, so that the wounds they gave each other might not be serious. Then he reserved a part of the enclosure for the old bulls and the old cows over 70 years of age. In fact, he did everything he could think of to improve the condition of the cattle, and when I asked him why he did not do the one obvious thing, break down the fence and let the cattle out, he answered, 'If I let the cattle out, I should no longer be able to milk them.'

My book was finished in October 1938. I was convinced that the betrayal at Munich had made war inevitable and I was deeply concerned, but I was also anxiously hoping that the book would appear before the war broke out. Such is human nature. It was published in March 1939.

During those immediate pre-war years I became more than ever convinced that the hope of a change to a social system which would at least begin to end poverty and exploitation, must lie with the trade unions and the Labour party, which the trades union created.

They were the inevitable weapon of the organised working class, allied with the cooperative movement representing them as consumers. At the same time the communist party, which seriously taught Marxism and published a fighting paper, the *Daily Worker*, was an important ally in the struggle. The right-wing leaders were more concerned with fighting communists than fascists, but this was not reflected in the rank and file.

8

The War Clouds Gather

As the war clouds gathered, Sydney Elliot – editor of *Reynolds* – took a courageous decision. He launched an appeal on his own initiative for the creation of a peace alliance against the danger of war and the appeasement policy of the government. It would include the Labour and Cooperative parties, the trade unions, the Liberals and communists.

The storm broke as soon as his appeal was published. The official Labour and trade union establishment was still more frightened of cooperating with the communists on the left, or the Liberals on the right, than of the mounting war danger.

The cooperative movement was divided and rather bewildered. But Alf Barnes backed the appeal and within the Cooperative party, and in the country, there was a spontaneous upsurge of support.

So much so that at the Easter conference of the Cooperative party in 1938, after an epic duel between Alf Barnes and A V Alexander, *Reynolds*'s peace alliance won the day.

But the Cooperative party was subordinate to the Cooperative congress and, in the interval between Easter, when the Cooperative party was held, and Whitsun, when the Cooperative congress met, there was a raging campaign to discredit the peace alliance. Congress defeated it by a two-to-one majority.

When the Cooperative party met the following year, Easter 1939, the war clouds were even darker and some delegates made an attempt to revise the decision to go back to the original endorsement of the peace alliance.

That conference opened with the announcement that Mussolini, the Italian *duce*, had invaded Albania. I cannot resist inserting here a remark made by Maisky, the Soviet ambassador, when he heard the news. He said, 'I see Hitler is leading from deuce.' Bridge players will understand the pun.

A resolution was moved referring to the grave international situation and the danger of world war. It instructed the Cooperative party 'to approach Labour with a view to entering an agreement with other progressive organisations opposed to the national government, whereby support will be given to agreed candidates in establishing in constituencies where only the combined progressive vote could defeat the national government along the lines of the peace alliance advocated by *Reynolds*.'

Mr D Wilson from Renfrew, Scotland, told the delegates, 'We believe that Mr Chamberlain and his government not only support fascism, but before long would be found with the possibility of fascism in this country.' Mr Dierman from Glasgow retorted, 'You passed a resolution a year ago adopting the peace alliance. It did not frighten Mr Chamberlain, all that resulted was a schism in our forces.'

Another delegate listed the drift to war – Spain, Austria and Czechoslovakia – but the debate was much more concerned with the electoral tactic of defeating the national government rather than the looming danger of war. But J Feeney, of Nottingham, who had fought in the International Brigade, said that there was an organised conspiracy in Transport House (the headquarters of the Labour party) to smother the rank and file support for the policy. The two main protagonists, Alfred Barnes for the peace alliance and A V Alexander, who was bitterly opposed, faced each other in the final debate. Alexander, who was also speaking for the national committee, said, 'We are convinced that the united peace alliance instead of being an electoral support is an electoral liability.'

Alexander went further, he showed how his bitter hostility

to the Soviet Union and to the communist party was his main motive. He said, *'Reynolds'*s articles were not a brilliant method of defeating the national government but had been borrowed from the communist international. It would split our movement from top to bottom.'

Alf Barnes said, 'When you move into the vortex of foreign affairs not a single man or woman knows what will come of it.' And he referred to the position Britain would be in if it was called upon to defend the frontiers of Poland. That was a prophetic reference. Again the peace alliance was defeated. Had the Labour leadership backed the peace alliance history might have been different. At one time it looked as if the Labour party might follow suit.

I was in the whips' room at the House of Commons. A Labour MP came in. 'I'm speaking this weekend,' he said. 'What's our line now on the popular front?' 'We're still agin' it,' was the reply.

Stafford Cripps launched a similar project as a member of the Labour party executive. And he circulated an appeal to constituency parties. That was judged to be a crime and, at the party conference of 1938, he was expelled together with Aneurin Bevan and George Strauss. George Brown, who later resigned in a huff from Harold Wilson's cabinet and later left the party, made a vicious speech supporting the expulsion, claiming to speak for the workers against rich men, like Cripps, infiltrating the party.

Cripps at a press conference angrily replied. He said something to the effect that they accused him of being rich, but were only too ready to take his money. I felt he had missed the opportunity to warn that the conference had evaded the real issue, that he was trying to pull back from the brink of war. But his anger was understandable. Bevan and Strauss ate humble pie and successfully applied to rejoin the party. Cripps remained outside until after the war, when the party pleaded with him to rejoin and take a post in the Labour government.

Looking back on those fateful years, as the plan of the Chamberlain government for an alliance with the fascist

57

dictators was more and more apparent, it is hard to understand the stubborn resistance to the *Reynolds*'s peace alliance and the Cripps plan for a popular front.

Those of us who were convinced that Chamberlain's appeasement policy was leading to war, watched the progress of events almost like a Greek tragedy. Others, of course, were deceived by Lord Beaverbrook's *Daily Express* which declared 'There will be no war this year or next,' and there were others whose sympathies with fascism led them to support Chamberlain's policy, whatever the consequences.

Seven months before the Munich Agreement Chamberlain had sacked Anthony Eden, and *Reynolds* recorded how Eden resigned, or was forced to resign, and in doing so, warned that Chamberlain's attempt to make agreements with the aggressors was bound to fail. Eden said, 'Agreements which are worthwhile are never made on the basis of a threat,' and his under-secretary, Lord Cranbourne, said the British government was yielding to blackmail.

We recorded how Chamberlain virtually admitted that his decision to sack Eden was influenced by an anonymous call warning him if he did not sack Eden he would incur the wrath of the dictators. Chamberlain admitted in the House of Commons on February 28th, 1938, that he could only guess at the identity of the friend who gave him this warning.

We recorded how Lennox Boyd, a junior minister, who was an open supporter of the organisation backing Franco in Spain, had said publicly, 'I do not think Mr Chamberlain would make a move to guarantee the frontiers of Czechoslovakia. Germany could absorb Czechoslovakia and Britain would remain safe and secure.' Chamberlain echoed that sentiment when, at the time of Munich, he said that Czechoslovakia was a 'far away land of which we knew nothing'.

In May of that year Austria was absorbed and Ward Price of the *Daily Mail* boasted how he rode with Hitler in his triumphal march through Austria.

Another incident which we recorded was how Chamberlain gave an interview, not to the British press but to Americans and Canadian reporters. He talked to these journalists at the home of Lady Astor, the headquarters of the pro-nazi Cliveden set. A remark by Lady Astor subsequently compelled her to make an explanation to the House otherwise the source of the interview, which was widely published in North America, would never have been known. This was how the *Montreal Star* interpreted the prime minister, 'Nothing seems clearer then that the British do not expect to fight for Czechoslovakia and do not anticipate that France or Russia will either. That being so then the Czechs must accede to the German demands if reasonable.' That was clearly a quote from the British prime minister.

Referring to this interview, Archibald Sinclair, in those days leader of the Liberal party, asked in the House, 'What would it matter if the demands were reasonable or were not, the Czechs will have to submit anyway.' Here is another quote from the interview with the American and Canadian journalists, 'This brings us to the question of a four power pact, the British prefer to label it something else because a four power pact might signify to some a dictators' committee to dictate to the rest of Europe. Soviet Russia is excluded on the grounds that it does not work well in harness.'

In the April prior to Munich Chamberlain had signed the treaty with Mussolini's Italy which sparked off Eden's dismissal, and once again *Reynolds* revealed the fact that Mussolini had promised Chamberlain a swift victory for Franco in Spain, and that he had refused to continue negotiating with France because France was in sympathy with the Spanish republic.

The agreement was to come into force when a settlement was reached in Spain. On May 3rd Hitler visited Mussolini, and from then onwards the Italian reinforcements were pouring in to support Franco in Spain while the Italian aeroplanes bombed British ships.

Just before the summer adjournment, Chamberlain attacked British shipowners who took food and other supplies to Spain 'because they made high profits', and he announced that Franco had promised to pay compensation for bombed British ships, obviously aware of the anger among the MPs. But the Foreign Office very shortly after had to deny the statement. It was clear that if Chamberlain had not deliberately deceived the House he had at least misinformed it.

Earlier we had revealed that Ribbentrop, the German Ambassador, was warned by both Chamberlain and Halifax that German intervention in Austria would destroy any hope of an Anglo-Italian rapprochement. Within 24 hours of that statement Hitler annexed Austria, but Chamberlain still went ahead with his appeasement plans with Italy.

On April 10th *Reynolds* published a programme which was drawn up at a meeting, again at Cliveden, attended by Chamberlain and Sir Thomas Inskip, the Attorney General. We quoted these main points: 'British support for France was to be dependent on commitments endorsed by Britain.' In other words, France would be forbidden to honour her pact with the Soviet Union to come to the defence of Czechoslovakia.

During Sydney Elliot's holiday I wrote the leaders, and what a joy to work on a paper with a policy you believed in. In August 14th, 1938, under the heading 'Fawning on Franco', I wrote this indictment. 'Since Mr Chamberlain threw overboard his Foreign Secretary at the request of his friends in Berlin and Rome, Britain has become accustomed to snubs from the fascist dictators.

'It is now no longer a matter of surprise that Britain should be treated with equal contempt in Rome, Berlin, Tokyo and Burgos (rebel-held Spain), and that the Union Jack in Mediterranean waters should be not a protection, but an invitation to attack.'

On August 7th I wrote about the Japanese attack on the Soviet frontier, 'The anti-Comintern Pact may look to a Japanese diversion in the East in order to prepare the way for a German assault on Czechoslovakia and the attempted realisation of Hitler's dream of a nazi Ukraine. Such is the final anarchy born seven years ago when Sir John Simon, delegate of the British "National" government, appeared at Geneva to defend Japan's annexation of Manchuria.'

So we watched the bastions falling one by one until the finale at Munich. Until then, *Reynolds* was not a lone voice in opposing Chamberlain's appeasement of the dictators and the drift to war. The *News Chronicle* and the *Daily Herald* were also critical.

The *Daily Worker* was in the forefront, but it did not have the same influence in the wider movement. *Reynolds* was the most outspoken. But when Chamberlain came back from Munich with his piece of paper proclaiming peace for our time, apart from the *Daily Worker*, we stood alone in proclaiming that the prime minister had brought not peace but the imminent threat of war.

The Spanish Civil War was always in the foreground, but we in *Reynolds* were trying all the time to warn that Spain was the first act in the nazi plan for world conquest. We exposed the Cliveden set, the group of pro-nazis, centred round Lady Astor, with links with Ribbentrop, the German Ambassador. It included Lindbergh, hero of the first direct flight from America to Paris, an admirer of the nazi regime who came to Britain with frightening stories of their vast air power.

We told how, in November 1937, Chamberlain sent Lord Halifax, the British Foreign secretary, on an appeasement visit to Germany. The pretext was an international hunting exhibition. He met Hitler, Goering and Goebbels, spending the first five hours of the talks alone with Hitler.

All that was said officially was that the visit had been valuable 'in furthering the desire felt in both countries for mutual understanding'. The news leaked out that in return for a free hand to annex Austria and Czechoslovakia, Germany would postpone discussion on the return of the colonies taken from her after the 1914–18 war for six years while it had a free hand in Eastern Europe.

Chamberlain was bent on following up talks with Mussolini. Anthony Eden, foreign secretary, protested that Italy must first fulfil its earlier pledges, including non-intervention in Spain. The German press launched a violent attack on him. Chamberlain accepted Eden's resignation in order to begin talks with Mussolini. The *Manchester Guardian* commented, 'European and American democracies interpret Mr Eden's resignation as a surrender to the dictatorships.'

Halifax told Hitler that he and other members of the British government were fully aware not only that the Fuehrer had achieved a great deal inside Germany, but that by destroying communism in his country he had barred its road to Western Europe and that Germany, therefore, could rightly be regarded as the bulwark of the West against bolshevism. Chamberlain believed it should be quite possible to find solutions by an open exchange of opinions.

That was after details of the nazi terror had been published. The world knew of the atrocities in the concentration camps when Germany intervened in Spain. But all this was far from the minds of the statesmen who were then discussing the situation. Hitler, during that conversation, talked about the 'prejudiced attitude towards the colonial question, arguing that it came entirely from the fact that it was well understood that America and Russia should possess great territories, that England should rule one quarter of the world, that France should have a colonial empire, and that Japan should at least not be prevented from expanding. It was also understood that little countries like Portugal and Spain should have colonies, only Germany was told that under no circumstances should she have colonies.'

In a conversation on March 3rd, 1938, between Hitler and Henderson, the British Ambassador, it is recorded in the archives that the latter pointed to a map and replied that the British government envisaged a system with principles similar to the Berlin Agreement of 1885, when the colonies in this region of Africa would be redistributed, and Germany would be considered in this redistribution and would therefore have a colonial possession under her sovereignty. At that point Hitler demanded Germany's former colonies be restored; that was the condition for Germany's cooperation in the new colonial regime.

There is a revealing record of a conversation between Bonnet, the French Foreign Minister and the Polish Ambassador in Paris, in which he said, 'The French government wanted to rely entirely on Poland and to cooperate with her, and Monsieur Bonnet would be very pleased after elucidating the question of collaborating with Poland, if he could tell the Soviets that France does not need their assistance.'

This was virtually a repudiation of the France–Soviet Pact. Then he went on to say, 'However, the positive side of the France–Soviet pact should not be overlooked. In the event of war with Germany the pact would serve as a basis for demanding of Moscow such assistance in the form of material and raw materials as might be needed. In certain circumstances Poland might utilise the pact to her advantage.' That is interesting because it explains why when there were conversations between the British mission and Moscow; the British said that they had no authority to agree to the Soviet Union taking the possible war against Germany on to Polish soil. The suggestion was that Moscow would be looked to for supplies but not for a military pact.

In the record of the discussions of the actual Munich meeting Chamberlain very mildly said that since the Czechs were being asked to make all these changes and concessions, it would be useful if one of them could be present at the discussions, but Hitler just brushed that on one side and got a meek agreement.

In the record published by the Soviet Union is a report made by Dr Hubert Masaryk of his arrival in Munich at 4 am on September 30th. He describes how when he arrived in Munich he was taken by police car and accompanied by members of the gestapo to the hotel Regina where the British delegate was staying. The conference was in progress, it was difficult to establish any contact with leading members of either the British or French delegations, and when he called by telephone he was told by a British official, Ashton-Gwatkin, that a plan (details of which could not be given to him) was already completed, and that it was much harsher than the Anglo-French proposals.

Gwatkin said that the conference would end at the latest the following day, and up until then only Czechoslovakia had been discussed. Gwatkin told Masaryk that he did not seem to realise how difficult the situation was for the Western powers, or how awkward it was to negotiate with Hitler. After saying this Gwatkin returned to the conference. At 10 pm that night, Masaryk was taken to see Sir Horace Wilson, Chamberlain's adviser, and Sir Horace told him the main lines of the new plan and handed him the map. Masaryk said, 'To my objection he replied twice with absolute formality that he had nothing to add to his statements. He paid no attention to what we said about places and areas of greatest importance to us.' At 1.30 am Czech delegates met Chamberlain, Daladier, Sir Horace Wilson, and Gwatkin. Masaryk's report stated, 'Mr Chamberlain's short introduction referred to the agreement and gave the text to be read out. Chamberlain showed no interest . . .'

There is a lot of talk today how the whole country believed Chamberlain when he came back from Munich, waving his piece of paper at the airport saying that it was 'peace for our time.'

In fact that had been his third visit. When he first went to talk to Hitler, British people on the side of Czechoslovakia stood packed in Whitehall shouting 'Stand by the Czechs.' I was there. Meanwhile the manoeuvres went on, digging trenches in Hyde Park, and evacuating children into the countryside, so that when he came back the third time most of the people fell for it.

The *Daily Worker* was alone on that Saturday, denouncing the agreement. In those days there was no television, but radio and newspapers followed the official line. I am very proud to have been a member of the staff of *Reynolds* on that Saturday after Munich.

My own article ran 'Peace or Surrender to Aggressors' Blackmail'. Sydney Elliot's leader under the heading 'Democracy in Danger' warned, 'As the history of the next few months will prove, a terrible price must be paid for the deliberate betrayal of the cause of collective peace. The price is being paid at this moment by Czechoslovakia, soon it will be paid by the men and women of Great Britain and by civilisation.'

H N Brailsford, one of the best known Labour publicists who had, through the columns of *Reynolds*, helped recruit for the International Brigade, wrote under the heading 'Why Britain Surrendered' that 'The Czechs will assess at its true value the signatures of the two dictators who raped Austria and Abyssinia, and the two democracies which deserted them after a pilgrimage to Bechtesgarden.'

He added, 'It was an Anglo-French plan of surrender that Mr Chamberlain and Daladier [prime minister of France] imposed on Prague, and neither of them thought about asking Moscow whether it consented to this capitulation.' Brailsford added, 'The Western General Staff has kept in touch but no one ever troubled to enquire what the Red Army was doing and was prepared to do.'

Reynolds carried a half page story of the economic resources which the Munich agreement had handed to Hitler, and on its back page was a picture of the Czech cavalry withdrawing under the heading 'Retreat with Honour'. There was also a picture of the demonstration in Whitehall calling for support for the Czechs, and another picture of the nazis beginning their occupation of the Sudetenland.

The front page news story told how Duff Cooper had resigned in protest at what he considered a surrender to the dictators. On the front page too was a story of how the League of Nations proposed to have a meeting at the Albert Hall to support Czechoslovakia and how it was informed it could not have the Hall unless there was a promise that no attack would be made on the government. The League of Nations Union refused to accept the condition, and they could not get another venue.

On a news page *Reynolds* faithfully reported the greetings that were given to Chamberlain, how there was a proposal from Sweden that he should receive the Nobel Peace Prize, how a little girl tripped up the steps of Downing Street to give Mrs Chamberlain a bouquet. The crowd outside shouted good old Neville and well done Chamberlain, and greetings were received at Downing Street from the Archbishop of Canterbury, the Lord Mayor of London, the City of Birmingham (from which Chamberlain came) and so on. This was the theme of the rest of the press. *Reynolds* stood alone and history proved we were right.

After we put the paper to bed that Saturday evening, Allen Hutt and I went to his flat nearby in order to write a pamphlet telling the whole story of betrayal. George Darling, the librarian, had gathered together all the cuttings for us. George subsequently became a member of the first post-war Labour government and finished up in the House of Lords. Allen and I worked virtually for three days with snatches of sleep and lashings of coffee. We told the whole story of the betrayal. It was a red-hot piece of work. It was the kind of story that you could never do afterwards because it would take months of research to put it all together.

We told how step by step the betrayal had been prepared. We told of the machinations of the Cliveden set. How influential circles in the City of London backed the dictators. How Runciman, the same Runciman who figured in the Post Office scare, was officially sent to find a peace settlement in Czechoslovakia but in effect to pressurise the Czechs into surrender. We told how at Geneva, Litvinov, the Soviet Foreign Minister, had proposed resisting nazi aggression and how he was spurned. We described the role of Sir Horace Wilson who was the man behind the scenes in Chamberlain's policies, and told how he was specially dispatched to Berlin to beg Hitler not to make things too hard for Mr Chamberlain while pledging that the Anglo-French Plan to dismember Czechoslovakia would be carried through with all reasonable speed.

We recorded the heart breaking reply by the Czech government to the first Anglo-French demands. 'The proposals go far beyond what we agreed on in the so-called Anglo-French Plan. They deprive us of every safeguard for our national existence. We are to yield up large portions of our carefully prepared defences and admit the German armies deep into our country before we've been able to organise it on the new basis or make any preparations for defence.

'Our national and economic independence will automatically disappear with the acceptance of Herr Hitler's plan. The whole process of moving the population is to be reduced to panic flight on the part of those who would not accept the German nazi regime. We rely upon the two great western democracies, whose wishes we've followed much against our own judgement, to stand by us in our hour of need.'

We recorded the futile protests of the Labour Party Executive and the TUC. I wrote the concluding paragraphs, 'The dictators bestride Europe. Unable to wage effective war until the diplomatic defeat of the democracies, they prepare to march forward to a point where they can back their challenge with real force.'

I continued,

> Vast new territories, economic resources essential to war are at their command. Britain's economy and standard of living are imperilled. Britain's ally, France, is gravely weakened. The Soviet Union, whose strength was at the service of democracy during the days of crisis, has been insulted and ignored. In every land the peoples, whose one desire is peace, watch fearfully for the moment when the armed truce will break into war.
>
> This is the end of a policy which, rejecting the principles on which British defence has traditionally been based, relies on a precarious friendship with avowed aggressors and treaty-breakers. The rule of law through the League of Nations has been repudiated, though the League's policy was endorsed through the peace ballot by the greatest democratic vote ever recorded in this country.
>
> This collective peace system which wielded a barrier against aggression while providing for the settlement of grievances, stood in the path of the dictators. Their ally in their work of destruction was the Prime Minister of

Great Britain. Mr Chamberlain assumes personal responsibility for this peace.

His plea, the only plea now seriously put forward, is
that the sole alternative was war. The facts afford him
no justification. Indeed, they support the charge that
both peace and democracy have been betrayed. Drawing the necessary conclusions may the British people,
who treasure their democracy, act swiftly and act
together.

May I add a footnote to this tragic story. Arthur Greenwood,
who was leading the Labour party in the absence of Attlee,
went with Hugh Dalton to see Chamberlain. Arthur, who
had become a very dear friend of mine, told me how he
asked at this interview, 'Mr Prime Minister, how do you
know this is Hitler's last territorial demand in Europe?'
Chamberlain stood up and said: 'But Herr Hitler told me so
personally.'

Sir Basil Liddell Hart in his book on the history of the
Second World War recalls what we suspected at the time:
that Hitler was convinced Britain would not oppose him
when he invaded the Soviet Union. Sir Basil wrote:

The escape of the British expeditionary force in 1940 was
largely due to Hitler's personal intervention. After his
tanks had overrun the North of France and cut the
British army from its base, Hitler held them up just as
they were about to sweep into Dunkirk which was the
last remaining port of escape left open to the British.
That meant that the bulk of the British Expeditionary
Force was still many miles distant from the port but
Hitler kept his tanks halted for three days. This action
preserved the British force when nothing else could
have saved them. Hitler, still thinking that Britain would
become an ally in his war against Russia.

In 1948, the Soviet Union published the archives of the
immediate period before Munich and the Munich Agreement
itself. It is a revealing picture: it shows quite clearly that the

policy of the Chamberlain government was to secure a four power pact against the Soviet Union, and that the German pressure was for colonies. The idea that the colonies could secure their freedom was completely absent from their minds.

9

Treasured Friendships

That Munich weekend was only 18 months since I had left my ivory tower at the PA. Looking back on those eventful months my abiding memory is of the comradeship of the progressive movement handed to me in full measure.

Perhaps I should list here some of the friends I made. There was Arthur Greenwood, one of the brains of the Labour party. He was the son of a Leeds painter and decorator, he won scholarships to the secondary school and Leeds University. He entered the Labour party through the Fabians and the Workers' Education Authority.

He took a degree in science and then switched to economics and political sciences. He taught for a time at an elementary school in Leeds but then became a university lecturer in economics. There he joined a strike for better wages and defied every university rule by speaking at open air meetings in favour of the strikers.

Parliamentary secretary to the Minister of Health John Wheatley in the 1923–24 Labour government, he was the first defeated minister to come back after the 1931 debacle when he won a by-election at Wakefield. Arthur regularly appears in my story.

Then there was Ebby Edwards whom I met through the National Council of Labour Colleges. This body differed from the Workers' Education Authority believing that education should offer a background explaining the class struggle. Ebby also comes into my later story, but I will recall here

70

how, after the nationalisation of the mines by the post-war Labour government, he was appointed labour officer to the newly created Coal Board. Ebby was bitter because within the movement some said he had sold out to what they regarded as the class enemy.

Ebby said to me, 'What nonsense, we fight for nationalisation and then, when we have a chance to administer a nationalised industry, we want to prevent our people from taking part in it.' He never liked Will Lawther, the then president of the Mineworkers' Union. He said to me, 'That bugger Lawther, he sits opposite me in the negotiating table. I am supposed to be representing the employers and I have to tell him what to say.'

George Tomlinson started work about the age of 12 in the mill and became Minister of Education in the post-war Labour government. After he retired he was a bitter man and he said to me, 'Gordon, there is one lesson I've learned in a long life in politics: we talk about the class war, the Tories wage it.'

Philip Noel-Baker talked to me many times about the failure of the first post-war Disarmament Conference of 1931–2 when Arthur Henderson, who had been Foreign Secretary in the Labour government, was chairman.

Philip always said that the turning point in world history came when the arms manufacturers sabotaged the hopes of peace at that conference. He told me how the American navy lobby launched an attack which destroyed the conference. He firmly believed that had it succeeded, the subsequent history, including the emergence of Hitler's fascism in Germany, would have been prevented.

Fenner Brockway, who started his struggle for peace in a cell at Dartmoor as a conscientious objector in World War I, ended on the scarlet benches of the House of Lords and never sacrificed a principle. When Harold Wilson asked him to go to the House of Lords he said, 'I'll go to it to help cut its throat.' He used the House of Lords to carry out his peace propaganda.

Fenner in those early years, when I first met him, was

71

busy in the Independent Labour party, and the campaign he constantly waged was against the 'merchants of death', the arms manufacturers who he believed were mainly responsible for the drift to war.

Hugh Dalton was Under-secretary of Foreign Affairs to Arthur Henderson in the 1929–31 government. He had taken the lead in a Labour party inquiry into the distressed areas which did much to awaken public attention to the tragedy of shattered lives which occurred during the years of Tory rule.

When the Labour party won its majority in 1945 everyone expected Dalton to become Foreign Secretary, and in fact, for an hour he *was*. Then the Foreign Office and the King objected to Dalton. Apparently the latter could stand Bevin who came from the working class but since Dalton was born in the purple (in other words came from the upper classes), considered that a betrayal.

The switch was made, Dalton became Chancellor of the Exchequer and Bevin Foreign Secretary. Bevin told me before the election that if they did win, he wanted to be Chancellor. Many things flowed in subsequent years from that decision.

Jack Tanner was President of the Amalgamated Engineering Union. On two occasions he came to my home at Kingston where we sat in the garden writing his presidential speech. Jack was on the left, and in the early days attended the meetings of the Communist International in Moscow. He argued with Lenin about whether the dictatorship of the proletariat meant the ordinary worker or the trained elite. He comes into my story later.

Aneurin Bevan, George Strauss, Ian Mikardo and Barbara Castle formed a left-wing group within the Labour party. I knew and respected them. I wonder whether Barbara remembers sitting in an air raid shelter with me, telling me to the sound of bombs, how she proposed to forge her career in the party beginning as a rank and file delegate to the conference. She did, and I admire her for it.

As political correspondent of *Reynolds* I met Clement Attlee regularly. I must say that I found him much more interested in the parliamentary struggle than the working class struggle, but nevertheless he gave his name to the International Brigade and in an introduction to one of the Left Book Club publications entitled *Road To War* he said, 'The present British [Chamberlain] government always has sympathy for reaction and dislike for what it considers to be left-wing governments. It is therefore hopeless to expect that it will put up a real resistance to fascism because to do so will be to weaken its own position.'

He added that 'The responsibility of all those who desire peace is to work to replace this government by one which really believes in rebuilding the League on a firm foundation of social justice, and which has a home policy in harmony with its international outlook.'

Fellow members of *Reynolds* staff, Allen Hutt, Monica Pearson and Howard Culpin, were all members of the Communist party. Sydney Elliot said, 'If they do their job, if they respect the policy of the paper their political viewpoint does not concern me.' They were very great friends and colleagues.

Then there was Arthur Horner, whose autobiography I ghosted at the end of his life many years later; Rajani Palme Dutt, the theoretician of the party at the time; Robin Page-Arnot with whom I served for many years on the Labour Research Department; Emile Burns, and so on. I was very flattered when I heard that Tom Mann, one of the leaders of the dock strike, had kept a file of my articles which they found after his death.

Some tried to persuade me to join the communist party but I always refused. I was convinced that, whatever its failures, the Labour party, having been created by the trade union movement, must be the vehicle for progress and the building of a new society in Britain.

And I must say too, and my subsequent story will give my reasons, that I would never accept the discipline of the communist party. I did not believe that the leadership was always right, and when I was told I could be a secret member, I said, 'I do not want to belong to a party when I do not have a voice in deciding policy.'

One of the most fascinating characters in this story is Geoffrey Pyke. A tall bearded figure, he came into my office at the height of the Spanish Civil War and asked whether I could spare the time to listen to a scheme which he was putting forward. I was fascinated.

He had the simple idea that if workers could not afford to give money they could give their most precious commodity – work. He formulated the plan that the workers in any given enterprise making goods of value to Spain should go to the boss and say, we are willing to work overtime, you will pay us at overtime rates, we will use that money to buy the goods we produce. We exchange our work for your goods and we send those goods to Spain. He called this organisation Voluntary Industrial Aid for Spain, and it succeeded.

It met with a lot of opposition but various unions, including the engineers union, backed him, and he sent drugs and food. He reconditioned lorries and other goods wanted by the Spanish Republic. He would have sent arms but for the arms embargo imposed by the so-called non-intervention agreement.

I got to know Geoffrey well. He was a fantastic character. In World War I he was a young student and got the idea that it would be valuable if he could find out how far the German people were backing the Kaiser. He decided to find an American sailor who carried a passport and who looked like him. (America was not then in the war.) So he went to Cardiff where the American ships landed and he could meet American sailors in pubs. He went around looking for the right man and nearly got arrested for soliciting! But he found his choice and got his passport and went to Copenhagen, but once he crossed the German frontier he was arrested and taken to a prisoner-of-war camp. He was the first prisoner to escape from Germany in World War I.

He again looked for the simple solution. He watched the sentries as they guarded the barbed-wire and noted there was one point which neither could see and managed to break it down and get out. He then decided people only got caught because they travelled by day and slept by night, so he did everything the other way round. It worked. Thinking he was still on the German side he had in fact got into Holland and was finally repatriated.

Once back in England he decided that the war must be ended by the peace forces, and he financed the *Cambridge Magazine*, a pacifist journal. He spent all his money on it because he decided, although he was the son of a rich lawyer, the money would be no good after the war. He concluded that he would have to earn money and again he sought the simple solution. How do people earn money?

They do not earn money by hard work, they earn it by speculating. So, he speculated in non-ferrous metals and was doing so well that he did not have to go to the Stock Exchange. He went to Switzerland and worked from there. But the big boys decided he was getting dangerous and broke him. That was the end of that venture.

Apparently he managed to retain some money and decided to start a college at Cambridge which was to provide the most advanced education ever. He put full page advertisements in the *Times* recruiting tutors but the venture failed and he lost his money. It was after these adventures that I met him. And later I tell of his most fantastic project – the construction of a battleship of ice during World War II.

10

Call for an Anti-Fascist War

I must go back to that tragic year between the betrayal of Munich and the outbreak of war on September 3rd, 1939.

Chamberlain had championed Hitler's pledge that he had no more territorial demands in Europe. That was broken in Spring 1939 when he marched into Prague and took Czechoslovakia.

Reynolds recorded how that Spring the cabinet made a half-hearted approach to Moscow in the face of this new nazi aggression, which even Chamberlain could not defend. The Russians proposed that all the countries menaced by Hitler's fascism should meet in order to forge combined resistance. Chamberlain said, 'The time wasn't ripe.'

During that summer I went to Zurich where the International Federation of Trades Unions was meeting. There, the British TUC pressed for the Soviet Trades Unions to be sent an invitation to join the Federation. That was resisted by the American Federation of Labour which represented America, instead of the Congress of Industrial Organisations, the fighting section founded by John L Lewis and other leaders.

It was a sad picture I had to paint for the paper. The delegates seemed to be unaware of the approaching tragedy, they were too much concerned with the anti-communism which obsessed the American delegation and which, in the end, prevented any progress being made.

Reynolds maintained, during those summer months, the

pressure for an alliance with the Soviet Union, which was clearly the only hope of preventing war.

Under pressure, Chamberlain pledged to assist Poland if it were attacked. When he was about to make this statement to the House of Commons, Halifax, then Foreign Secretary, called the Soviet Ambassador, Ivan Maisky, to the Foreign Office. He read the government's statement about Poland. Halifax said, 'I assume your government will support that.' Maisky replied, 'But my government has not been asked.' 'Ah well,' said Halifax, 'it's in line with your policy.' Maisky said, 'My government does not accept commitments when it does not know how it can fulfil them. How will you fulfil this pledge?' Lloyd George in the House of Commons asked the same question.

The British government at last agreed to send two missions to Moscow. The most important was the Strang mission. Strang was a minor foreign office official. He and his staff went by boat rather than plane, and it turned out when they got there they had no real authority to take decisions.

The Russians stressed the need, in their view, to define aggression. Not just armed aggression but indirect aggression. They were referring particularly to the Baltic states. These states were part of Tsarist Russia and many of their leaders took an active part in the revolution and in the War of Intervention, but like half of Poland, the Bolsheviks had to secede these territories during the struggle for survival.

The Soviet negotiators then produced a map and said, 'In the event of nazi aggression we propose to move our forces to this and that point to stop the nazi advance.' The British said, 'We can't agree to that because that needs the consent of the Poles, and the Poles have refused to have any Soviet troops in their territory. And they could stop the Germans themselves. No doubt with their cavalry!' The Russians said, 'What are we discussing?' And that is how the negotiations broke down.

That is why I believed then, and still believe, that the Russians signed the Non-Aggression Pact with Germany because they saw it as the only way they could stop the Four Power Pact operating against them.

The Pact came as a bombshell. Ernie Hunter, who was the political correspondent of the *Daily Herald*, went to see Arthur Greenwood. They agreed that the bottom of the world had fallen out. There was a general condemnation of the Russians. But to me it was the inevitable result of the failure of the British to take seriously the negotiations for a pact against the nazis.

I was away on holiday in France that weekend with Tony Field, a friend on the *Daily Mirror*. I said, 'This means war, I am going home.' Tony said, 'I am going to finish the holiday.' I got back quite comfortably, Tony just struggled back on the last boat. Events moved very fast after that. When the nazis invaded Poland the die was cast.

I was in the House of Commons on Saturday, September 2nd. It was a special session, and we were all waiting for Chamberlain to come and make a statement. All sorts of rumours were going around the House. Ellen Wilkinson came into Annie's Bar, the little bar in the inner lobby which is now the whips office, and said, 'I know what's happened; Stalin has given all the allied plans to Hitler.' There were other rumours and we just had to sit and wait.

I wrote in *Reynolds*,

> When Mr Chamberlain entered amid cheers from the Tory benches, he began with the suggestion that the failure of Herr Hitler to answer the British ultimatum might be due to the efforts of Mussolini to secure a conference between Britain, France, Poland, Germany and Italy. The House listened in silence. Only when the Prime Minister emphasised that Britain would be bound to take action unless the German forces were withdrawn [from Poland] did a roar of applause sweep round the Chamber. As Mr Arthur Greenwood, acting leader of the Labour Party, rose to speak, a Conservative shouted 'Speak for England!' The cry was taken up by other members and for a time Mr Greenwood stood with bowed head at the despatch box waiting to make his

voice heard. 'I believe the whole House is perturbed by the Prime Minister's statement,' he said measuring every word. 'There is a growing feeling that this incessant strain must end sooner or later, in a sense, the sooner the better.' Again the cheers came from the Conservative as well as Labour benches. 'I hope therefore that tomorrow, however hard it may be for the Prime Minister – and no one would care to be in his shoes tonight – that we should know the mind of the British Government and that there should be no more devices for dragging out what has been dragged out.' Again the whole House cheered.

The Prime Minister, clearly aware of the feeling of the House, hurried to explain that there was not the slightest weakening in the attitude of Britain and France. The French Cabinet was in session and he hoped to have a reply within a few hours. Tomorrow he hoped to give the House a definite statement. War was declared at 11 am the next morning. It was a very courageous speech by Greenwood. I met him shortly after and Arthur said to me 'If Chamberlain hadn't declared war I would have crossed the floor and we would have had another government.'

In the same issue of *Reynolds* I recalled that the Labour party had decided against an invitation from Chamberlain to join his government. That decision was taken by a joint meeting of the National Executive of the Labour party and the Executive of the Parliamentary party. Arthur Greenwood, leading the party, took the decision to Downing Street. I commented, 'The party feels that in present circumstances it would be more in accordance with the spirit of the constitution if the Labour party held itself free to offer constructive criticism on matters of detail while giving every support to the struggle against aggression.' I added, 'It must also be stressed that many Labour and Cooperative members are unconvinced that the government under present leadership is capable of showing the necessary energy and initiative in facing their difficult task.'

I must tell you one funny story. On the Sunday morning after Chamberlain made his speech declaring war, which came over the radio, the air-raid sirens sounded. It turned out afterwards that it was a false alarm. I was going back to the office in Gray's Inn Road. The air-raid shelter was in a church hall with a few sand bags and there was a poor little woman weeping bitterly. I said to her, 'What's the matter my dear?' She said, 'I've forgotten my gas mask,' and I replied, 'Don't worry, he is not going to use gas this time,' and she said, 'Oh, thank you Sir.' As if I knew, but I comforted her.

My attitude to the war was summed up in a letter which I drafted for the Richmond Labour party (I was then vice-president) which we sent to our members two days before war broke out. I am quoting it in full because I think it is a valuable indication of the attitude of many of us:

Dear Comrade,

Before this message reaches members of the branch, the world may be plunged into the disaster of war against which for 20 years we who believe in Socialism have fought constantly.

In our view it is essential that at this moment of crisis, certain fundamental facts of Labour policy should be stated, not only to our own members but to as wide a circle as possible.

In the first place, Labour officially stands behind the government in fulfilling the pledge to protect British integrity from attacks by German fascism. That does not mean that we have any illusions as to the record and construction of the Polish State.

It does mean that we are left with no alternative if the world is to be saved from the rule of the nazi storm trooper and the gestapo, under whose grip hundreds of thousands of our comrades are now suffering.

At the same time we set on record that war need never have come if the League of Nations, for which men died in the last war, had not been sabotaged and destroyed by a British government, which, until the final phase, did not disguise its sympathy with the fascist aggressors. We Socialists were accused of being warmongers when we said that the battle of democracy against fascism was being fought in Abyssinia, China, and, above all, in Spain. Now the disastrous results of the foreign policy of the National Government and in particular the personal policy of Mr Chamberlain are revealed.

When sanctions were applied against Italy, 52 nations stood behind us. If we had stood firm when democratic Czechoslovakia was attacked, the Soviet Union, France and Great Britain could have defeated Hitler without war. We fight under far more dangerous circumstances and remember that whatever view history may take of the Russian non-aggression pact with Germany it was the British government which deliberately delayed and finally smashed the negotiations.

A Peace Pact with Russia, offered after the invasion of Austria, before Munich and after the invasion of Czechoslovakia, would have saved the world. The British government made no effort to conclude this pact. It sought for a Four Power Pact with the dictators. Its object was to turn German armed force against the Soviet Union.

The responsibility of the Chamberlain government must not be forgotten, even if, as a united nation we march to war. Socialists fight, not against the German people but against fascism. We do not surrender our belief that a heavy measure of responsibility lies with the Western powers who refused to assist democratic Germany. When they have overthrown their fascist aggressors, we are ready with them to build a new world. We will have no part in redividing the world for the benefit of international capitalism.

Labour opposed the vindictive Versailles Treaty out of which came Hitler and the present tragedy.

In war, if it comes, or in peace, burdened by the intolerable weight of arms expenditure, the principles of Socialism must be kept alive. Only in these principles lies the hope of building a world from which the shadow of war is removed and in which the vast resources of all countries are utilised for the well-being of the common people. Whatever suffering lies before us, that will be our task.

11

Strange Happenings in the Phoney War

We were at war. No one noticed it. French and Germans faced each other on the Maginot and Siegfried lines. The papers, which told us sunshine stories about the invulnerable Maginot line, did not tell us that it had not been finished. Stories went the rounds, about behind the scenes peace negotiations. Some, no doubt, were true.

It was during that phoney war that the communist party made its extraordinary somersault. When the war started it was broadly in the same position as I had outlined in my letter to the Richmond Labour party. But then it suddenly announced this was an imperialist war. I was flabbergasted, and shocked when some of my party friends followed the party line. One story was that Springhall, who later was imprisoned for spying, had brought the instructions from Moscow. I said this is not democratic centralism; this is dictatorship. They said, 'We can't trust Chamberlain to fight an anti-fascist war.' I said, 'We've got to make it into an anti-fascist war.'

The communist party and some supporters formed a Peoples Congress. It was supposed to call over the heads of the leaders for a people's peace. D N Pritt, to my surprise, asked me if I would be a sponsor. I said, 'In heaven's name, no!' Harry Pollitt, who had resigned the party secretaryship over the imperialist war decision, did not support the congress, nor did Arthur Horner, or Johnny Campbell. But other leaders did, and the *Daily Worker* was more concerned with trumpeting the congress than fighting the war. That was their position until June 1941 when the nazis attacked the Soviet Union. Then the communist party was 100 per cent behind the war.

The phoney war ended when the nazis launched their offensive against Belgium and the Netherlands, and their air offensive against Britain. The German bombers came with monotonous regularity. At home we had an air-raid shelter – a dug-out with a protection of brick and earth, fitted with bunks for Rosie, myself, and our children Rupert, 8, and Geoffrey, 5. Our little terrier was always the first to hear the sirens and waited at the entrance to the shelter. Our Kingston home was a few hundred feet from the Thames, and the bombers used to follow its path to London.

I had to go to a job in the north and, as the nightly attacks were growing fiercer, decided that Rosie and the boys should go to a lodging in Southport. The bombers constantly attacked nearby Liverpool, but Southport had been left alone. There was a raid on as we were due to travel and we waited in *Reynolds*'s air-raid shelter. The train was full and we travelled in the guards van with the soldiers. The boys sat on their knees and we sang the new war songs, though *We'll hang up our washing on the Siegfried line* was perhaps then a little optimistic. Rosie, who had qualified as state registered nurse, midwife and health visitor, soon got a job in the local hospital and the boys found school places. Back in London the Battle of Britain grew fiercer. I spent one or two nights in the underground. Originally the government wanted to close them at night. They had built steel doors to seal the tunnels should a bomb go through the bed of the Thames, flooding the underground system. But the people would have none of it. They stormed the underground stations. There was a wonderful sense of comradeship among those underground communities. People shared their rationed food and everyone cared for the children and the old.

One evening I got to Richmond station on my way home to Kingston, and found that incendiary bombs had set fire to a big store opposite. On the pavement a soldier and his girl were standing. I said, 'What are you waiting for?' The soldier said, 'A bus!' I said, 'He's lit that fire and he's coming back with bombs. Let's get out of here.' We reached a side turning when six bombs came down. We lay on our bellies, and I thought, 'What an undignified way to die.'

We reached Richmond Hill and went into an air-raid shelter. The raid went on. A little old lady came gingerly down the steps. 'Threw me out of bed three times,' she said, 'this Hitler is a fidget!'

The Battle of Britain was becoming a war of attrition between the nazi bombers and the fighters manned by the few, to whom Churchill paid his immortal tribute. I remember meeting Arthur Greenwood in a sombre mood. They were taking the fighter aircraft, the hurricanes and spitfires, straight from the factories. The airfields for the fighters' take-off were becoming unusable. I wrote a front page for the following Sunday saying it was now or never if the nazis were going to invade. 'Zero Hour, now or never,' I wrote.

Sept 15th, 1940

Britain faces zero hour. All indications reaching official circles last night confirm the view expressed by the prime minister in his broadcast speech, that Hitler must make his invasion attempt soon or abandon his plans. Goering's Blitzkrieg on London has a dual object. First, to smash communications and disorganise public services in the capital; and second, to confront the Government with the problem of a demoralised and panic-stricken population. Despite the heavy damage of the last few days both these preliminaries to invasion have failed. But on the other side of the channel the preparations go on. Barges, troops, including it is reported, 100,000 Italians and mechanised equipment are massing at strategic points. These are Hitler's invasion weapons. Britain's counter-measures are no less formidable. Mr Churchill has personally inspected the defence preparations on the coasts.

Later evidence proved I was right.

But at that point the German strategy changed. They stopped the battle of attrition and concentrated on the terror-bombing of London. Historians have mulled over that decision. Some hold the view that Hitler believed the British would support him when he turned on the Soviet Union, and that an invasion would be counter-productive. The same explanation is given by some for his failure to prevent the escape of much of the British army from Dunkirk.

Whatever the reason, it was a nazi miscalculation. The bombers took a heavy toll, but there was no breakdown in morale. Some dived for the shelters directly the warning sirens went; others carried on, confident that, whoever got killed it would not be them.

We were desperately working to rebuild the equipment and weapons lost at Dunkirk and (this is not a *Dad's Army* joke) the Home Guard were practising with pikes because rifles were unavailable.

Stafford Cripps, our Ambassador in Moscow, met Stalin, who assured him that no arms were included in the German–Soviet pact, but that the Soviet Union would be willing to sell rifles to Britain. Before the deal went through Britain seized the gold reserves of the Baltic states, which by then had joined the Soviet Union. The gold was deposited in London and the deal lapsed.

Two other episodes during the phoney war were significant. First, when Yugoslavia overthrew its pro-fascist government and was threatened by the nazis, Moscow recognised the new government. Second, Moscow offered to conclude a pact with Bulgaria promising assistance in the event of a German attack. It was reliably reported that the offer was refused on advice from London.

News came through that Molotov, Soviet Foreign Secretary, was visiting Berlin. Churchill said to the Cabinet let's teach him a lesson. Arthur Greenwood told me that side of the story. The other side is told by the American journalist William L Shirer. He describes how Hitler said that Britain was defeated, and their job was to divide the British Empire.

The sirens sounded and they took to the shelter. Molotov said, 'If Britain's defeated, who do those bombers belong to?'

When France fell I wrote an article in *Reynolds* saying that the nazis had won because the French leaders were not willing to mobilise the people and the working class against the enemy. I gave a broad hint that there were some people in Britain who had been friendly with the nazis before the war who might behave the same way.

I have often asked myself, how many of us who lived through those years when the bombers came every night, and far superior German forces were massed along the Channel, really believed our country could suffer the same fate as France. Reports went the rounds of would-be invading ships being destroyed. We knew that we were prepared to use gas if the Germans landed.

A Home Guards officer came to the office and warned that London was virtually defenceless. If one German armoured column got across the Channel then London, he said, would be at its mercy. He thought we could publish a warning to wake up the authorities. I told him it would never pass the censor.

It is very funny how, amid the most world shaking events, one's personal problems intervene. I hoped that if the nazis did arrive, Rosie and the boys would be as safe as any other non-combatants. I knew that my anti-nazi articles meant I was on Hitler's blacklist. At that critical time when I thought that Hitler might get here I learned a lot of poetry when I was riding around on buses, and in spare moments. I thought that if they did not kill me and I were put in jail, I could at least recite poetry to myself. I still remember most of the pieces that I learned, in addition to those I learned earlier at school. Our hope was that the Soviet Union would join in the anti-fascist struggle.

Meanwhile the Chamberlain government was fast losing support. The failed invasion of Narvik was making the country realise the danger. A move was made for Churchill to take over. The crisis led to a vote of confidence in the

House of Commons on 8th May, 1940. Normally the government could count on its 200 majority, but now, following the vote, it held on to just 81 MPs. Churchill voted for Chamberlain. But as Arthur Greenwood said to me at the time, it was the Tory abstentions which defeated him. Churchill formed a new cabinet two days later, but Chamberlain hung on and did not resign till October, 1940. Cripps was sent to Moscow to make contact with the Soviet Union.

In my report of the Bournemouth Labour party conference of 19th May, 1940, I said, 'Bournemouth has changed the face of wartime Britain. Labour men have been called in to carry through the tasks on the home front in which Chamberlain has failed – they included Ernest Bevin, Herbert Morrison, G R Grenfell and Hugh Dalton. Attlee and Greenwood had already joined.' I pointed out that the key positions, especially at the exchequer, were still in the hands of the discredited Chamberlain ministers. I went on,

> The facts must be faced at once, these leaders will be compelled to ask for the widest concessions in order to keep the war industries going to the maximum of human endurance. There will be a new approach to the question of distribution of available manpower, to the allocation of skilled labour, to the balance between industries for home consumption and those devoted to the urgent production of war material.

The Labour conference did not take decisions on these matters and I added,

> I believe that the Labour and trade union movement will make any necessary sacrifice to provide the means of victory. It will do so provided trade union rights are ensured, and this is the vital point, provided there is a real conviction that sacrifices are equal.
>
> Amid the heat of the struggle, which all realised was now a matter of life or death, the conference had the duty of safeguarding the principle of socialism and inter-

88

nationalism for which the party stands and for which it fights both at home and on the battle front. The Bournemouth conference disappointed because, while stating these principles, it did not get down to brass tacks on how they are to be achieved. Yet the stark facts emerged from every phase of the conference, from the urgency of Mr Attlee's speech, to the fervent appeal of Blum, French Socialist leader, for more soldiers, more supplies, so that men and women working up to 70 hours a week in French factories, could be relieved.

At the end I said,

The conference which appeared to be collapsing after giving a mandate to its leaders to join the government, sprang to life when Harold Laski made his appeal for socialism. All through the discussions, and in spite of one or two attempts to stimulate war-hatred, delegates expressed their hope that eventually the German working people would join in rebuilding the new world. The conference did not blindly accept the job of building for victory where Toryism has failed. Delegates were bewildered sometimes by the swift rush of events, but 20 years of struggle and propaganda since Britain won the last war and lost the peace, had not been wasted. They believe in socialism as an integral part of the struggle for victory. They will not allow even heavier taxation to fall on the poor while capital is untouched, and a minority of the population is still allowed to draw vast unearned income at the expense of the war effort. They know that socialism is not a mere matter of state control but involves a shift of control from the monopolists to the people.

Brave hopes in 1940, when we were at the critical moment of the war. At the press table, when they had all finished, I turned and said the one thing they failed to do was to pass a resolution saying the Soviet Union does not exist. At no point in the conference was there any belief that the Soviet

Union would come in on our side. Before the next Labour party conference it had.

At the Cooperative party conference the same year, A V Alexander and I were in a group and he turned to me, his voice dripping with sarcasm, and said, 'What's the great Schaffer have to say?' I said, 'Until we have the Russians on our side, we can't win.'

On May 12th, 1941, Hess, Hitler's deputy, landed in Scotland. He wanted to meet members of the Ribbentrop pre-war group, but was arrested. Those of us who knew the perilous situation facing the country concluded that this was some sort of peace mission. It was inconceivable that the deputy fuehrer could have defected by air without official knowledge or permission. When Greenwood gave me the official version, 'the rat escaping the sinking ship?', I said, 'Arthur, pull the other leg.' Actually, Hess came with a message that the fuehrer was about to attack the real enemy, and offering Britain a generous peace.

After Hitler's defeat the British prosecutor at Nuremburg revealed that Hess had come to Britain with a proposal that Hitler should be given a free hand in Europe, while Britain was to retain her Empire but former German colonies must be returned. The British prosecutor also said that Hess's proposal for peace with Britain was aimed at securing a one-front war against Russia.

Ernest Bevin, a minister in the Coalition government, said on 15th May, 1941, at a meeting of the Holborn Chamber of Commerce, 'Hess is a murderer. He was the man who collected every index card of every trade union leader in Germany and those of the Social Democrats, and when the time came they were either sent to concentration camps or murdered. I do not believe that Herr Hitler did not know that Hess was coming to England.' The Hess mission coincided with one of the heaviest raids on London. The bombing started in the early Saturday evening and went on, hour after hour. The tape machines in the *Reynolds* building bringing in the agency news were cut off one by one. Then the phone link with the branch office in Leeds went down.

We were isolated except for our reporter at the Ministry of Information in the London University building in Blooms-bury. He told us that a bomb had gone through the pavement at Kings Cross on to the Metropolitan railway and that they were pulling bodies out of nearby buildings. We were work-ing with the emergency printing machines on the ground floor and changed the pages on the stone as news came through, but the roof spotters would not allow the depart-ment making the moulds and the plates for the rotary machines to work on the upper floors.

Towards dawn the all clear sounded. The reporter came in with the official hand-out that 32 nazi planes had been brought down. I wrote the headline and soon the papers were pouring out. That Sunday morning I walked round the bombed streets within range of the office. It was like a scene I had witnessed in Barcelona. A woman emerged weeping from a wrecked building. She held a dead cat in her arms. The horror of war strikes in many ways.

After the war, among the captured German documents was an order to be issued by the commander of the occupy-ing German troops in England. It was in German and English and, with German efficiency, announced the exchange rate between the pound and the mark. It set out the penalties under military law for failing to hand in radio sets, for pos-sessing arms, for fomenting strikes and other offences. A facsimile was published in the Soviet magazine *New Times*.

The Hess mission set off a spate of rumours about an impending nazi attack on the Soviet Union. We know now that Stalin had been warned that the nazi onslaught was indeed imminent. Cripps, presumably on information from Hess, had conveyed the warning. It also came from a Russian spy, Richard Sorge, in Japan. Some officers came over from the German lines with the same information. Stalin would have none of it. Did he believe that his non-aggression pact would hold? More likely he believed there was a plot to force him into a pre-emptive strike, when the Western powers would accuse him of aggression and thus justify the German counter-attack. Whatever the reason or the motive, the

91

Geheime Kommandosache

Bekanntmachung

für das besetzte Gebiet.

Auf Grund der mir vom Oberbefehlshaber des Heeres erteilten Ermächtigung mache ich bekannt:

I. Gewalttaten und Sabotageakte sind mit schwersten Strafen bedroht. Als Sabotage wird auch jede Beschädigung oder Entziehung von Ernteerzeugnissen, kriegswichtigen Vorräten und Anlagen aller Art sowie das Abreißen und Beschädigen angeschlagener Bekanntmachungen gewertet. Unter dem besonderen Schutz der deutschen Wehrmacht stehen: Gas-, Wasser- und Elektrizitätswerke, Eisenbahnen, Kanäle und Schleusenanlagen sowie Kunstschätze.

II. Die Abgabe von Schußwaffen (einschl. der Jagdwaffen) und Kriegsgerät ist durch besondere Bekanntmachung angeordnet.

III. Kriegsgerichtlich geahndet wird:

1. jede Unterstützung nichtdeutscher Militärpersonen im besetzten Gebiet,
2. jede Hilfe bei der Flucht von Zivilpersonen in das nichtbesetzte Gebiet,
3. jede Nachrichtenübermittlung an Personen oder Behörden außerhalb des besetzten Gebiets zum Schaden der deutschen Wehrmacht und des Reiches,
4. jeder Verkehr mit Kriegsgefangenen,
5. jede Beleidigung der deutschen Wehrmacht und ihrer Befehlshaber,
6. das Zusammenrotten auf der Straße, das Verbreiten von Flugschriften, die Veranstaltung von öffentlichen Versammlungen und Aufzügen, die nicht vorher von einem deutschen Befehlshaber genehmigt worden sind, sowie jede andere deutschfeindliche Kundgebung,
7. Verleitung zur Arbeitseinstellung, böswillige Arbeitseinstellung, Streik und Aussperrung.

IV. Alle gewerblichen Betriebe, Handelsgeschäfte und Banken sind offen zu halten. Grundloses Schließen wird geahndet. Produzenten und Händler mit Waren des täglichen Bedarfs haben ihre Tätigkeit fortzusetzen und die Waren dem Verbrauch zuzuführen.

V. Die Erhöhung von Preisen und Entgelten jeder Art sowie von Löhnen über den Stand vom Tage der Besetzung hinaus ist verboten, soweit nicht Ausnahmen ausdrücklich zugelassen sind.

VI. Für deutsche und landeseigene Währung besteht Annahmezwang. Das Umrechnungsverhältnis beträgt: 1 engl. Pfund = 9,60 Reichsmark.

Die Anwendung eines anderen Umrechnungskurses ist strafbar.

Gesetzliche Zahlungsmittel sind neben den englischen Zahlungsmitteln die deutschen Reichskreditkassenscheine und Reichskreditkassenmünzen. Daneben sind deutsche Scheidemünzen im Werte von 1 und 2 Pfennig sowie 1, 2, 5 und 10 Reichspfennig oder Rentenpfennig im Zahlungsverkehr zugelassen. Die im Gebiet des Deutschen Reichs geltenden Reichsbanknoten, Rentenbankscheine und Scheidemünzen im Werte von 50 Reichspfennig und mehr sind nicht gesetzliche Zahlungsmittel im besetzten Gebiet. Sie dürfen daher weder in Verkehr gebracht noch angenommen werden.

VII. Die deutschen Soldaten und Reichsangehörigen werden ihre Käufe und ihre Arbeitsaufträge bar bezahlen. Die Truppe stellt an Stelle der Barzahlung Leistungsbescheinigungen aus.

Der Oberbefehlshaber der Armee.

Notice
for the occupied Territories.

By virtue of the powers vested in me by the Commander-in-Chief of the Army I issue the following Notice.

I. Acts of violence and sabotage are liable to the most severe punishment. Any damage to, or removal of, harvest produce, supplies and stores of military importance, and the tearing down or defacement of Notices will be regarded as acts of sabotage. The following stand under the particular protection of the German Armed Forces: Gas and Waterworks, electric power stations, railways, oilreservoirs, locks, art treasures.

II. The surrender of fire-arms (including sporting guns) and war material has been the subject of a Special Notice.

III. The following will be punished under Martial Law:
   (1) Any assistance to non-German military personnel in the occupied territories.
   (2) Any assistance to civilians in attempted flight into non occupied territory.
   (3) The transmission, to individuals or authorities outside the occupied territories, of information to the detriment of the German Armed Forces or of the German Empire.
   (4) Any dealings or relations with prisoners of war.
   (5) Any insult to the German Armed Forces.
   (6) Assembly in the streets, distribution of leaflets, organisation of public gatherings and processions which have not previously received the sanction of the German Commander, and any other form of anti-German demonstration.
   (7) Inducement or incitement to a stoppage of work, malevolent stoppage of work, strikes and lock-outs.

IV. All industrial undertakings, trading establishments and banks will remain open. Unjustifiable closing will be prosecuted. Producers and dealers in goods of everyday requirement will continue to function and to supply consumers.

V The raising of prices and payments of all sorts, including salaries, above those in force on the day of occupation is forbidden, except in cases where an exception has been expressly authorized.

VI The acceptance of German and of local currency is compulsory. The rate of exchange is
$$L. 1 = 9.60 \text{ RM.}$$

Acceptance or offer of any other rate of exchange constitutes a punishable offence.
   Legal tender, in addition to English currency, will be:
Reichskredit notes and coinage (Reichskreditkassenschein),
German coinage in the values of 1 and 2 Pfennig,
Reichspfennig and Rentenpfennig in the values of 1, 2, 5, and 10 Pfennig.
   The Reichsbank notes. Rentenbank notes and coinage in the values of 50 Reichspfennig and over, which are in current circulation in the German Empire, are not legal currency in the occupied territories. They must therefore neither be put into circulation nor be accepted.

VII German nationals, soldiers and civilians, will pay cash for their purchases or orders. Military units will issue Certificates of Value Payable in lieu of cash payment.

The Army Commander.

Russians suffered grievously for the lack of preparation.

Maisky, the Soviet ambassador in London, had been ordered to ignore the rumours and he was away on a 'bicycling weekend'. When on 22nd June, 1941, the nazis invaded he returned to London. That afternoon Churchill and Maisky wrote the speech that was to change history. I record Maisky's version as he told it to Pat Coates.

Churchill did not consult the Cabinet or the Foreign Office. It was to be a full-blooded denunciation of the nazis and an assertion that the Soviet Union was our friend. At one point Churchill said, 'I shall have to say I don't like the communists!' 'That's all right,' said Maisky, 'as long as you don't like the nazis.'

At my home in Kingston I sat waiting for the speech, waiting and hoping. When those ringing tones came over the radio, 'Whoever fights the nazis is our ally', I was convinced we were saved.

That was Churchill's finest hour. There were certainly voices in the Cabinet who, if Churchill had not taken the initiative, would have wanted to discuss Hess's terms. I doubt whether any of the Labour leaders would have carried it off. But Churchill could not be an appeasement prime minister.

12

Russia – Our Ally

During the discussion on the content of the paper following the nazi attack I said I want to write a piece entitled 'The Red Army Will Win'. Sydney Elliot retorted, 'If you want to make a fool of yourself, you can. You're not going to make a fool of the paper.' Almost everybody would have agreed with that assessment.

Why was I so confident? I have asked myself that question many times for, as it turned out, I was right and they were wrong.

I have already told of my visit to the Soviet Union in 1935, and my conviction that they were building a more equitable socialist society. The Webbs saw the defects, but they reached the same conclusions. It was difficult in those years for the sympathetic observer to understand the dual nature of Stalin. The elimination of many of the Bolshevik leaders, the exile of Trotsky, the trials; we were worried, we were shocked, but we recalled that the English and French revolutions had also been far from bloodless.

We were convinced that in the new socialist Soviet Union, and in the development of the republics (some of them having their languages written for the first time) was what Marx called 'the creative genius of the awakened masses'.

We were convinced that the Soviet Union was in the forefront of the struggle against fascism and for peace, and that the capitalist powers were intent on its destruction, an aim they had failed to achieve by the war of intervention.

Stalin's speeches, ignored now in the Soviet Union as well as in the West, were those of a statesman, not of a paranoid dictator like Hitler. He said in 1931, in a speech to business executives, 'We are 50 or 100 years behind the advanced countries. We must make good this distance in ten years. Either we do it, or they crush us.' Exactly ten years before the nazi attack! And in those ten years, the Soviet Union built an industry which played a major part in the Allied victory.

I had read the analysis of the Red army's potential by Max Werner, the American expert, and Major Hooper's assessment of the winter war by the Russians against Finland which smashed the Mannerheim line, the strongest in Europe. I asked myself why, if they were not preparing to resist a nazi attack, the Russians should have smashed the Mannerheim line which, in German hands, would have made the defence of Leningrad impossible.

Why did they defy the nazis by recovering from Poland the area accepted as Russian when the Curzon line was drawn? Why include the Baltic states in the Union? It only made sense if it was part of a defensive strategy.

Incidentally, during the war we were very conscious that many among the Polish military units stationed in Britain were hostile to the allied cause. I had a spectacular example when one day three Polish soldiers, in uniform, came into *Reynolds*'s office. They told me that they were Jewish and subject to persecution. Two of them were academics and had been given the most menial jobs. They told me that in the evenings the Polish soldiers sang the nazi *Horst Wessel* song.

It was of course an offence in wartime to give shelter to escaped soldiers. I got in touch with the National Council for Civil Liberties, or 'Liberty' as it is called today, and they gave these men a haven. I also received information that they had been given permission to transfer to the British army. That episode is significant in view of some things that happened after the war in Poland.

Stalin's speech to the Communist party congress in 1939 was seen by some of us as a warning to the western powers

that the Russians were aware that their policy of appeasement might have been designed to isolate the Soviet Union,
and assist aggression by Germany and Japan, but could be
disastrous for them.

He said, 'Combined, the non-aggressive democratic states
are unquestionably stronger than the fascist states both economically and in the military sense.' He referred to the way
non-intervention was applied in the Spanish Civil War and
added, 'Non-intervention may be defined as follows: Let
each country defend itself from the aggressor, as it likes, or
as best it can, but actually speaking, the policy of non-
intervention means conniving at aggression being given a
free hand to make war. A desire not to hinder, say, Japan
from embroiling itself in a war with the Soviet Union, to
allow all the belligerents to sink deeply into the mire of war,
to allow them to weaken, and then to appear on the scene
with fresh strength, to appear, of course, in the interests of
peace, and to dictate conditions to enfeebled belligerents,
cheap and easy.'

I saw the events leading up to war in the light of that
speech. For me, it explained the replacement of Litvinov,
who had fought for so long for coexistence through the
League of Nations, by Molotov, who believed with Stalin
that they faced the danger of a nazi onslaught, with the
western powers standing on the sidelines.

I saw the Soviet–German non-aggression pact, which
many peace workers regarded as a betrayal, as a logical
sequel. The execution of the Soviet generals shocked and
worried me. I was convinced they were not traitors. The
explanation I gave myself then, which I still believe, was
that the Russian officer class retained its respect for their
counterparts in the German army from the time of the
Rapallo Treaty (1922).

Both realised Hitler was hell-bent on war and there was a
joint move to stop him. We know he could have been
stopped. Stalin would have regarded that as treason. At the
time of writing, the Russian authorities have given no explanation of that tragic episode.

On the day after the Russians became our ally, I wrote to Rosie saying they should come home. I was convinced the nazis would be too involved on their Eastern front to go on bombing Britain. I was right. There were no more serious air attacks until the doodle bugs towards the end of the war. In those first months after the nazi attack the Russians were in retreat. It looked as if Hitler's gamble would pay off, for there was little support from the British ally. The tide turned within sight of Moscow. Today, the spot where the Germans were halted is marked by a memorial.

Ilya Ehrenburg told me some time after the war that, in those first days, when the Soviet armies were being decimated and large areas occupied, Stalin lost his nerve. But he was still revered by millions. He went public a fortnight after the nazi attack with a radio address. It was no doubt written by the Political Committee. It was a message of defiance, an admission of grave defeats, but a declaration that the German fascists could and would be defeated. It called for a scorched earth policy if land had to be abandoned to the invaders, and the formation of guerrilla bands behind enemy lines.

He sent this message to the world, 'In this great war of liberation we shall not be alone. We shall have true allies in the peoples of Europe and America, including the German people enslaved by Hitler's fascist armies.' It was, he said, a 'patriotic war against German fascism'.

Looking back on those months and years when the Soviet armies and the guerrillas behind the lines held the might of the nazi forces, backed by the machine power and slave labour of occupied Europe, one recaptures something of the awe and admiration which those achievements inspired.

Mrs Churchill headed an aid for Russia fund. Lord Beaverbrook, in charge of arms production, launched a tanks for Russia week. The workers responded with such enthusiasm that they ran out of spare parts. The Amalgamated Engineering Union, created jointly with the employers production committees with the sole object of increasing output, they exceeded all expectations. An appeal for people to hand in their aluminium pots and pans met with an overwhelming response.

Britain and the Soviet Union cemented the alliance with a pledge that neither would conclude a separate peace. I had the story that Stalin had written to Churchill saying that if a second front were opened in Europe, the war could be won in 1942. To my surprise my story was killed by the censor. How could its publication help the enemy? Later the reason became clear. The political battle was to centre round the demand for the second front.

The Stalin–Churchill letters released in Moscow are very revealing. There is one in particular in which Franco wrote in 1945 to 'our good friend the British Prime Minister'. The letter attacked the Soviet Union and suggested a rapprochement between Britain and Spain aimed at resisting the Soviet Union. Churchill sent Franco's letter to Stalin together with his reply. He told Franco, 'I should be seriously misleading you if I did not at once remove any misconception that His Majesty's Government are prepared to consider any grouping of powers in Western Europe or elsewhere on the basis of hostility towards, or of the alleged necessity of defence against, our Russian allies. The policy of HMG remains based on the Anglo–Soviet Treaty of 1942 and the continuance of Anglo–Russian collaboration within the framework of the future world organisation as essential not only in our own interests but also for future peace and prosperity of Europe as a whole.'

When this correspondence was published I wrote a review in the Indian daily *Patriot*. I commented, 'Had that policy been adhered to there'd be a different world today. But a little more than a year after victory had been achieved Churchill betrayed this pledge in the Fulton speech calling for an alliance against the Soviet Union.'

On February 27th, 1945, Churchill said in parliament, 'Sombre indeed would be the fortunes of mankind if some awful schism arose between the Western democracies and the Russian Soviet Union. If all the future world organisations were rent asunder and if new cataclysms of inconceivable violence destroyed all that is left of the treasures and liberties of mankind.' He added, 'I know of no government which stands to its obligations, even to its own disadvantage, more solidly than the Russian Soviet Government.'

On November 15th, 1944, Eisenhower replied to a red-baiting speech by a Congress representative, 'Russia has not the slightest thing to gain by a war with the United States. I believe Russia's policy is friendship with the United States. There is in Russia a desperate and continuing concern for the lot of the common man and they want to be friends with the United States.'

Sydney Elliot decided that *Reynolds* would support the second front demand. America was in the war, having been brought in by the Japanese attack on Pearl Harbour in December 1941.

The allies met in America and agreed on the urgent necessity for a second front in Europe in 1942. There was a demonstration backing the second front in Trafalgar Square. The crowd was massed from the plinth and up to the steps of the National Gallery. It stretched half-way up Whitehall. Older hands said it was the biggest in memory.

I was one of the speakers. I was conscious that we were asking our forces to face dangers far greater than those we endured at home. My theme was: I am not a military expert. Those who do know the situation have given the pledge. Its fulfilment will shorten this war and will relieve the burden on our Soviet ally which is holding the frontline for us all at immeasurable cost. The second front did not come till D-day in 1944 when the German armies were in full retreat from the Soviet armies.

The preparations for the invasion of northern Europe were in the hands of Lord Mountbatten, and among his team were two friends of mine, J D Bernal and Geoffrey Pyke. Geoffrey had come to me when war broke out and expressed his doubts about giving support. I said we've got to make it into a war against fascism. Mountbatten swept aside the protests that they were pro-communist. In fact, Geoffrey told me that

Mountbatten was enthused by the achievement of the Soviet ally and they discussed the works of Marx and Engels on several occasions. Geoffrey, incidentally, was never a communist.

For a time Geoffrey and I met openly. Then he was told I was a security risk. Friendship with the ally, who was enduring the main burden of the common struggle, was somehow suspect! He told me later about one of the most fantastic events of the war. It is mentioned briefly in Churchill's memoirs. A scheme to build an ice battleship. Geoffrey had found that in very deep mines with below zero temperatures and a peat rich soil, pit-props were not needed. He experimented with mixtures of water and peat. When frozen the material was as hard as steel. He suggested that it could be used for various types of construction. The military were not interested, but Churchill was fascinated. They called the material pycrete. Churchill fired a revolver at it in a Downing Street test and it proved resistant.

The idea that pycrete could be used to build a ship capable of carrying men and armaments across the Channel for the second front emerged. Geoffrey went to Canada and secured permission from the Canadian government to make the material with wood pulp from Newfoundland trees. Tests had shown that with refrigeration installed the vessel would be able to sail in all waters. Geoffrey had an operation while in Canada, and refused an anaesthetic because he feared he might give away his secret while under its influence. He told me they lost a year because of the opposition of the brasshats and, before the work could be completed, the second front was launched.

Geoffrey had been working on ways in which the German occupation could be undermined before the second front. He produced a design for a vehicle which could run on snow in Norway. The idea was not to drive the Germans out but to attract them in! These vehicles could operate on snow and become a thorn in the Germans' chest. That too was delayed by the War Office, and eventually the result was seen not on the snow of Norway but in the mud of Flanders after the second front.

After the war Geoffrey became an 'adviser' to Alf Barnes, a Labour government minister. He investigated the shortage of nurses and their professional status. I found that he was going back to the times of the Greeks and Romans which seemed a bit mad. He also investigated ways of dealing with the shortage of transport in liberated Europe. He looked at various schemes for using man-power. On the last occasion I met him it was quite obvious he was suffering mental trouble. I wished I had persuaded him to come with me to Kingston – he had visited me several times – but the next I heard was that he had committed suicide. It was a very sad occasion. When I think of Geoffrey I think of the old saying, 'Great minds to madness sure are near allied and thin partitions do their bounds divide.' I think at the end Geoffrey did lose his reason.

My own job involved gathering news from all sources. My main contact with our Soviet ally was Pat Coates, Secretary of the Anglo–Russian Parliamentary Committee. I met Maisky occasionally. Some of the minor Soviet officials sometimes tried to pump me. I would reply, 'If you want to know about our war effort, OK, but I don't know any secrets, and if I did I wouldn't tell you.'

Actually the Soviet embassy relied on its agreement for cooperation in the joint struggle. This was exemplified in the case of Springhall. He was tried and convicted at the Old Bailey. The case was in camera, but Len White, Secretary of the Civil Service Clerical Association, was in court because one of his members was involved.

Springhall had a girl-friend working in a government department. Springhall apparently had no intention or opportunity to spy. But he was suspect. MI5 arranged for one of their young women members to strike up a friendship with Springhall's girlfriend and eventually they shared a flat.

At one point Springhall's girlfriend left in the flat some planted material, which was considered useful to the Soviet ally. The MI5 girl had it copied. Springhall took it to the

Soviet embassy. They said, 'We have an arrangement to share information with our British ally.' Springhall was arrested and imprisoned.

For me it was a new experience to be *persona grata* with the establishment. I was invited to write a weekly article on Britain's war effort for the Ministry of Information. I was told it went to more than 1,000 outlets round the world. The ministry asked *Reynolds* to provide 200 pictures of me. I wondered later in the cold war days where they were filed!

I had a weekly BBC overseas programme for the war effort, and I made periodic contributions to the news services and to radio newsreel. I was also asked to take over from a colleague, who had joined the forces, as the London correspondent on the *Johannesburg Sunday Express*.

South Africa under General Smuts was on our side. The apartheid leaders who later gained power were either interned or under surveillance. I had the front page lead under the name of Gordon Jones from 1941 until near the end of the war, when the *Express* amalgamated with *The Times*.

I forecast the imminence of a Japanese attack in a despatch which appeared the morning before Pearl Harbor. The paper carried a panel in the next issue dubbing me a news wizard.

Early in the war I was elected editor of the *Journalist*, the organ of my union, and I regarded its main job to keep contact with our members in the forces. Giles, *Reynolds*'s cartoonist, gladly agreed to do a cartoon for each issue. They always had a newspaper angle. The first was of a little soldier subbing copy and looking over his shoulder at a general, with the words, 'This has got to come down by half.' The others were similar and were eagerly read in Fleet Street and by our members worldwide.

Giles, who like me was unfit for military service, was offered jobs by a number of papers. Whenever he was tempted, particularly by Lord Beaverbrook's *Express*, I would go out with him for an evening's drinking and he would agree not to leave *Reynolds*.

Then Arnold Russell, the news editor, cut his cartoon

down from three to two columns. That did it. He went to the *Express* with the promise of a free hand. Sydney Elliot was also approached by Lord Beaverbrook, who flattered him, often telling him *Reynolds*'s leader page was the best in Fleet Street. I was shocked when he called me into his room to tell me he had agreed to accept. He said, 'I've got to think of my family.' I said, 'I know we are not getting Fleet Street salaries, but in terms of the average worker, we are well off.' Sydney was browned off by the failure of the directors to appreciate the problems of running a newspaper.

He told me that, on one occasion, when they discussed the cost of news agency services, one director had said, 'Our reporters know shorthand, couldn't they take the news down from the radio!' Sydney told me, 'You'll be offered the editorship.' I was doubtful and when it came to the appointment, there was a majority for Bill Richardson, editor of the *Cooperative News*. Sydney joined Michael Foot on the London *Evening Standard*. Later he joined the *Daily Mirror* and was then brought in to try to save the *Daily Herald*. But it was too late. The *Herald* sold out and became the pornographic *Sun* and disappeared from the scene.

I went to see Bill before he moved from Southport to London and assured him he had my support in his difficult task. There was no difference of policy. *Reynolds* supported the anti-fascist war 100 per cent. But it did not accept that the electoral truce precluded our right to criticise and, if necessary, attack the government in which the Tories had a substantial majority.

13

Greenwood Inspires Beveridge

Attlee and Greenwood, the first to join the Coalition Cabinet, were soon joined by Bevin, Dalton and Morrison and some junior ministers. Arthur Greenwood was in charge of production in the first days, but was soon shifted by Churchill to a new post – Minister of Post-War Reconstruction.

Arthur, who from his earliest days was bitterly aware of the sufferings of the poorest sections of the community was determined to use the common sacrifices of the war to inspire a new sense of responsibility for all the people. He secured a Cabinet minute authorising him to tidy up social services. He announced that Sir William Beveridge had agreed to chair the committee.

In answer to a House of Commons question on whether death benefit was within the purview of the committee, he said, 'That and all related questions are within its purview.' He told me step by step how the work was progressing. I gave a hint of what was coming on the Sunday before the Beveridge report was published.

To the media it was manna from heaven. It was published in December 1942. Here was Britain with her back to the wall, preparing for a world after victory when the people would be rewarded for their sacrifices, and for the first time there would be a policy aimed at combating the poverty, unemployment and avoidable disease which had overshadowed their past.

The report was named by the press from the womb to the

tomb. Churchill was furious. He had not paid any attention to Arthur Greenwood's activities. The War Office initially banned the Army Bureau of Current Affairs from organising discussions on the report.

But it could not be suppressed. I told the story of Arthur's contribution on the radio and through my articles for the Ministry of Information. Arthur was sacked and returned to the backbenches to lead the parliamentary Labour party. It was in this capacity that he initiated a three-day debate in the Commons calling on the government to accept the report 'as the policy to be pursued in post-war reconstruction'.

After hearing the government's reply, the Labour party added an amendment 'expressing dissatisfaction at the government's declared policy and urging the early implementation of the plan'.

Opening the debate, Arthur said, 'No document within living memory has made such a powerful impression or inspired such hopes as the Beveridge report. The people have made up their minds to see the plan in its broad outline carried into effect and nothing will shift them.

'They feel in their hearts, quite rightly, that it is their due. They have responded to the principles of a plan that would begin to disperse the dark, sombre, sinister clouds of insecurity which are shadowing millions of homes in this country. They also challenge the government and this House.'

The main reply for the government came from Herbert Morrison. The impression on the Labour benches was that he was avoiding firm commitments, and was damning with faint praise. Labour pressed the amendment to a division. Arthur said that though he moved the original resolution, the House would understand that he would support the amendment. It was defeated by 338 to 121 votes.

Reynolds published a summary of the debate because this clash was significant. As the immediate dangers were receding, Labour supporters, while accepting the wartime coalition, were becoming suspicious of the Tory motives. Incidentally, the clash had an interesting sequel. Arthur was approached to stand as treasurer of the Labour party in

106

opposition to Morrison, the sitting holder. Arthur told me he would not accept unless he first got the nomination of an important union.

I went to see Jack Tanner, AEU President, and he agreed to persuade his union to nominate Greenwood. I explained it was not a personal contest, but was based on the opposing attitudes to the Beveridge report.

Arthur won with the Labour conference vote. To secure Morrisons' continued membership of the party executive the deputy leader of the parliamentary party was given an automatic seat on the executive. That had repercussions in later years.

Despite the cracks in the coalition, the Labour party stuck to the electoral truce, but there was nothing to stop other parties or individuals taking part in by-elections. That was how Commonwealth emerged under the leadership of Sir Richard Acland, who had set out a policy under the title of *Unser Kampf* (Our Struggle).

It was a good progressive programme, but I could not see what its place would be in the political scene, particularly in relation to the trade unions. Looking back on those years, I think it did a useful job in refusing to be bound by the electoral truce which, in effect, *Reynolds* was also doing.

The Tory dominated government, it is true, abandoned some of the Tory policies of the past and in a white paper supported public works schemes to reduce unemployment, and admitted that it could not be solved by cutting wages and curtailing production.

I commented on this 'amazing discovery' and added, 'They admitted all their mistakes: all they asked was that the same people and the same methods should be retained and that private enterprise, in the hands of the big monopolists which had turned Britain into a land of distressed areas and unemployment, should remain in power.'

Ernest Bevin brought before parliament a bill setting up machinery to ensure a minimum wage standard for the catering industry which had been grossly sweated in the pre-war years. A total of 111 Tory MPs voted against it. I commented,

'They talk about their intentions to give a square deal to the people after victory. They prove by their votes that they will fight to preserve profits even at the expense of underpaid waiters and chambermaids.' (True to form in 1993 they resisted the Social Chapter.)

I gave a reminder that 'even when the nation faced disaster in 1940, the Tories ensured a majority of 81 for Neville Chamberlain.' It was the Tory abstentions and the Labour votes which made Chamberlain's hold on office untenable and ensured Churchill's succession.

I was invited to a meeting of Commonwealth leaders at Acland's flat near the House of Commons. J B Priestley was in the chair. The discussion hinged on various ideas for improving conditions after the war. Towards the end, Priestley pointed to me, 'You haven't given us your views.' I said, 'All evening you have been sympathising with the working class. The last thing you seem ready to do is join them in doing the job for themselves.'

I'm not so sure now, but at that time my attitude was conditioned by the conviction that the Labour party, as the political child of the trade unions, was the only body that could change capitalist society. Priestley, who was making heart-warming radio addresses on the war effort at the time, was very much the prima donna. I could not help thinking at that meeting how, before he wrote an article for *Reynolds*, he demanded a fee some four times my weekly salary.

Sometime after that meeting, I was invited to lunch by a Commonwealth leader. They were looking for candidates to fight a by-election. I refused. My place, I said, was with the Labour party. Tom Driberg, who by that time was doing a column for *Reynolds*, won the seat. He later transferred to the Labour party, was elected to the national executive, and ended up in the House of Lords.

Years after the war I was Chairman of the Political Committee of the London Cooperative Society. We gave a party at the Labour party conference. Party leaders dropped in during the evening. Harold Wilson, then leader of the opposition arrived, after doing the rounds of the other functions.

I welcomed him and, in a brief speech, he made a crack about my blue pencilling his articles. As I escorted him to the door he said, 'See where his connection with *Reynolds* got that fellow Driberg, you could have done that.' Harold was always the pragmatist!

Tim Shane, assistant TUC press officer, rang me to say 'There's a rather sinister character named Sir Edward Jones trying to get TUC approval for a cartel which he is planning.' I investigated.

I found that Sir Edward had been responsible for the pre-war tin cartel. His plan aimed at stabilising export prices through a series of export product committees. There was to be a world clearing bureau with the task of planning exchange of goods, and a central world development commission to assist the backward countries.

Two right-wing trade union leaders backed the plan. Otherwise it was supported by leaders of big business. I commented that it was similar to a declaration by 120 British industrialists which made concessions to the public demand for new policies, but made no suggestion that the power of private enterprise should be curtailed. The Cooperative movement rejected the scheme.

Sir Edward Jones invited me to lunch at the Savoy. I said I could not make lunch, but I would call at his office. He assured me the TUC General Council was backing the plan and asked whether I would be prepared to discuss it with selected groups of trade unionists. 'I know you are a busy man,' he said, 'but I am sure we could make a satisfactory arrangement.'

I said I was not convinced. 'I had seen the results of power in the hands of the monopolists in the pre-war years and I would never trust them.' Sir Edward snarled, 'How do you spell your name?' I told him. 'German of course,' he said. 'Yes,' I said, 'but my family has been over here for about 150 years, longer than His Majesty the King's.' The subsequent meeting of the TUC referred the proposal back and I heard no more about it.

The attitude of the ordinary people to the German refugees

was an indication that there was an awareness that we were fighting the nazi regime, not the German people. During World War I shops with German names were looted. Some of my relatives changed their name. In the second war you could talk German openly. At the beginning of the war, the Chamberlain government panicked and arrested all Germans, including anti-fascists who had long been nazi opponents.

Reynolds launched a campaign demanding the release of the Germans who were our allies in an anti-fascist war. This did not stop many of them being deported. Some perished when the *Arandora Star* was torpedoed. Others were transported to Australia and others interned in the Isle of Man.

After a time tribunals were set up to assess whether detainees should be released. Many were, but one of the questions was, 'If this country is at war with the Soviet Union, whose side will you be on?' Those who would not commit themselves, mostly the communists, were kept behind bars. They were released when the Soviet Union became our ally.

Those detained in Australia were brought back. Siegbert Kahn, one of them, set to work organising the anti-nazi Germans. I took part in organising a British group called Allies Inside Germany. We secured the sponsorship of leading figures from virtually all sections of society. We organised meetings and exhibitions, providing information that had leaked out of Germany and occupied Europe about anti-nazi resistance. We organised opposition to the Vansittartists – taking their name from Lord Vansittart who proclaimed that the history of Germany proved it is 'aggressive and predatory by nature of its people'. Anti-Hitler forces in Germany, it declared, were negligible. Vansittart's book, *Black Record*, was used by the nazis to discredit opposition.

The voice of sanity on this issue came from Moscow. In February 1942, when the Red army was facing heavy odds, Stalin, in an order to his troops, said, 'The foreign press sometimes carries such twaddle as that the Red army aims at exterminating the German people and destroying the Ger-

110

man state. This is a senseless lie and a senseless slander. It would be ludicrous to identify Hitler's clique with the German people, with the German state. The experience of history indicates that Hitlers come and go, but the German people and the German state remain.'

At a TUC Congress Jack Tanner, President of the AEU, told me that two of his shop stewards had attended a meeting at which Moore Brabazon, a member of the government, had said that the best solution would be for the Russians and the Germans to weaken each other to the point when the Western powers would dictate the peace. Truman said the same in America, which was what Stalin had warned in his speech in March 1939.

Jack was determined to raise what he regarded as a betrayal of the anti-fascist alliance at the next day's session. We went over the day's agenda. There seemed no opportunity. I said, 'Get in on standing orders. Suggest it's a matter of urgency. Tell the delegates what it's about before the president rules you out of order.' It worked. Walter Citrine tried to wave it on one side, but the press reported it. Moore Brabazon had to resign.

One Saturday evening I came into the office to be met by Allen Hutt, who showed me the proof of a piece by Bill Bliss, *Reynolds*'s foreign editor, which said that if the allies went on delaying the second front, the Soviet Union was ready to listen to the peace doves of Berlin.

'Richardson won't listen,' said Allen. I went into Richardson's room. He was angry. 'Now you are going to start. Don't you see this is the way to make them open the second front?' I said, 'Bill, there's a solemn agreement between the allies that none would make a separate peace. *Reynolds*, which has been in the forefront of the anti-fascist war, now suggests the Soviet Union is about to break that pledge. I think that will be seen as a stab in the back.'

He was quiet for a few moments and then he said, 'You are right.' He took out the offending paragraph. Bill Bliss got information from the Turkish embassy. The Turks were nominally neutral. More significant, the censor passed the report.

One Sunday evening I picked up an American station on my short-wave radio. The speaker was talking about America's post-war plans. Jobs for all, milk for the children, and so on. I was thrilled. Then came the announcer's voice. 'You have been listening to Henry Wallace, Vice-president of the United States.' Next day, I asked whether the American embassy could send a copy of the speech. Not only had they no copy, they had no knowledge of the speech. our Washington correspondent managed to secure a copy and *Reynolds* had a scoop. We gave the full report.

It was rather like the reaction in Britain to the Beveridge report. Once made public, it was taken up and used all over the world as the promise of a better life for the people after victory.

One of the weaknesses of the American constitution is that the vice-president is chosen by the presidential candidate, for political reasons. Roosevelt dropped Henry Wallace for his last term and brought in Harry Truman. A strange idea of democracy! Would we have avoided McCarthyism and the cold war if Wallace had followed Roosevelt?

An innocent sounding question in the House of Commons aroused my interest in the activities of international cartels. 'Could a copy of an American book called *Germany's Master Plan* be placed in the House of Commons Library?' The reply was non-committal. What was this mysterious book? I intended to wire our New York correspondent to ask him to investigate. But, lo and behold, during my lunch hour, I found it on sale in a Charing Cross Road bookshop. It was a mine of information.

It was published by John Long, which had offices in London, New York and Melbourne. The English edition had a note saying that the American text had been retained almost entirely in its original form. This was obviously due to wartime restrictions. The strange part was that it had received no publicity in Britain and, as far as I could trace, none in America. It was written by two officials of the Anti-

Trust Division of the American Department of Justice, Joseph Borkin and Charles A Welsh, with an introduction by Thurman Arnold, the Assistant Attorney General. The sources quoted by the authors left no doubt of its authenticity.

I wrote a series of articles in *Reynolds* based on the material and enlarged them into a pamphlet, *The Secret Empire*, which sold 120,000 copies at 3d. On the cover I quoted Vice-president Henry Wallace, 'These groups which rule over economic empires have usurped the sovereignty of the people in international relations.'

I also quoted Herbert Morrison, Labour member of the cabinet, 'Cartels and trusts have within their grasp powers over fields of public wellbeing and public policy far greater in practice than parliament itself wields.' Both comments were made in the autumn of 1943, at the height of the war.

I quote here only the opening of my pamphlet (but the whole story of how the international cartels agreed that war would only interrupt their cooperation, and of how nazi Germany cornered materials essential to war, needs retelling today. The international capitalist monopolies still dominate our lives).

I wrote, 'While the common people of Germany were celebrating the foundation of the Weimar Republic in which they hoped to find peace and freedom, the German industrialists and militarists began to plan for the day of revenge. With cold-blooded genius they set out to find a counter-weapon to the British blockade' which defeated Germany in the 1914–18 war.'

I often wondered, during the McCarthy witch-hunts in America, whether the authors of this book, or indeed Thurman Arnold, were immune from attack.

As the fighting grew fiercer, more news came through of the resistance movements against the nazi occupation. I received one such message from Yugoslavia describing how Tito was mobilising guerrilla fighters in the mountains. I submitted my story to the censor. It came back, killed. I raised the matter with the central London branch of my union. We decided to ask Admiral Thompson, the chief censor, to meet a deputation. He immediately agreed.

We asked how it could possibly be that a proved fighter against the common enemy was refused assistance, while a so-called ally, Mikhailovich, who if not collaborating with the Germans was certainly not fighting, was recognised. Admiral Thompson explained that Britain recognised Mikhailovich and if others were involved that was a matter for the Yugoslavs. We went on talking. Then I said, 'At what point do we change our allegiance from the so-called ally, who is *not* fighting, to an ally who *is* fighting?' Admiral Thompson smiled. 'Don't ask me,' he said, 'ask the government.'

Some time later I got a message from the censor inviting me to resubmit my story. It was passed. As the war developed, Tito became an important ally with a high level British mission cooperating.

It was a very different story in the case of Greece. The allies had agreed on a programme for liberating the territories which had suffered under the nazis. Britain was responsible for Greece. Churchill had long since lost the fervour of the early days of the anti-nazi alliance. He went to Athens in 1944 to put the collaborators back in power and the resistance fighters in jail. That began the tragic story of post-war Greece and the struggle against the dictatorship. There were protests against the British action. Many asked why the Soviet Union made no protest, but Stalin stuck to the agreement. Progessives carried on with the fight. We put wreaths on the statue of Byron. We took deputations to the Greek embassy. I did a talk on the illegal Greek radio. For many of us, that betrayal was the shape of things to come.

Another background battle was in India. I used to meet Krishna Menon in a cafe near the office of the India League in the Strand. Nehru was in jail when war broke out, and his impassioned plea from the dock ranks as one of the great moments of the liberation struggle.

He was released, and supported the anti-fascist war. Another Indian group, however, saw their liberation

114

struggle as the only objective, with the claims of the opposing sides of war as irrelevant.

This group asked me to speak at a meeting to celebrate Nehru's birthday. I rang Krishna, 'I want to join in honouring Nehru,' I said, 'but I cannot appear on a platform opposing the anti-fascist alliance.' Krishna said, 'We'll organise our own meeting.'

Looking ahead to the early days of the post-war Labour government, I recall another India League meeting. Harold Laski, member of the Labour party EC, and I were speakers. Harold spoke first and ended his speech with the words, 'So, I demand that Britain give India her freedom *now*.' I started my speech, 'I must disagree with those last words of Harold Laski.' There was an awkward silence. Then I said, 'Give India freedom! What an impertinence. What Britain must do is to cease depriving India of the freedom which is her right.'

Some Labour leaders found it difficult to forget the imperialist past. Many of us who had worked through the years for India's freedom were convinced that, far from supporting Congress as a body embracing both Moslems and Hindus, the Cripps mission, which was sent to India by the Labour government to prepare the way for independence, encouraged Jinnah, first ruler of Pakistan, and his Moslem separatists. The tragic consequences of that division are still with us.

I treasure the memory of my first visit to India House. Here, in the former home of the British Raj, the Indians had taken their rightful place. Nehru was on a brief visit. The waiting room was full of visitors hoping to meet him. An official came in and said, 'The Prime Minister will see Mr Gordon Schaffer.'

Krishna did not neglect his comrades in the liberation struggle when he became the first High Commissioner. Later he was Defence Minister. 'The old story,' he told me, 'I was sabotaged on one side by the generals and on the other by the arms manufacturers.' Later he took a prominent part in the activities of the World Peace Council. I record here as a matter of interest a story which appeared in *Patriot* quoted from a provincial paper.

Jinnah told Ali Khan, Pakistan's first Prime Minister, 'You have started thinking of yourself as a big man, you are nothing. I have made you the Prime Minister of Pakistan. You think you have made Pakistan, I have made it, but I'm now convinced that I've committed the biggest blunder of my life. If I get well I will tell Nehru about the follies of the past and become friends again.'

14

When the Devil was Sick, a Devil the Monk Would Be

To return to the war. The Soviet armies, having encircled the Germans at Stalingrad, were poised for victory. The second front in Europe was, at last, launched.

The people enthused by the Beveridge report were beginning to demand concrete evidence that their leaders were genuinely determined not to return to the unemployment and the pre-war conditions of riches and poverty. The government, in which the Tories had a big majority, were conscious of this demand. In May 1944 they published a white paper setting out plans to prevent a return to unemployment. It was a spectacular repudiation of their pre-war policies.

I commented in *Reynolds*, 'All the things the Tory party, the Federation of British Industries and the Bank of England told you in 1931 were wrong. The Labour ministers who refused to cure unemployment by cutting unemployment pay and cancelling schemes of public works were right.'

The white paper outlined plans to steer industry to the former distressed areas, and to encourage local authorities to accelerate or slow down public works in the light of the unemployment situation. Emphasis should be placed on using periods of recession to provide more houses, better transport and improvement of power and water supplies.

The paper accepted the principle that if unemployment developed in one section of industry it leads to a reduction in purchasing power which has repercussions in other sections.

I commented 'Principles are stated, but there is no real suggestion of action to deal with the people who created unemployment in the past and, unless controlled, will recreate it in the future.' I said that the Labour party had given the answer that 'every extension of socialism makes it easier to plan employment as a whole. The Tories,' I added, 'cannot operate this policy, but they will try to persuade you that they can. And they will sell you down the river as they did in 1931.'

In June 1944, the Coalition government published a white paper on control of land use. Here too, it repudiated the pre-war policies. It asserted that all the measures of reconstruction needed after the war involved the use of land. 'It is essential that the various claims to land should be harmonised to ensure for the people of the country the greatest possible measure of individual well-being and national prosperity.'

It accepted many of the recommendations of the Uthwatt Committee, which had been appointed in January 1941, 'to make an objective analysis of the payment of compensation and the recovery of betterment in respect of public control of the use of land, and to advise on what steps should be taken to prevent the work of reconstruction being prejudiced.'

With victory in sight, the world trade union movement also moved into action. A conference in County Hall, Westminster, forged the unity denied by the pre-war conference at Zurich. The Soviet trades unions were equal participants, but this time America was represented by the Congress of Industrial Organisations, rather than the American Federation of Labour, which still remained aloof.

The first action of the new organisation was to demand a place at the peace conference planned for San Francisco in April 1945. Incidentally, at this conference, the roses on the table were called 'Peace'. It had been bred by the French breeder Meilland, and the buds were kept through the early part of the occupation and smuggled to America. They were placed on the peace table when the treaty was signed.

Hitler was not admitting defeat. He launched his new weapons, the flying bomb and the rocket, primitive and horrifying. The flying-bombs or doodle-bugs were frightening. When the engine stopped, you knew they were coming down, and you hoped one would not hit you. Which reminds me. Two old ladies were drinking their beer in a pub near the office. I heard one of them say, 'I preferred the blitz. It was more natural!'

I also remember the story of a Jersey man who went to the German occupying officers. He hated the British, he said, and offered his help. The Germans fell for it and sent him to Germany for training. Later they landed him on the English north coast with money and a transmitter. He went straight to Scotland Yard, and acted on official instructions.

He transmitted enough information so as to prevent the Germans becoming suspicious. He was ordered back to Germany for special instructions. His job was to report where the rockets fell. As a result of his misinformation most of the first rockets fell outside London. Only later did they start reaching the centre with heavy damage.

15

Brave Hopes – Labour in Power

The election campaign of 1945 will always be one among my happiest memories. I addressed about 30 meetings in various parts of the country during that campaign, also writing the weekly lead story in the paper. You could smell victory: I never had a bad meeting. The enthusiasm was there.

Just before the election I had a conversation with Jimmy Shields, International Secretary of the British communist party who told me they were thinking of supporting the continuance of the Coalition government because it was the only way to preserve the anti-fascist alliance. I said, 'Jimmy, the people would never stand for it, they hate the Tories.' Strangely enough, Arthur Greenwood approached me with the same idea. He said, 'What do you think of the idea of retaining the coalition with each party putting forward its own programme?' I repeated the people would never stand it.

The *Sunday Express* tried a dirty trick during the campaign. It published a picture of a hill on Wandsworth common with a handful of people and a couple of cyclists, and Ernie Bevin. The caption read 'Ernest Bevin addresses his constituents.' I knew the picture was a fake. So I checked up and found it had been taken on the slope of the hill, hiding the main audience. I exposed this in the early edition of *Reynolds* and the picture disappeared from later copies of the *Express*.

I opened the election campaign in Portsmouth where we won two seats. The chairman held up my pamphlets, *The*

Secret Empire and *Who Owns Britain?* and said, 'This is the policy we are fighting this election on.' One felt that *Reynolds* and my share in it was part of that victory. I will go further and say that *Reynolds* played a major part because it kept up the campaign all through the war – backing the war effort, backing the government (in so far as it was supporting the war effort) – but indicating that we were fighting to defeat fascist Germany and to build a new world after victory.

The Sunday before the election I met Clement Attlee in Peterborough, where Stan Tiffany won the seat for Labour. We met in the hotel later that evening. I said to Attlee, 'If what I've seen in various parts of the country is typical, we are in with a big majority.' He put his hand on my shoulder and said, 'My boy, I've been in politics a lot longer than you have and it's not the people who come to election meetings who win elections; the people will come out on Thursday and vote for Mr Churchill.' Attlee had no idea he was on the verge of victory. He was a good politician but never a leader of the people in any real sense. There were no opinion polls then.

When the election came and the results were declared – and we had to wait some weeks for the Service vote – I shall never forget listening to the radio, reporting that Tory minister after minister in the government had fallen. It was the reverse of 1931 when the Labour ministers were wiped out. So the new Parliament was elected, I had some regrets then because I could have been one of that victorious number. This is the story. I was approached by the London Cooperative Political Committee which offered to nominate me for various seats. As it happens they were all won. I was also approached by the miners in Cannock Chase to stand as a candidate. I was tempted. I told Bill Richardson, *Reynolds*'s editor, about it and he was quite worried. 'No, don't do it,' he said. 'you're going to have so many better opportunities to do all the things you believe in. We're not only going to have the Sunday *Reynolds*, we're going to have a daily paper. You'll be editor of either the Sunday or the daily.' Almost without further discussion or consideration I said, 'Okay Bill' and abandoned the idea.

My life would have been very different because I would certainly have got a seat in the 1945 parliament. There were hints that I would be offered a post if they got in. Maybe I would have met the same sad fate as the other left-wingers.

On the Sunday before the results were declared, *Reynolds*, under my by-line, forecast a victory! We were alone in the Sunday press. I also gave a warning on 5th August, 1945, in *Reynolds* under the heading 'Monopolists Stunned But Not Yet Beaten'. I said, 'Vast power is still in the hands of the reactionaries and they will fight as every ruling class in history has fought with every weapon that they possess.'

Immediately after Labour won I wrote a topical short book. It was published by Musearts, a firm founded by David Martin, the poet who fought in the Spanish Civil War. I told the story of how the Labour party was born out of the struggle of the trades unions and the socialist societies, and the story of its failure in 1931, and the final victory in 1945. I set out the difficulties which it had faced. I wrote, 'I have recounted this story of a 45-year struggle because it is impossible to assess the tasks of the new Labour government, and the results it will achieve, without taking into consideration the soil from which it has sprung. The Labour party is a working-class party; its claim at the same time to be a national party rests on the simple fact that more than 90 per cent of the people of Britain earn their living by hand and brain.' I set out the task facing the Labour government in this way, 'The Labour government sets out on the great crusade to change the economic basis of society, to lay the foundations on which later parliaments can build the structure of socialism, to show the world that a great industrial state can carry through economic reforms constitutionally and peacefully, that democracy can produce revolutionary changes without violence and without bloodshed.'

I pointed out that the Labour government was in a better position to carry out its tasks because not only had it an overwhelming majority, but it was able to take over a number of war-time powers and they were sufficient to prevent sabotage. I said, 'In normal times reactionaries would have started sending capital abroad as soon as the first results came over the tapes. The value of the pound would have been forced down in every capital. Foreign capitalists would have started taking their money away from London. Loans would have been called in from home enterprises in order to create unemployment and undermine the prestige of the new government. None of these lines of attack was possible in 1945. War-time controls forbade all exports of funds. Issues of all new capital were subject to strict government control, so that even if the financiers were to take their money out of existing enterprises, they would have no haven for it except government loans, which had been held at low rates of interest. New factories could only be built under licence and supplies of raw materials and most grades of labour were strictly controlled.'

I also quoted Oliver Littleton, who was one of the organisers of the pre-war cartels, and a typical spokesman of British big business. He said of the King's speech, when the Labour programme was introduced: 'The standard of life for every citizen in the country, and nearly every citizen of the British Empire and Commonwealth, depends on our receiving sympathetic help and the largest measure of financial aid from the United States. I challenge anyone in the House to deny that without American aid our standard of life is bound to fall, and will fall even below that austerity to which it has been reduced in the war. If you wish to obtain assistance from the United States you must be careful about the critical things you say about private enterprise.'

I cited the government's plan for an Investment Board which would seek to direct the nation's savings into the channels most useful to the nation's well-being. 'Finance,' I said, 'will be available for building houses, for re-equipping basic industries, for construction work. It will not be forthcoming for the speculators who caused so much suffering in the years between the wars, and which brought some of the more honest speculators to the House of Lords and some of the more dishonest to Dartmoor.' I set out the various nationalisation proposals contained in the King's speech which ushered in the Labour government, and I made this reference to the problem of land:

In the last coalition government, very moderate proposals were put before parliament to permit land to be acquired for town planning at prices related to 1939. The Tory majority fought desperately to secure every possible modification in favour of the land owners. Now, for the first time, the majority of the House of Commons is strong enough to deal with the land owners. Immediate steps will have to be taken to speed up the acquisition of land by local authorities, to collect for the community the betterment value created by community enterprise, and to devise some scheme of land purchase which will allow local authorities to buy land at a value related to the use for which it is to be put, rather than its value as a site in a particularly expensive area. In other words, if the workers require houses they should not have to pay inflated rents to meet the high cost of the land, if a local authority wishes to set out local gardens and swimming pools in the centre of a town they should not have to buy the land at the price which would have to be paid if expensive offices at high rentals were being erected. Block purchase of available sites by the state and resale to the local authorities and private enterprise at prices related to the use of land would do a great deal towards making a housing drive possible.

Turning to foreign policy I wrote,

If Britain, even under Labour leadership, allows herself to play the game of the reactionaries she will become an appendage of the United States, the last great citadel of private enterprise. She will lose every historical or geographical claim to be a great power. If she marches with the progressive forces in Europe and Asia, the progressive forces in our own Commonwealth, as well as those which have been thrown up by the war and which will go forward, whatever obstacle may be placed in their way, she can play a leading part in building the new world for which the people suffered and fought through the long years of war.

I added,

The Labour party is pledged to assist the former subject races to build their own lands in freedom under governments of their own choice. There can be no place in Labour controlled Britain for the policy of colonial exploitation from which British capitalism drew vast sources of wealth in pre-war years.

I concluded:

Thus Labour sets out on the great adventure. In recounting the task that lies ahead, both at home and abroad, I have not attempted to minimise the difficulties. The hopes of millions could be frustrated. Failure could come, not because the Labour government was unable to provide quick and easy prosperity, for no one expects miracles, but because it faltered in applying the basic principles on which the Labour movement has been built. I do not believe that the men and women who form Labour's first majority government will falter, nor do I believe that the great Labour cooperative and trade union movements which sustain a Labour government will allow them to fail. The world which hovered so long on the brink of a cataclysm threatening to envelop mankind in generations of fascist reaction now faces limitless prospects for the advancement of the whole human race. In our time the peoples of the world can abolish war. They can mobilise the vast resources at the service of mankind for the good of all peoples everywhere. They can usher in the century of the common man.

That is dated October 1945.

Starry-eyed no doubt, but millions shared my dream. In the sad aftermath of today (and I write in 1995), we have a right and a duty to examine why the dream faded.

On November 25th, 1945, I wrote an article headed 'Why Tories are Scared' with sub-heads 'Speculators are doomed', 'Land Profits to be cut, 'Bankers to get less'. In the article I said,

> Is it any wonder that the Tories are frightened? Labour measures do not constitute a Socialist revolution. As yet there is no real shift in economic power from the few who exploit to the many who are exploited, but the government is laying the foundations on which subsequent parliaments can build a socialist economy. The Tories, like every ruling class in history, are going to fight to retain their power and privilege. They cannot challenge the mandate of the government to carry through these measures. The battle will be fought in the country rather than in parliament; all the vast press resources controlled by the Tories will swing into action; certain industrialists have already hinted that they are ready to adopt a policy of non cooperation.
>
> One noble lord has tried to stop the people lending to the government while Labour is in power . . . The Tories want controls removed so that the vast funds now being forced into government loans with low rates of interest can be turned into 'get rich quick' enterprises. They moan that the government's export policy is depriving the people of motor cars, they never bother to calculate what percentage of the total population has ever been able to afford a motor car. They talk about the need for economy, they do not mention that the government's policy of keeping down interest rates, controlling the prices of essential commodities, and preventing speculation disrupting the national economy, has already done more to put the nation on an even keel than all the slashes in the standards of the people proposed by the national government of 1931. The one simple act of cutting interest on treasury deposit receipts has saved the nation more than £12 million a year.

I went on to express the hope, that the people would not be stampeded by Tory propaganda.

> They know that the years ahead are likely to be grim. The Labour government standing firmly on election policies and 'taking the people into its confidence as a partner in a great enterprise' can go forward undeterred by the flamboyant utterances by men whose every action in the past denies their right to speak for the common people.

I wrote in *Reynolds* about the first TUC after the Labour victory, that it was untrue the Labour ministers were dominated by them. But 'The Labour party will head for disaster if it once forgets that it is the political instrument of the trade union movement and the weapon of the working class. Although it rightly claims to be a national party it is national only because the great majority of the people earn their living by hand or brain. The leaders of the trade unions are living much nearer to the bitter and intensifying fight with privilege and monopoly, and there I do not think that the TUC will have the same honeymoon atmosphere as the last victory conference at Bournemouth.' I went on to say, 'The trade unions are realising that although Labour rules at Westminster, economic power is still firmly in the hands of Labour's enemies and the fight against reaction will not be confined to parliament.' I warned, 'In the field of foreign affairs anxiety is growing at the trend of British policy.' I also wrote 'There is another problem far removed from those that dominated the trade union congress in the years of slump and depression. The new economic situation, in which the key is the need for increased production, rather than the failure of industry to distribute its produce, has overturned all the old values. The trade unions are demanding the right to act as equal partners in dealing with the new problems involved.'

When the Tories came back in 1951 the shadow of unemployment was already looming. I wrote a piece in

Reynolds which tried to point out that even in a Tory Britain, only by increasing the consuming power of the mass of the people could you remedy unemployment. This is still true today. I started my article,

> How many women would like new summer frocks? How many men could do with a new suit? How many children need new clothes? How many homes would like new curtains, carpets and furniture? If need were the only test, the shops now stocked with textiles, the warehouses crammed to the roof with goods which shops cannot take, would be empty in a matter of days. The looms of Lancashire and Bradford are idle, not because there is overproduction but because the people cannot afford to buy. After paying the rent and the necessities of life the majority of the people have nothing left for clothes, furniture or any of the other consumer goods which are now cramming the shops. And so the mills come to a full stop. Hundreds of thousands of men and women are either out of work or on short time. Forced to live on the pittance of unemployment pay, they cut down purchases even further and add to the crisis of underconsumption. This is a story as old as capitalism itself – a picture of an unemployed shoe-worker whose children are barefoot, symbolising an economic system which cannot consume the goods it produces.

I suggested that the credits which were collected during the war – called post-war credits – should be released immediately and earmarked for purchases for consumer goods.

The tragic fact about the Labour programme all those years later, in the disastrous election of 1992, was that it failed to deal with the underclass as it was called. It failed to press for an increase in the people's purchasing power as the way to end the slump. But then it had abandoned any demand for a planned economy.

From this point, my story divides into several streams. First there is the story of the Labour government, its very great success and its failure; within less than five years an election reduced the majority to a handful and a year later, another election wiped out the majority and ushered in 13 Tory years. Another stream is the story of *Reynolds* which is so much my own personal story; the way in which high hopes of an invigorated Sunday and daily paper under the ownership of the cooperative movement was dissipated by the men and women of little vision, who were in charge, and thought the only way of running a paper meant emulating the sex and crime sensationalism of their rivals.

The other stream tells of the international struggle exemplified in the cold war on one side, and the nuclear arms race and the efforts of the peoples in various peace movements to save the world from another catastrophe, on the other.

16

Studying War's Aftermath

In the summer of 1946 the British-Soviet Friendship Society was invited to send a delegation to the Soviet Union. I (Vice-Chairman), the Rev. Stanley Evans (Chairman), Julian Silverman MP (who later became Father of the House), a cooperative member from Edinburgh, a Liberal MP, and Sarah Wesker (a trade union organiser, and aunt of the playwright Arnold) made up the delegation.

We were there five weeks and given every facility. I wrote a series of articles for *Reynolds* which were syndicated all over the world by Reuters (and subsequently published as a booklet by *Reynolds* and the British-Soviet Friendship Society). I think it gave a pretty good picture of the Soviet people emerging from the agonies of war, beginning to build the peace with the same determination they had shown in the years after the civil war and the War of Intervention in their country.

When I returned I wrote in *Reynolds*, 'Since I've returned from my tour, I have been asked a hundred times, "What does Russia want?" and "Why are the Russians so difficult?" My brief reply is that the Soviet Union wants above all a settled peace and is sometimes difficult in the international field because she fears that peace is being jeopardised. "Why," they ask, "are Britain and America supporting reaction wherever they find it? Why do these countries who were our allies in the common struggle against fascism, now seek every opportunity to quarrel with governments that are friendly to us?"' That sounds a bit naive now, but if you look back that really explains the situation. If friendship with the Soviet Union had continued into the post-war period, the world would have been a very different place today.

Looking back on my reports in the light of the disintegration of the Soviet Union in the 1990s, I still say that I gave an accurate assessment. The Soviet people, despite the tyrannies (and no doubt I did not make sufficient enquiries into these allegations) had achieved the unity and the devotion which during the war surprised and saved the world. And I was convinced that this same determination and willingness to sacrifice was apparent among the ordinary people in those first years of peace.

I will deal with two of my reports because they do have some relevance to later events. Latvia did vote to join the Soviet Union in the crisis years of 1940. I saw what was happening in Latvia after the liberation. I wrote, 'The Soviet central government is pumping assistance into the Baltic countries on a terrific scale. For the next five years Latvia will receive coal, oil, grain and factory equipment in a constant flow. During all that time her exports back to the other Soviet states will be negligible.

'Latvia is being kept for a period of years in terms of raw material, machines and other industrial equipment by her fellow Soviet republics, until both her industry and her agriculture have recovered. Divorced from the Soviet Union she would have been unable to secure any substantial industrial help from any of the countries which formerly bought her dairy products. Her recovery, at best, would have been slow and painful.'

When Latvia and the other Baltic states left the union their industrial production was many times greater than before the war.

Stalingrad told the same story. I recorded how, since liberation, it had built eight hospitals with 3,200 beds, opened 32 schools for 62,000 children and established special trade schools to train building workers. The Red October factory, left an empty shell after the fighting, was employing 10,000

131

workers, and was already turning out steel. I visited Stalingrad (or Volgograd as it has become) some 19 years later and
found a rebuilt city. There were beautiful boulevards along
the river, public buildings, hundreds of thousands of flats
and trees. The chalk cliffs nearby had preserved the writing
of the soldiers during the Battle of Stalingrad, their messages
of defiance, and of love. It was a moving experience. Whatever the later failures I shall never cease to pay tribute to the
men and women who waged the battle and rebuilt the city
with such devotion in the aftermath of war. I held in my
hand the Sword of Honour given by George VI to the 'heroic
city and people of Stalingrad'.

In the Urals I saw a scientific research station set up by
order of Lenin in 1920. There they had been charting the
mineral wealth of the Urals. I am quoting from my article,
'I asked one of the scientists if they had found uranium.
"No," he said, "but we have all the uranium we need in the
Soviet Union." Everyone in Russia,' I wrote, 'knows that
intensive work is going on into atomic energy. I was told,
though I could not check it officially, that Soviet science had
already released electricity from atomic power.' This was
written at the beginning of 1947. No one took any notice but
it was something of a scoop.

After my visit to Russia I desperately wanted to see how
eastern Germany was developing. I told Willy Richardson
that I was determined to go to Germany and I put my job
on the line. Later, when the Cold War had developed, it
would have been a very risky thing to do. But at that time I
was indispensable to the paper. In July 1948 for example,
the *Daily Worker* had reported my speech to a conference in
London. I had said:

Straight from another sector of the world front, from Berlin
itself, Gordon Schaffer of *Reynolds* spoke with gravity and
urgency as a representative of the British Council for German
Democracy. From what he had seen in Berlin he believed
that there were people on the Western side who really were
toying with the possibility of a third world war. "We must
not minimise the danger," he said, "but if we could put the

132

facts across, we can win the fight for peace. The fight for a united democratic Germany was at the very centre of the fight for peace."'

I got credentials as a war correspondent, and permission from the Soviet embassy in London to enter their zone. I was rigged up in khaki because you could not travel unless you were a war correspondent and in uniform. You had the rank of lieutenant-colonel, not that you had an officer's authority, but had priority on aircraft, etc.

When I got to Calais, I wandered along the quayside looking for the train. I heard a voice saying, 'Hi, soldier.' I took no notice, and then someone got hold of my shoulder and said, 'Hi, you're wanted.' And I realised that in my uniform, I *was* a soldier!

I travelled on the train to Berlin and saw the kind of economy that had developed. On the train from Hamburg a young man was openly boasting about his black market activities. He was buying up food in the countryside. I do not know what he paid with, it certainly was not official marks. He was one of the many who at that time were living on the black market. Cigarettes were currency and passed hands at so many marks a piece, sometimes falling apart without ever being smoked.

I got another insight into the atmosphere that was developing when sitting in a restaurant in west Berlin (the city was not divided then, but this happened to be in the west) and a group of people opposite were drinking champagne. You did not buy champagne on any legitimate income at that time.

One of them called me over, and said, 'You are English?' I admitted it. He said, 'Do you remember when our armies were fighting at Stalingrad?' I said, 'Yes.' He said, 'If we'd been together then we could have smashed them. Now you want to smash them and we want to smash them. Weren't you fools to allow our army to be destroyed?' I said, 'If your German armies had got to my country you would have sent our men and women to work in your war factories and when we were too tired to go on working, you would have gassed us as you gassed millions of others.' I wasn't offered any champagne!

I stayed at the Amzoo hotel where the press correspondents were staying and we had a bottle of whisky a week for 7s 6d and all the food in the world. The German people were very near starvation.

While arrangements were being made for me to visit the Russian zone I found the Russians had printed 18 million new school books for the zone because the existing books were full of nazi propaganda. I told one of the other reporters this story and said, 'Get a cab to the Ministry of Education, I'll give you the name of the person in charge, it's a very good story.' He said, 'Don't be silly, if I sent that over they'd bring me back for putting over communist propaganda.' Already this was the line the hostile press was taking.

I wrote a series of articles about my ten week stay in the Russian zone and expanded them into a book published by Allen and Unwin at a cost of 10s 6d. I tried to give a picture of all the developments in agriculture, industry, denazification, education, and so on, but I cannot do better here than to quote two of my conclusions:

> In this fascinating bit of Europe in which almost unnoticed by the rest of the world, social and economic changes of the most far reaching importance are taking place, you can gain a different impression every day.
>
> Talk to an ardent anti-fascist in charge of some measure of social and economic reform and he will almost persuade you a new Germany has already been born. Spend an hour listening to the cross-talk in a barber's shop and you will come out convinced that these people can never be redeemed.
>
> Examine the work put in by the Soviet administration, see how the Russians are sending the best products of their technical colleges and universities to help raise Germany to her feet, and you will be lost in admiration at the creative drive and sense of purpose of a people who can register such achievements after a devastating war and the loss of millions of their best citizens.

Check up some act of bureaucracy or petty tyranny by some unimaginative Russian official and you wonder how such folly can be allowed to jeopardize the work to which their country is devoting so much effort.

I emphasised that the elimination of fascism, and the causes of fascism, was the major objective in the Soviet zone. I added,

The eastern zone of Germany has operated on the assumption that the war was caused by fascism, and that therefore the main task of the democratic forces must be to eliminate fascism from the whole national life.

In the west of Germany, generally speaking, this has not been the case. Whatever machinery has been operated for the de-nazification of the country, there has been no basic policy of creating, in place of the old administration, a new anti-fascist administration.

I went on,

The Russians believe that attempts to set up federal states with a weak and ineffective social administration would not only play into the hand of the reactionaries but would also eventually provoke the united opposition of the German people.'

It is important to remember that the Soviet Union was not in favour of dividing Germany. It stood for a united Germany, on the basis of the agreed decisions reached at Potsdam. After NATO was formed they offered to join NATO. It was only when the division was clear that the Warsaw Pact was established and the military division of the continent became absolute.

The later story of divided Germany, the economic progress of the German Democratic Republic, as it became, the building of the wall, which was the only way to prevent the economy being destroyed, and the part played by two Germanies in their respective spheres comes later into my story, as does the final catastrophe, when Germany was united, but united in a very different way from what we had visualised after the allied victory.

The Council for German Democracy published a newsletter, *Searchlight on Germany*, and I wrote in the first issue of April 1945,

> We cannot forget the lessons of the last 12 years. We know that it was the steel kings of the Ruhr who brought Hitler to power. We know that German capitalism nurtured and used the nazis, for it feared that a democratic Germany would attack their power and privilege. We remember the support given to Germany by the great trusts and the other reactionary sections in the western democracies, and we are well aware that the battle for the final destruction of nazism will not be fought in Germany alone. The battle for a free Germany is in essence the continuance of the common struggle waged on the battlefield. Therefore we will do everything in our power to resist the attempts to divide the allies. In Germany the allied powers are pledged to retain the unity which alone brought victory in war. Enemies of the cause, for which the United Nations fought, are busy in Germany as in the rest of the world trying to drive a wedge between Britain and America on the one side, and the Soviet Union on the other. To allow these manoeuvres to succeed will be to throw away the fruits of all the sacrifices endured in the long bloody struggle against fascism.

My article in *Reynolds*, summing up my experiences in the Soviet zone in Germany in 1946, said quite clearly, 'The economic unity of Germany, like the political unity of Germany, is historically inevitable.' I added,

> But in the discussions on unity, the Soviet zone is by no means the humble supplicant at the allies' table. The Soviet zone is a going concern even after the dismantlement of factories for reparations which has now

136

ceased; its industrial potential is enormous. In the years
of the Weimar Republic, the machine-tool works, the
textile mills, and the many other industrial enterprises
in what is now the zone, never worked to capacity
because of slump and unemployment.

During the Hitler regime this vast capacity was geared
for war. Today, for the first time, it is engaged on an
all-out production drive. Out of a total working population of 10 million, unemployment figures are less than
90,000, and thousands of jobs are waiting to be filled.
A scheme for training craftsmen and technicians is
operating throughout the zone and, as in Britain,
employers are forced to take on a proportion of the dis-
abled. The zone is working on an economic plan, a plan
which it is true is often a makeshift affair because of the
need to improvise to make up the shortages.

Nevertheless it is a plan which keeps a tight hold on
materials and the labour force and checks, if it doesn't
entirely prevent, the flow of goods to the black market
. . . Russian policy, and I saw it in action, is to give to
the Germans a chance to rebuild a democratic nation.
The Russians know that to deny Germany's right to be
a nation is to fly in the face of history. They believe that
after purging Germany of nazism, the next step must
be to trust the democratic movements of the people.

That sounds very visionary in the light of the collapse of the
Soviet Union in 1991, but it did represent a policy which
would, I believe, have prevented the Cold War division of
Europe and made possible the peaceful reunification of
Germany.

The policy laid down at Potsdam to eliminate nazism, and
to end the domination of cartels was not carried out in the
west, and the subsequent development of the two sides of
Germany is in many ways a microcosm of the world in which
the two social systems were competing. It is beside the point
in this discussion that the failures in most cases were not of
communism or socialism as a system, but of the communists
and socialists who purported to put theory into practice.

The two social systems were different. In the east, rents

137

were so low that they could be afforded by any family; education was up to the age of 16 with career opportunities offered, and the health service was certainly as good as anywhere else in Europe. Economically the GDR had some powerful achievements. It was almost self-sufficient in agriculture; the cooperative system worked – I saw it in action. Their research stations in agriculture and horticulture, which was my special field, were certainly as efficient as any I saw in the west – in fact I saw many developments going on side by side, and I thought what a pity they weren't cooperating. But you must understand if you have two social systems of this kind, you have different conceptions.

They used to say to me that the difference between the east and the west zones of Germany was that in the east they did not work so hard. I replied that was fine, that is exactly what I hoped would happen! As a socialist I want people to work shorter hours, to have more time to enjoy what they produced. There was no unemployment. Of course, a lot of jobs could have been eliminated, but was that necessary? Was it necessary to carry out modernisation with the sole object of saving labour? I cite the recent case of the London Underground where they installed machines instead of ticket collectors, and presumably the ticket collectors went on the dole being financed by the state, while the enterprise declared that everything is much more efficient!

You have to have a different way of thinking to understand what happened in the socialist countries. I am not going to deny the failures, or how brave hopes disappeared in many cases – and I am not only now talking of the GDR – because I was conscious in the Soviet Union during my later visits, how the attitude was different. The enthusiasm which I saw in the 1930s and in the early days after the war was disappearing, and the lure of the West was accentuated on television and had an effect on morale.

On the other hand, the idea that the socialist countries – and I am thinking particularly of the GDR, Hungary and Czechoslovakia – were sunk in poverty just is not true. The shops were full of goods though many luxuries were in short

138

supply. If you wanted a car in East Germany you had to pay in cash and have one of their Trabants, but the cars worked. The technical level, of the people who went from East to West after the wall came down, was high. Some were unable to get jobs because they were of a higher technical level! Others took jobs from local workers for the same reason.

Looking at this sad world we have a great need to study in much more detail the reasons for the failure of socialism.

17

The Great Programme and the Defeat

The first job of the 1945 Labour government was to get its legislation on the statute book. My friend, Arthur Greenwood, was Minister for Post-war Reconstruction, and his immediate job was to organise legislation. He was short of parliamentary draughtsmen, and found that one was on a warship in the Far East. He had him brought home. I interviewed him two months and eleven days after the Labour government took power. In that time 22 bills had gone through. He said it was a session's work unparalleled in history. He expected the next session to deal with industrial injuries, to nationalise the Bank of England, and to pass the Dock Workers Regulation Bill. The other bills which Arthur looked forward to would nationalise the mines and begin the creation of the National Health Service, first of all with a National Insurance Bill and improved old age pensions, and most important perhaps, to control land values.

I was particularly concerned with the latter, partly because my brother Frank had been the Acting Secretary for the Uthwatt Commission and was in charge of the Town and Country Planning Bill under Lewis Silkin in the Department of Planning.

This bill, as I wrote in *Reynolds*, would, for the first time, tackle the problem. I recalled how various attempts had been made, right back to the beginning of the century, by Lloyd George, and by Philip Snowden, to deal with the scandal of profits made for land owners by a community effort.

140

The bill laid down that in areas cleared by the blitz, or in areas where slum buildings or obsolete property had to be demolished, the planning authority would have to pay only the site value of the land at 1939 valuation with some discount for owner-occupiers. The slum landlord would get only the value of the land in its slum condition.

The bill also provided that any town in Britain would have the power to schedule a Green Belt for preservation, and owners would have no right to compensation if they were refused the right to develop their property in the Green Belt. It also provided that when a new railway line opened, and sites for housing or other developments were available, the builders would have to pay a Central Land Board the differences between the value of the land for agriculture and its new value for building. A fund of some £300 million was created for compensating land owners in cases of hardship.

My brother Frank drafted the bill and was in charge of briefing ministers as it went through the Commons and Lords, where one expected the opposition to be centred. I was told by the ministers concerned that they could always depend on Frank to supply answers to any supplementary questions that might be hurled at them. On one occasion I was walking through the lobby and met Prime Minister Attlee with a friend. Attlee introduced us and the friend asked, 'Are you any relation to the Schaffer at the Ministry of Town and Country Planning?' I said, 'Yes, he's my brother,' and Attlee said, 'Brilliant fellow, brilliant fellow.'

The Labour government also planned to nationalise the mines. In those days coal was the gold of recovery; by taking over the pits the Labour government saved our economy. If the coal owners had still been able to dictate their terms, many of the older pits would never have been reopened, and the owners would have concentrated on getting quick profits because coal was in such short supply. Instead coal was given a plan.

I recalled an idea which the owners issued just before the election which proposed concentrating increasing power in the hands of the big firms to make the coal industry safe for the monopolists. I argued, 'The course that they had set themselves would have led not only to a decline in manpower, but to wage clashes similar to those forced on the country by the coal owners in the years after World War I.'

Even at that time some of us criticised the method of nationalisation (chiefly the responsibility of Herbert Morrison) because it was quite clear that a state-owned industry in the hands of a government hostile to socialism could use it to attack wage standards and the principle of national ownership. That is what happened years later. A group of us discussed a scheme whereby there would be a nationally owned industry, but the individual pits would be organised as cooperatives, with a structure similar to that of the wider cooperative movement. But the Labour leaders were not interested.

In my article setting out the first year's work I put in my own philosophy. I wrote,

> The test to be applied to the state owned mines is not whether they make a profit in the old capitalist sense, but whether they achieved their task of making the maximum contribution by the mines to a national economy. The value of coal in the present situation cannot be calculated purely in terms of pounds, shillings, and pence. If it comes to a calculation of profit or loss under nationalisation it is perfectly legitimate to balance the £20 million profits of the state owned Post Office with the losses incurred by the state owned mines. In fact it is questionable whether the government was right in insisting on each nationalised industry being self-supporting. [I inserted the comment that dentists in the new health service were drawing very high salaries and added] if you pay the men who drill the nation's teeth many times more than the men who drill the nation's coal you are heading for trouble.

I found that comment on the notice board of one of the miners' institutes.

The Health Service was one of the great achievements of

the first Labour government and many of us had worked years to achieve it. We had a body called the Socialist Medical Association and when I was campaigning, I used to put the demand very simply. I used to say, 'We give the government the duty to defend us, and we provide all the money they need for our defence. In the same way we say the responsibility of the government must also be the defence of the health of the people and we, the people, provide the finance.' That was the basis of the free health service, and it was that principle for which Bevan fought; he fought against the mandarins of the British Medical Association; he was the object of a virulent press campaign – I do not think any other minister would have fought as he did – but he would not give up on the principle, and in the end he won.

It was the decision of Hugh Gaitskell, Chancellor of the Exchequer in the 1950 Labour government, to put a 1s charge on prescriptions that precipitated the resignations of Nye Bevan, Harold Wilson and John Freeman. When they stated their full reasons they also included their opposition to arms expenditure, which they said was jeopardising the whole social policy of the government, but it was this attack on the Health Service which precipitated their resignations. It is a sad comment that prescription charges are more than £5, and many of the poorer patients have to ask their pharmacist which of their medicines are essential because they cannot afford them all.

Ernest Bevin, though he was Foreign Secretary, was the major force calling for the complete repeal of the Tory anti-trades union legislation. The TUC, including Sir Walter Citrine, TUC General Secretary, had been lukewarm about the project. They were willing to accept the clauses limiting trades union power provided they got the Civil Service Unions back into the fold, and some of the worst elements of Tory legislation wiped out. But Bevin would have none of it. He said the whole thing must go, and with a majority in the House of Commons it was easy to get the bill through.

In November 1947, when the government was getting into its stride, Hugh Dalton resigned. Looking back I cannot

143

believe that the only reason was an indiscretion committed on the way to the House of Commons when he said a few words to the correspondent of one of the evening papers not realising that there was still time for the paper to go to press that evening. One of his budget proposals was published. It had no serious effect, but Dalton resigned. I wrote at the time that 'He made a foolish and pathetically silly mistake and he paid the penalty.' But I wonder now what pressures were exerted. During the time of Thatcher and her press secretary there were leaks all the time, and even with the worst of them, no minister was forced to resign.

Dalton opposed the new trends of the Labour leadership in two ways. First, he was an inveterate opponent of the gathering plans to rearm the Germans. He said, 'Rearmament of West Germany is the road to Hell.' Second, and perhaps this was more important, he insisted on a 2.5 per cent interest rate. That meant that funds for reconstruction, house building and a whole range of activities which were so essential to the recovery after the war, were financed without an intolerable burden of interest. Both of those policies were anathema to the right wing, and I think that the pressure behind the scenes must have been on Dalton. This strange schoolboy honour business was invoked and he went.

I think too that the sacking of Arthur Greenwood in a Cabinet reshuffle was due to the same pressures. I recounted earlier the clash between Morrison and Greenwood. Morrison was the prototype of the compromise section of the Labour party; the idea of making capitalism work rather than changing it. Arthur was very much nearer to the rank and file, and the heart of the Labour movement, and some of his critics complained that he was too ready to mix with ordinary people. He would go into one of the House of Commons bars and have a drink with the staff, or with anybody; I remember once when we were having a drink in 'Annie's Bar' he suddenly said, 'Good heavens, I've got an appointment with the King,' and off he went.

Talking to fellow journalists in the horticultural press, 1960

Hyde Park. Ex-servicemen in the fight against German rearmament

Soviet visit 1946. Visit to children's play school

Reporting for *Reynolds* on conditions in the East End of London

The author (centre) with Sarah Wesker on his right. Soviet Delegation, 1946.

Meeting of the World Peace Council. The author on the left with Paul Robeson on Ivor Montagu's left

The author, invited as the London representative of *Patriot*, meets Mrs Ghandi shortly before her assassination

Grafting the tree of friendship on a visit to Sochi. Twenty years later it was producing fruit.

I referred to Arthur in an article about the fall of Dalton. I wrote,

> Arthur Greenwood who is still the best-loved leader in the Labour movement was the victim of a Cabinet reshuffle in which he was too proud and too loyal to fight for his own hand, or even to enlist the support of the party, by letting it be known how much the success of the government in carrying through their legislative programme depended on his efforts and his unfailing tact. Dalton is in a different category. Until that fatal moment in the House of Commons when he admitted his responsibility, his position in the government was unchallenged. [I recorded that his successor was to be Sir Stafford Cripps, and added] I always remember Cripps on the platform at Southport defying an angry Labour party conference which expelled him because he wanted a popular front against Chamberlain and the threat of war. For Cripps the wheel has come full circle. It will revolve again for Hugh Dalton.

Greenwood was offered a hereditary viscountcy. He asked me what I thought. I said what about Tony, his son, who was embarking on a career as an MP. Arthur refused. Later Tony became a Lord.

At this point I'd like to talk more about Arthur. I spoke at one of his election meetings when he was defending his seat in Wakefield during the 1945 election, and I referred to the speech he made in the House of Commons on September 3rd, 1939, on the eve of war. I said, 'I watched Arthur Greenwood making that speech. Never in the whole history of our country has a statesman been faced with a greater responsibility. His was indeed the voice of England because he expressed with complete sincerity and simplicity the determination of the British people to have done with the blackmail of the fascist powers, and to follow the only path consistent with honour.'

I added, 'I believe that when the history of this war is finally written the part that he played will be shown in its true greatness. In the first war cabinet after the fall of Chamberlain I would say without any fear of contradiction, and from a pretty close knowledge of the inside story of those desperate days, that the man who did most to sustain Churchill, the Prime Minister, and to mobilise the people for war during the dark months of 1940 was Arthur Greenwood.'

When he was Minister of War Production I said

> he had to fight the service departments to get cement to build the shelters because the Tories had failed not only to produce sufficient weapons but had even neglected the protection of the civilian population. Some ministers would have lost themselves in an approach like that for it was no easy matter to think about peace in those grim days of unceasing blitz. Nevertheless he did think ahead and laid the foundations of international plans for the relief of war victims for civil aviation and for a score of other post-war developments. [I referred to his transfer to the Ministry of Post-war Reconstruction and added] Because social security is at the root of all our domestic problems he appointed Sir William Beveridge to carry on his enquiry. If Greenwood had stayed in office there would have been another bombshell because he contemplated appointing another committee to investigate the question of full employment. The Tories were afraid of Greenwood's activities on behalf of the common people. That was why he was pushed out of his post.

I've often wondered whether the sacking of Greenwood from the post-war Labour government was part of the shift of right-wing leaders away from the ideals expressed in the 1945 election. Arthur was never a left-winger, but he was always firm on the basic ideas of the labour and socialist movement. I recall an interview I had with Arthur in November 1946. He said,

> You will see that we have not yet completed our election promise of jobs for all. A year is but a short time in

146

which to destroy the mainspring of capitalism, a reservoir of idle labour, or to eliminate the profit-making motive. We have already taken over the Bank of England and passed legislation to control the investment of capital. Many administrative steps have been made to further the policy of full employment.

Our election programme dealt with "industry in the service of the nation" which is part of our plan for "jobs for all". We have already nationalised the coal mines; we still have to deal with the electricity and gas industries, with inland transport and iron and the steel industry. We shall fulfil our pledges for these great industries and services before the next general election. We shall, as we promised, face the menace of monopolies and cartels and develop our plans for the organisation and development of the export trade.

Arthur was pressing for that full programme; the right wing leaders – Morrison in particular – were determined to push him out.

The story of the post-war Labour government needs to be retold today at a time when all the nationalised industries are being handed back to private enterprise by the Tory government. Saddest of all is that full employment, which was at the heart of the Labour government's policy, has been abandoned. No one, either in opposition or in government, seriously talks about the possibility of removing from our country this terrible blot, victims are now called an underclass.

To return to the story of the other members of that government. Stafford Cripps took over at a difficult period. His job was to hold down wages against trade unions who were expecting, at long last, to reap the benefits of their sacrifices during the war. I remember one press conference when he put forward his plan to freeze wages. When it came to questions I said, 'There are, I think, two million workers in this country who have agreements under which their wages change with the cost of living index, and if the index is rising they are entitled to wage increases to match. Are they to be

147

the most favoured of His Majesty's subjects?' There was a whole row of officials along the table with Cripps. There was a hurried consultation, and Cripps had to reply that there was no intention to interfere with trade union agreements. That was the sort of dilemma which he faced.

In many ways the nationalisation of the mines epitomised the struggle which the Labour government waged, and the way in which it organised national resources in order to save the country from the devastating effects of the war. In 1948, I summed it up like this. 'There can be no doubt that if the coal owners had remained in charge, there would have been a steady decline in coal production. The years of mismanagement in the coal fields had stopped the flow of recruits to the industry. But for the joint efforts of the Board and the National Union of Mineworkers to improve the conditions and to assure a career to the entrants, the 94,000 recruits now working in the pits would not have been there.'

I interviewed Manny Shinwell who was in charge when the mines were nationalised, and was now transferred to the War Office. What he said then sums up, in many ways, the triumph and the tragedy of the post-war government:

> Where difficulties have arisen, the practical idealism of the Labour party fortified its members, but there are large numbers of people in the country who are not influenced by ideals; they are much more concerned about material things. In the face of food, housing and other shortages, it is not surprising that among such folk the enthusiasm of 1945 has waned. Nevertheless, it is true to say that the government has as much solid support as when it was first elected and the strength of feeling amongst the workers against the Tory party is as strong as ever. The future depends, in a very big degree, on the direction and purpose of our policy. It may not be possible to provide all the houses people want, but when it is appreciated that everyone gets a fair share of what is going, and that rents are adjusted to meet income, and there is a determined resolve to stamp out racketeering in rents, irritation disappears. It

148

is the same with food or clothing or anything else. There is no use in talking about fair shares for all unless we make a determined effort to apply that principle. Indeed, there is more socialism in fair shares for all than there is in nationalisation of industry.

That quotation explains very largely why, when abandonment of that support for fair shares for all resulted in the resignations from the Labour government, the party was defeated. It is a lesson which should be learned today by the present leaders of the Labour party who, in the 1992 election, thought in terms of looking after the people who earned £20,000 a year or more, forgetting the people who were living on the edge of poverty. Sadly they still do.

Manny was one of the generation who had come up through the struggle. He was involved in the battles in Glasgow after World War I, and was regarded then as a revolutionary. He was now ensconced in all the grandeur of the War Office. When he said in an aside, 'These generals aren't bad chaps,' I thought, 'Manny, they've captured you.' Later, in the Lords, he lost all his revolutionary ardour.

I interviewed Shinwell's successor at mines in April 1951. Philip Noel-Baker told me how, when they had talks at Downing Street in January, the problem of the shortage of coal was very very grim.

We asked the miners to give us three million tons more in the first four months of 1950. We also asked consumers to help us by economising in the use of fuel. The miners responded splendidly. There were better attendances on week days, and Saturday shifts were accepted everywhere. There was a fall during January and the first weeks of February because absenteeism was high, but that was due to the influenza epidemic which affected all sections of the people. The men responded and weekly output went up. During the week before Easter, the men dug 300,000 tons more coal than in the previous year. Yes the miners have earned the gratitude of us all. Coal today, as in the past, is

149

the foundation of our economy. Full employment has steadily pushed up the demand. Today more than ever Europe needs our coal, and we must recreate a flourishing export trade.

Rather sad words when one thinks how, today, our coal industry has been decimated and pits closed. We are dependent on oil wells, which would not survive a modern war, and the pursuit of the private electricity companies for more profits results in imported foreign coal which only puts miners on the dole.

Another episode concerning the Labour government was the ground nuts fiasco and that strange statement by John Strachey that 'it takes a Labour government to run an Empire.' Contrast that with a statement by George Tomlinson who left school at 14, began life in the cotton mill and became a minister in the Labour government. I went to see him when he was near to death. He said, 'Gordon, there's one lesson I've learned in my long life in politics; we talk about class war, the Tories wage it.'

Earl Bertrand Russell, one of our most famous mathematicians and scientists, made a statement during this period in which he said, 'The United States owns and controls nearly two-thirds of the world's resources, but it contains only 6 per cent of the world's population. This is the basic reason for the starvation level of existence experienced by nearly two thirds of the people of the world. To protect this cruel system of plunder, the United States has created an unparalleled war machine. 3,300 US military bases are spread over the globe to prevent the victims of exploitation from resisting the domination of US capitalism over the wealth of their people.'

I quoted that statement in the articles I sent to various countries overseas, and I also paid tribute to Barbara Castle who was in charge of the Ministry of Overseas Development. I said of her then, 'She worked hard to secure assistance for a number of the newly independent countries, but these were no more than ambulance measures. There has been no

150

serious attempt to deal with the real problem. A rise in only 4 per cent of world prices for the primary commodities produced in the under-developed countries would be of immeasurably greater value than all the "aid" given by the capitalist countries. But this would mean seriously challenging the grip of the great monopolies, and they will fight to the end to prevent this.'

I might add that William Graham, who was in charge of the Board of Trade in the Labour government of 1929–31, said that the solution to the economic problem of the world was to raise the price of primary commodities so that the colonial countries which were producing them would get a fair price.

I interviewed Ellen Wilkinson, Labour Minister of Education, within a few months of her taking office. There she was bubbling with enthusiasm and determination. She talked of the very grave difficulties as a result of the war. She said, 'We are determined to ensure that no child is debarred by lack of means from taking a course in education for which he or she is qualified. As part of this policy we shall see that full effect is given to the decision of parliament that admission to all grant-aided schools are made on the basis of merit. We are out to increase and improve technical education not only as a service to the people, but equally as a vital measure for the successful reconversion of our industry and for the expansion of our export trade.

'We have the duty of improving and extending the training of teachers and ensuring steady improvement and development in the standard of education in all our schools. That is a pretty big job for a country just emerging from the grimmest war in history.'

She told me how educational authorities had been asked to submit their development plans which she hoped to receive in the new year of 1946. She went on, 'We also aim at a steady increase in the number of nursery schools and nursery classes. We are working closely with the Ministry of Health and are discussing with them the division of responsibility for the children under five. Here again short-ages of staff and building facilities are a big obstacle.'

Finally, Ellen told me, 'I would add that this great campaign to build a better and fuller education system is one in which all the people should take part. I hope the citizens everywhere will show their interest in the work we are trying to do. I think in this connection that the formation of parent teacher associations is a very useful method of bringing the mothers and fathers as well as the children into our work.' Ellen died tragically and much of the work which she looked forward to, in those very desperate days, has still not been accomplished.

Looking through my articles which appeared in *Reynolds* almost every week of that first Labour government, except when I was away on visits to the Soviet Union and the Soviet zone of Germany, no one could say that I did not give full and warm support to the government. It was on the question of foreign affairs that differences emerged, and I was not alone. Harold Wilson, Nye Bevan, and others were far more critical than I. I wrote an article about the Labour party conference in 1947, and the heading was, 'Ghost delegate at Margate was the US Loan'. I pointed out that the economic crisis was behind every discussion. I wrote, 'Put bluntly it is this: either, in the next 12 months Britain makes herself independent of the new American loan or by next year, the Labour party conference will have to decide between two alternatives – drastically cut the standard of living of the British people within two years of a general election, or prepare the nation to accept renewed assistance on whatever terms Wall Street may lay down.'

In January 1946, when the Labour government was just getting into its stride, I wrote how representatives of the Farm Workers' Union were about to see George Isaacs, the minister in charge. I wrote, 'They are putting to him this simple issue. If the government cannot guarantee to the men on the land, wages comparable with those paid in industry, will you remove the order which still ties farm workers to their jobs.' I went on to explain,

152

When many of the controls on movement of workers from one job to another were relaxed by Mr Isaacs, farm workers were excluded because the nation had to prevent any further reduction in the dwindling manpower resources of the countryside.

There can be no dispute about the justice of the farm workers' demand, but their problem goes far deeper. It will force the nation to face up to the economic situation created by the determination of all parties in the state to ensure a policy of full employment. The plain fact is that once there are more jobs than workers, the industries, which in former times permitted sweated rates of pay, must, as a condition of survival, offer wages capable of attracting a sufficient number of employees.

Full employment is elevating the dirty and unattractive jobs to a new and honoured place in the national life. It means ending for good the present situation in which cheap food for the towns is secured at the expense of sweated labour in the countryside.

The Agricultural Wages Board was made up of employees, trade union representatives and also independent members. The independent members, I wrote, voted against a pay increase for farm workers. At that time they were getting £3.50 a week and the farm workers proposed putting it up by 60p. The independent members said this would mean an increase in the price of farm produce which, if the cost of living was to remain stable, would have to be met by the government at the expense of the taxpayer. I wrote,

Here is a repetition of the same old argument used before the war to hold down the Cinderellas of the national economy. The coal owners could not afford to pay a proper wage to the men who had spent their lives toiling in the bowels of the earth. The farmers could only afford such a low rate of pay that the governments' insurance scheme had to be modified to prevent a farm worker with several children getting more for being unemployed than for working all day in the fields. The nurses had to be paid wages which made a mockery of their great profession because the hospitals could not afford to be decent employers. There is no place for any of these arguments today. If we are going back to the cut-throat methods of uncontrolled capitalism the farm workers, at this particular moment, are perfectly entitled to say that they cannot afford to remain on the land at the rates of pay offered by the farmers. The fact is that we cannot go back to the old capitalist methods because if they are allowed to operate unchecked we shall achieve not full employment but a repetition of the unemployment and the poverty of pre-war years.

I linked this report of the agricultural workers' demand with some of the other things that were being done by the Labour government. I said,

> The National Insurance Bill together with the Industrial Injuries Bill and the new rates of pay and pensions for the forces are designed to provide a minimum income below which no citizen will be allowed to fall. The Catering Act and the Wages Councils Act go far beyond the old trade boards in ensuring minimum wages for industries formerly at the mercy of unscrupulous employers. These measures represent the foundation on which a sane post-war economy can be built, but more remains to be done.
>
> When the Tory party, in fear of the electors, gave its blessing to a policy of achieving full employment it had no intention of carrying the pledge into effect. The Labour party intends to achieve full employment and that would mean many changes which the reactionaries will not like and which they will resist with all the power at their command.

The Labour party with its majority in the House of Commons was at least laying down in the post-war Labour government the right of every citizen to a job and a decent standard of living. The Tory government has not only abolished the Wages Councils which gave a measure of protection to workers who had no trade union power, they actually resist the Social Chapter in the Maastricht Treaty which would at least guarantee some minimum standards.

Another measure which was put forward in those first fruitful years of the Labour government was by Chuter Ede, the Home Secretary. In his Criminal Justice Bill he set out plans for penal reform. They abolished corporal punishment, including flogging in the prisons. Birching of boys, which could be ordered by magistrates, was abolished. Announcing this measure in *Reynolds* I said the pre-war Tory dominated coalition had proposed some measures for penal reform. It said that prisons should be places for reform and training rather than punishment. But it never went so far as to abolish corporal punishment because of revolts by the Tory party. I recalled how, at a Conservative womens' conference in May 1938, there were angry demands for the continuance of flogging. Speakers attempting to defend the Tory proposals were howled down. As a result the measure was withdrawn.

Then I said that in 1933 a bill had also been brought forward by the Tories with a clause abolishing birching, but the House of Lords insisted on retaining it. And the Tory government of the day gave in. I added that the Labour party bill would replace penal servitude with a provision under which the courts would be able to order a stipulated term of punishment. The prison authorities would determine the form of work and training which had to be undertaken. Hard labour, which at one time included the treadmill and the picking of okum, would be abolished.

Judging by the reaction of post-war Conservative party conferences, if the rank and file had its way, most of these punishments – including capital punishment, birching and flogging – would be reintroduced. It is a sad commentary again, with these hopes of real penal reform, that the situation in the prisons is now little better than at the time when the Labour government's measures were introduced.

In another article I described the situation of industry like this,

Once the whip of unemployment has been removed,

the essential workers who were formerly the most depressed, assume a new status which can only be assessed in terms of their contribution to the national economy and not solely in relation to the economic position of their particular industries. For example, the wages of the land workers must be examined in the future, in the light of a desperate need for more food, and not from the viewpoint of prices or the farmers' profits . . . The problem of relating wages to contribution to society, and not to the economic situation of a particular industry, was inseparable from the task of creating a planned economy within a predominantly capitalist society. It will produce many grave problems in the coming months, but it must be resolved if we are not to lose the battle of production. It means not less but more socialism.

The issue of the arms programme and the foreign policy of the Labour government came to a head with the resignation of the three ministers, Harold Wilson, Aneurin Bevan and John Freeman. They published a pamphlet for *Tribune*, the Labour weekly, which was an emphatic denunciation of Hugh Gaitskell's budget.

The immediate reason was not only the imposition of the health prescription charges, but the whole course of his policy. The three authors labelled it the budget nobody loves and said that 'Gaitskell's child has become an outcast, even his father can't love it.' They said that the budget and the rearmament programme were intertwined, and argued that the rearmament programme was based on an incorrect analysis of a long-term danger to peace on an overestimated Russian military strength, and on a false picture of our relations with America.

They quoted Harold Wilson in his resignation speech when he said that the country could carry either the burden of the arms programme or the export drive, but it could not do both. Harold Wilson also argued that the £4,700 million arms programme could not be achieved without irreparable damage to the economy of the country and the world, and

therefore the arms programme put forward by Hugh Gaitskell was already invalidated. Wilson added, 'If the financial
programme for rearmament runs beyond the physical
resources which can be made available, then rearmament
itself becomes the first casualty. The basis of our economy
is disrupted and the standard of living including the social
service of the people is endangered.' That is a warning that
should be heeded today.

The government's term ended and in the general election
Labour came back with only a tenuous majority which survived by carrying sick members through the division lobby.
After a year, Attlee called for a dissolution. There were some
who criticised him because it was obvious that it was the
lowest ebb of the party's fortunes. According to the story at
the time, the King knew that he was near death and he told
Attlee that he wanted to see a secure parliament when his
daughter took over. Attlee was criticised in some circles but
I doubt whether any sensitive human being could have
refused such a request. That was the end, for the time being,
of the great experiment.

The two general elections of 1950 and 1951 symbolised the
tragedy of the Labour party, for it was almost impossible for
it to win having rejected three leaders of the left. And it was
impossible for them to offer any real solution to the economic
problems once they had committed themselves to a massive
rearmament programme, and once Hugh Gaitskell was in
the saddle.

When Attlee reformed his cabinet after the 1950 election he
pointedly left out members of the left-wing pressure group;
Richard Crossman, Michael Foot and Ian Mikardo. The fierce
right-winger, Aiden Crawley, was promoted. He declared
there was no longer a class struggle and that capitalist society
had been replaced by 'pressure groups' in which the TUC
and the Federation of British Industries, who were on an
equal footing, had replaced the class struggle.

Two former left wingers, John Strachey and Manny Shinwell, had been given jobs in the defence department where

they could resist the growing volume of protest against the crippling burden of rearmament.

In January 1949 I wrote a piece in *Reynolds* which is ironic in view of the situation today. 'One of the most influential deputations ever to approach the government from both sides of industry is seeing Mr Harold Wilson, President of the Board of Trade, to discuss the growing menace of German competition. There is complete agreement between both employers and trade union leaders on the need to take action at once to stop the development of the German export industry on the basis of wage rates which are no more than half those paid in Britain.

'Unofficial hints are being constantly given by leading employers that unless something is done to stop this unfair competition, wage rates in the engineering industry will have to come down.'

In 1993 the Tories were fighting against the Social Chapter because they want to keep British wage rates down while those on the continent, including Germany, are being governed by the Social Chapter clause in the Maastricht Treaty which provides for minimum standards.

I wrote in *Reynolds* on December 28th, 1952,

> The Tories have only been back in power for a few months and the Tory policy of pushing up interest rates has meant that those who own capital can be assured a greater share of the national resources. The ordinary people have paid for dearer money in higher rents for council houses, in increased fares and in steeply rising living costs. The campaign is being devised to convince the people that it is in their interests that we should cut our social services and reduce the taxation on the rich. The Federation of British Industry has sent to Mr Rab Butler, Chancellor of the Exchequer, a memorandum headed 'Budget 1953' which quite bluntly asserts the view that our only hope of competing in the export markets is to cut taxation on the rich so that they can invest more in industry, and to slash social services in order to reduce national expenditure.

As I look at the situation today, I cannot help recalling 1931. The 1995 Tory government is studying various proposals to cut social services and other forms of national expenditure. Will there be similar panic measures to those imposed in 1931? Will the electors succumb in the same way?

18

The Battle for Land

Of all the shattered dreams of my story, the failure to deal with land profiteering and the collapse of the new towns (one of the most progressive experiments of modern times) rank as the saddest. My brother Frank, who was five years younger than me, was very much concerned with that great experiment.

Frank was seconded from his civil service job to be Secretary of the Uthwatt Commission, which was set up early in the war to analyse the problem of the land and the many problems associated with it. I described earlier how Lloyd George ran a campaign under the slogan 'God gave the land to the people' and how Philip Snowden, in that bitter speech in the House of Lords, said land profiteering was at the heart of many of the evils of our modern times. The legislation which was carried through from 1945–1950 by the majority Labour government was repealed by the following Tory governments. As a result we were back again to the profiteering, racketeering, Rachmanism (the name given to profiteering in the slums) and the ever mounting costs of houses.

Some years before, the wartime coalition acted quickly when the land issue arose. Lord Reith agreed to set up a central planning authority which was to take over all planning functions from the Ministry of Health. Then, in 1943, the new Ministry of Town and Country Planning was created with W S Morrison as the first Minister. His job was to secure consistency and continuity in the framing and execution of a national policy with respect to the use and development of land throughout England and Wales. Very shortly after that, legislation was introduced, as recommended by the Uthwatt Committee, and a year later the new Town and Country Planning Act (1944) – still under the coalition government – was passed. It made new and far-reaching arrangements for post-war reconstruction by enabling areas of severe war damage and obsolete development to be bought compulsorily by the local authority, replanned and leased out for rebuilding.

The Uthwatt Committee had recommended, as an essential minimum for the successful carrying through of these reforms, the transfer to the state of all development rights and values on land not built on. Four years of study, during the coalition government, had produced no more than a half-hearted white paper recognising the need for control and for some form of central machinery for balancing compensation payments with the collection of the betterment value of the land.

Frank was very much in the lead in planning the new legislation when the Labour government took over, and later on he described some of it in his book *The New Towns Story*. He wrote that Lewis Silkin laid down the three-stage programme for dealing first with new towns, then with planning and compensation betterment, and finally with the problem of the countryside.

This programme was to embrace a complete set of powers covering the whole needs of physical development for the foreseeable future. A simpler and more flexible system of planning control was to be applied to the whole country under the overall direction of the government. Development values would be vested in the state with once and for all compensation to the owners. Future building and other changes in the use of land could then be properly planned with a development charge paid where development was allowed. Local authorities could buy land and carry out comprehensive development in place of the piecemeal and spasmodic efforts of the past. New towns could be built in areas selected by the government. Stretches of our most beautiful countryside and coastline could be protected for the enjoyment of all.

All this, however, was purely a framework for administration, a mechanism for implementing policies which the government or local authorities wished to achieve. The actual decisions were to be left to ordinary democratic processes. Under these powers there could be built the new Jerusalem or a new round of slums. Under them, private enterprise could be allowed to play a major or a minor role. Under them, the owners of land selected for development could reap large profits or could have the profit reduced according to the amount of the development charge. Public purchase of land could be operated on a large or small scale according to the needs of the area, and the policies it was desired to secure.

These measures eventually reached the statute book as the New Towns Act 1946, the Town and Country Planning Act 1947, and the National Parks Act 1948. Perhaps the most courageous and far reaching series of bills ever to pass through parliament in such a short period. This famous trio earned for Lewis Silkin permanent recognition in the social history of our time. I might add they should have earned my brother Frank recognition too.

With the defeat of the Labour government in 1951 one of the first acts of the Tory government was to repeal those measures which impinged on the ownership and monopoly power of the landowners. When he was asked to draw up repeal legislation, Frank said he could not destroy his own baby. He was in too senior a position to be sacked so he was made Secretary of the New Towns Commission. That had a proud history too. But, today, it has been virtually demolished. The dreams have faded and the racketeering goes on. House prices soared and soared beyond the reach of a worker's wage.

Frank commented bitterly in his book *The New Towns Story*, 'The land system has run amok and prices are now completely out of hand. There are no published statistics from which the total burden can be accurately calculated but some £20–30,000 million in half a generation is a likely estimate . . . That has to be carried on the economy and born mainly by the taxpayer or by the tenants or purchasers of new houses . . . In a century in which Britain can pride herself on steady progress in the sphere of social legislation it is a major tragedy that the land reforms of 1947, broadly accepted by all parties as the essential minimum for the post-war reconstruction and the proper ordering of our economy, were so hastily swept away under pressure from the professional and other interested landowning organisations to open the way for one of the most fantastic property booms in our history.'

19

Shadow of Ethelred the Unready

I was not only involved in recording the work of the new Labour government, but also in developments in my home town, Kingston-on-Thames. Kingston had always been ruled by the Tories. As I used to say, 'since Ethelred the Unready was crowned in the market place'. In the halcyon years just after the war, the Labour party had high hopes in the local elections, and I was nominated a candidate. At that time the Kingston Tories split. There was the original Conservative organisation and the Chamber of Commerce, broadly run by Bentall's, the large store.

After the election – and I was a successful candidate – the Council was divided 16:16, which meant that the Mayor, a Tory, had the casting vote. But we soon discovered that two elderly Tory members had to be in bed sometime after 9.30pm. The Tories formerly met at teatime, having cosy little meetings, but we changed the rules so that those who had to earn their living could get to council meetings. If we wanted to be certain of getting something through we would just carry on talking until these two members had gone home.

When the election results were declared we sang the *Red Flag* on the town hall steps and were not ashamed of it. After all, the Labour party, in its manifesto for the election, *Let us Face the Future* said, 'We're socialist and proud of it.' We were also socialists and proud of it. In the long term we could not do a lot, but we did build some of the best post-war blocks of flats at Kingston Hill, an area which our opponents would have kept for temporary accommodation, and we did quite a few things for the Borough. A particular incident concerned Sunday games. For years, whenever anyone suggested the recreation grounds should be open for games on a Sunday, there was a massive campaign against it by religious extremists and the Council succumbed.

A colleague on the property committee and I were invited to meet Bentall's representative (the Mayor and Town Clerk were also there). Bentall's man put across his proposal: the Council owned some tennis courts. The club which had them before the war had disappeared and they were more or less derelict. The idea was that Bentall's would take them over, would rebuild the pavilion and restore the courts. I turned to the Mayor and said, 'What about Sunday games, Mr Mayor?' 'Oh,' he said, 'that's a matter for Bentall's.' The Bentall's man said, 'Of course, we want to play on Sundays, that's when our workers are off-duty.' Having got that out of them, we broke the news that only over our dead bodies would we hand over the municipal tennis courts to Bentall's.

We suggested that there should be a system under which business houses could book some hours for their staff, and the rest of the time it would be open to the public. Bentall's grudgingly accepted and I told the Town Clerk to put down the issue of Sunday games on the agenda for our next committee. When the committee met, I moved that all our recreation grounds be open on Sunday, and no one opposed. When it came before the full council nobody opposed either. They knew that if they had I would have told the story of that interview.

At my end of the Borough there was no library for the children. The only one was on the other side of the main road from my home area, and I was very anxious to use my time on the Council to get a local library. I found a piece of land and got the Council to issue a compulsory order giving permission to build. I also found that we had a caravan which had been given to us by the people of Kingston, Ontario, for use during the war. I suggested that we use this as a travelling library. The Tories opposed, one saying, 'We can't do that, we might need it for taking cups of tea around the Borough sometime.' At that time we had British restaurants set up by the local authorities during the war to provide cheap meals. I replied, 'You want to take cups of tea around the Borough, but you're intent on abolishing the British restaurants!'

Anyway, I got my travelling library and it was very popular. The plan for a library building also went ahead, but on another piece of land. The piece of land I had wanted mysteriously fell into the hands of the developers. I had lost my seat on the council and my opponent opened the library and took all the credit. That's local government!

In Kingston we built one of the first post-war power stations. It was on a site by the river. The sewage beds had to be removed while the power station was built. For a time the sewage was being discharged without proper purification, into the river. I heard about this and I raised it at a Council meeting. There was consternation. The Medical Officer told me, 'It's quite all right, it's not dangerous.' I said, 'But it must be dangerous. My children swim in that river and I'm very worried.' I suppose in the end the two enterprises caught up with each other, but rather interestingly, my protest was not reported in the local press.

Eventually the power station was built and the sewage beds were moved to Mogden. We had a ceremonial opening. King George VI and the Queen (now the Queen Mother) were the guests. At a Council meeting before the ceremony I left immediately after the proceedings, but many of the councillors remained practising curtsying and bowing. I was very amused to hear about this display of sycophancy. When we were introduced to the royals at the ceremony I simply shook hands and the King said, 'How do you do?' and that was that. Afterwards the Town Clerk gave the King and Queen tea in a separate room, and after they had gone he said, 'Do you know, the King, when he took his jam, instead of putting it on his plate, put it straight on his bread and butter!' I imagine half the people in Kingston were putting

166

their jam on their bread and butter instead of on their plate after that!

When we lost our majority, and I my seat at the next election, I was flattered to be invited to the dinner before the new Council met. I was asked to propose the toast of 'Kingston'. You can make a half-hour speech with a few notes, but if you are only given ten minutes you have to be very careful with your words.

So I really took a lot of pains with this speech. I spoke about our lovely Borough by the river, and our history, and it went very well. Afterwards, while we were having a final drink, one of the councillors said to me, 'You know, Gordon, you're wasting your time with the Labour party, why don't you come in with us?' I said, 'If I want to sell out to Tories, I know a lot more expensive ones than the ones at Kingston!' But we had good comradeship on that Council. We were bitterly opposed politically, but there was a genuine devotion by most of the Tories to the welfare of the Borough.

20

Not Nazis – Businessmen

The story of Labour's attempt to change Britain in the interests of the people must be set against the formidable power of their enemies fettered for a time, but by no means defeated.

'Let Us Face The Future', the programme on which Labour won its great victory, was forthright in its determination to destroy the fascist policies which had led to war, and its determination to deal with the economic basis of fascism. Ernest Bevan made this clear in almost his first speech as Foreign Secretary. He said,

> We have to consider the ownership of the basic German industries. These industries were previously in the hands of magnates, who were closely allied to the German military machine which financed Hitler and which, in two wars, were part and parcel of Germany's aggressive policy. We have no desire to see these gentlemen or their like to return to a position which they have abused with such tragic results. As an interim measure we have taken over the possession and the control of the coal and steel industries and vested them in the Commander-in-Chief. We shall shortly take similar action in the case of the heavy chemical industry and the mechanical engineering industry.
>
> Our intention is that these industries should be owned and controlled in the future by the public. The exact form of this public ownership and control is now

being worked out. They should be owned and worked by the German people but subject to such international control that they cannot again be a threat to their neighbours. The case for public ownership of heavy industries was never stronger than it is in Germany today. I am satisfied that this statement in the House today will give hope to those Germans who never again want to see themselves the victims of these cartels and trusts which led them to disaster, those magnates who used the labour and skill of the German workman with such ingenuity and with such disastrous results for them and for the whole world.

They were brave hopes but in early 1952 another book was published which continued the story of the cartels, which I recounted earlier in my review of *Germany's Master Plan*. This book was by James Stewart Martin entitled *All Honorable Men* and was published by Little, Brown of Boston. He tells how, so soon after the war, the interests and even the men responsible for the pre-war German trusts were coming back to power. Martin describes how he was nominated by Roosevelt to prepare the break-up of the pre-war nazi trusts, how he photostated some 4,000 documents at the Luxembourg headquarters of the International Steel Cartel. This is how he described his find, 'Four thousand documents had opened up a panorama of international ties among all the major steel firms of the world, including the details of their working relations with the Germans at the time the cartel was organised.'

Martin tells how a member of his team interviewed the financier Dr Schacht who engineered Hitler's plan to gear Germany's economy for war. Schacht, who was earlier on trial before the International Court as a nazi war criminal and was in prison at the time, explained that he had a plan to make Germany the international centre of an economic federation formed with other European countries. Martin writes, 'Though Schacht's plan was not immediately accepted, the position taken by the Western German government in negotiations in France over the Schuman plan bore a striking resemblance to Schacht's.' If he were here today Schacht would probably say they had been achieved in the EEC.

The story of how Standard Oil of America and I G Farben met at the Hague after war broke out to find a way of maintaining their contacts during hostilities, and preparing for resumption after the war, was told by the American Antitrust Department. During the war Martin found the documents. They were marked by one of the I G Farben executives with the label 'Post-war camouflage'. The documents showed that Flick, one of the steel magnates, had been given special terms because of his contributions to Himmler's funds for the hire of slave labourers from the concentration camps. This was run by a nazi corporation set up specially to deal with slave labour.

Martin's first realisation of the difficulties he was to face came when he met Sir Percy Mills of the British Control Commission. One of his colleagues complained that while domestic servants who had been members of the nazi party were being removed, men like Dinkelbach and Stinnes, the Ruhr industrialists, were running loose. Sir Percy Mills wheeled on him, 'What's wrong with them?' he asked. 'They're not nazis, they are businessmen.'

Martin found that the Dresdner Bank granted five million reichmarks to the special organisation which supplied 'cheap expendable slave labour' to heavy industry, while the Reich Bank had special arrangements to receive and dispose of carefully inventoried bags of gold teeth, jewellery and other valuables shipped from Auschwitz and the other concentration camps. Through the Reich Bank (a member of the Bank of International Settlements), this loot was disposed of. Martin recalls that at the time of his visit, there was a directive from President Roosevelt for the break-up of the nazi cartels, and France and the Soviet Union agreed a draft law to break up the monopolies in their zones. It was vetoed by Sir Percy Mills of Britain. In the end, Martin threw up his hand and resigned his job because he said that his job was to break up the cartels in Germany but 'all threads led to New York and Washington'.

In an article for various overseas and American newspapers I filled in the background to Martin's book. I said,

> Now go back for a moment to the events in America in 1946 which set the capitalist world back on the course which has led so swiftly to the re-creation of the economic policies which prepared for war before 1939. In 1946 Leo D Welch, Secretary Treasurer of Standard Oil of New Jersey, gave the signal for the destruction of Roosevelt's policy of peaceful competition and coexistence between the socialist and the capitalist worlds. Welch said, 'As the largest producer, the biggest source of capital, and the biggest contributor to the global mechanism, we must set the pace and assume the responsibility of the majority stock-holder in this corporation known as the world.' He went on to call for an all-out struggle by private capital to save its position in the world. From that time the men who opposed Roosevelt, the men who had built up the nazi economy through the interlinking of world capitalism gradually assumed power.

I cannot resist putting on record a statement made at the time by Senator Stamford, a delegate from the Republic of Ireland to the Consultative Assembly of the Council of Europe, which met at Strasbourg. He told the Assembly, 'The American representatives do not seem to understand what it means to be a European. They do not seem to understand what we live for and sometimes die for. They think they are rich and we are poor, in fact in relation to the things that matter, to the things that many of us value most, they are still our undischarged debtors.'

Stamford went on to ask if the Americans would like all the European Gothic cathedrals to be streamlined into functional skyscrapers, whether they would like Shakespeare and Dante to be reduced to official condensations in the *Reader's Digest*. He said that the argument that if we do not talk

American we get no dollars was crude, 'The reply should be made that if the Americans shut off their dollar fund, Europe should close their art galleries and museums against them.'

In the early 1950s when the Cold War was at its height, and the McCarthy witch-hunt against all progressives was being intensified in America, Professor Brady (who had been a member of President Roosevelt's Brains Trust) told me this story,

> As the war was drawing to its close and Vice-President Henry Wallace had stirred the nation with his call for an end to poverty and for measures to prevent a return to the unemployment of the pre-war years, Roosevelt endorsed a memorandum outlining the part America must play in reconstructing the war-shattered world. This memorandum pointed out that alone of the warring nations America would emerge with a vastly increased productive capacity but also with an industry geared to production of armaments. To maintain this productive capacity, and thereby counter the danger of unemployment, there were two alternatives – either to continue arms production or to switch to producing the goods of peace. The memorandum said that the switch to peace production will involve finding overseas markets and this must be met by vast dollar loans to the countries that needed the goods but could not afford to pay for them. It advocated loans on a massive scale, particularly to the Soviet Union, China and India.

It may be that Roosevelt would not have been able to carry out this policy. Certainly, his replacement of Wallace for Truman in his last election was a sign that he was giving way to pressure from the reactionaries. When Roosevelt died in April 1945, on the eve of the San Francisco peace conference, Truman reversed the pledge of post-war collaboration between the wartime allies and set the western world on the course of Cold War. And the proof that Truman's America was taking the other alternative set out in the Roosevelt memorandum, continuance of arms production, came in an item in the diaries of James Forrestal, Truman's Secretary of Defence, on 14th November, 1945. 'Admiral Edwards advised me that the army is in pell-mell haste to equip all the South American countries with armaments, ground forces, air and navy on the ground that this is necessary to carry out the concept of regional arrangements for reciprocal defence.'

21

Whose 'Cards on the Table'?

As tension grew between the left wing and the post-war Labour government leadership, Ernest Bevin tried to challenge his opponents with the demand 'Put your cards on the table – face upwards.' I wonder whether he was quoting from a little known pamphlet which was published two years after the general election called *Cards on the Table*. Strangely enough it came from the headquarters of the Labour party but with no author.

It was clearly an attempt to stem what it realised was a legitimate anxiety on the part of the rank and file. The pamphlet began by saying a minority of Labour's own supporters were sincerely disturbed about the government's activities abroad. 'Apart from disagreement on particular issues like Palestine, Greece and Spain, which are not discussed in this pamphlet, some loyal members of the party are genuinely concerned about the general line of Labour's foreign policy, because it is held to take sides with a capitalist America against a socialist Russia, or to entail a diversion of men and money from home production which this country cannot afford.'

There was the clear voice of the Foreign Office in the phrase 'Until international relations can be conducted entirely under a guaranteed rule of law, the effectiveness of Britain's part in this international activity depends on her power whether her policy is capitalist, socialist, communist or fascist.'

Then the anonymous author said, 'Socialism can only be achieved at home if the Labour party stays in office and if the country's economy is put on its feet as a going concern. It is easier to forget that a socialist foreign policy equally depends on the material support of the British electorate. The maintenance of Britain as a world power is more than the precondition of a socialist foreign policy. At the present time when the world is torn between the economic attractions of capitalist America and the ideological appeal of Soviet Russia, democratic socialism will only survive as an alternative to these extremes if Labour Britain survives as a world power.'

This was the pamphlet's description of Europe in 1945.

> The whole of Europe was in a state of moral, social and economic collapse. The physical destruction alone was immense, cities laid waste, ports destroyed, railways and bridges shattered, harvests ruined.
>
> In addition, the wreckage of the fascist new order was not yet replaced by stable democratic governments; the black market was rampant; violence and fraud were taken for granted; vast armies of occupation were scattered far from their own homes. Twelve million displaced persons presented an urgent human and economic problem. In the absence of peace treaties, frontier questions threaten a new outbreak of war in a dozen places. Europe trembled at the approach of famine and disease . . .
>
> The elimination of Germany, Japan and Italy, the weakness of France and China, reduced the number of effective world powers to three: Soviet Russia, the USA and Britain. Yet the absolute power of each of these was increased by new technical developments to such an extent that any one in the absence of the other, might have controlled the world. The victorious powers were like three elephants in a boat.

The whole tenor of the pamphlet was to blame the Soviet Union slightly more than America. Yet the objective picture of the world in 1947 intended to indicate that America was completely dominant, and that the Soviet Union was virtually on the ropes.

The pamphlet added,

> The United States ended the war with prodigious assets, unchallengeable control of all the oceans, a great long-range bomber force, sole possession of the atom bomb, 70 per cent of the world's productive capacity, great surpluses of all products in a world of scarcity.
>
> Few people outside Russia realise the cost of her victory and the Russians themselves prefer to minimise their crippling losses. But in fact the development of the Soviet Union had been set back ten years. Her dead were estimated at seven million, her homeless at 30 million, the destruction of a third of European Russia and the dislocation of Soviet industry were made worse by a serious weakening of communist discipline.
>
> The collective farm system was menaced not only by individualistic peasants but by the illegal encroachment of public organisations. Contact with European civilisation had disturbed the army. The war had disclosed serious minority problems. Two autonomous republics in the Crimea and the Caucasus were degraded in status, their populations deported for fighting with the nazis. New forms of nationalism, stimulated by the war, threatened Bolshevik ideology.

The pamphlet was at pains to answer the allegation that Ernest Bevin, under a Labour government, was pursuing the Fulton policy of Churchill in calling for an alliance, if necessary war, against the Soviet Union.

To me, the contradiction was that having given this description of the overwhelming power of the Americans and the impossible military situation of the Soviet Union immediately after the war, the whole tenor of the policy was still that the threat of war came not from America but Russia. In this way the calamitous arms bill was sustained.

If the Tory party under Churchill had been in power after

1945, the danger of war would have been very much greater. Also the pamphlet said correctly that the Labour government's measures to control the economy would mean that 'a few million tonnes of coal for export would change the face of our European policy in a night'. The mobilisation of resources did enable the country to recover and exert some influence in foreign policy.

I could not accept the black and white picture of the world situation given in this pamphlet. On the other hand there were all sorts of factors which left me confused although, by and large, I was convinced that the Soviet Union wanted peace and that America was preparing for the eventuality of war.

One thing is clear. There was no war threat from the Soviet Union. The threat, from the American viewpoint, was of the success of socialist planning. American policy was to force the Soviet Union into an arms competition which it could not sustain. But who would say that with the collapse of the socialist countries, the world is a safer or better place?

22

World Peace Forces Unite

*'I will dare, dare, dare, until I die. I will go out now to the common
people. Let the love in their eyes comfort me for the hate in yours.'*
Bernard Shaw, quoting St Joan of Arc, as she was about to
face her executioners.

I was not alone in believing that, on balance, the danger
of war and of a new period of rearmament came from the
Americans and not from the Soviet Union. That was the
motive for the setting up a peace organisation based on the
belief that coexistence and cooperation between the powers
was possible, and that the rule of law through the United
Nations could be achieved. It found its expression in the
great peace conference of 1950.

The conference was scheduled to be held in Sheffield. The
British Peace Committee had written to the Prime Minister,
Clement Attlee, informing him of the conference, and
requesting that overseas' delegates would be allowed in the
country. The initial reply was that 'in this free country' there
is no power that would forbid such a conference, but in
actuality so many people were refused entry at the ports that
the conference became impossible. The Polish government
then offered to host the conference in Warsaw, a city still
bearing the scars of war, and travel was organised by plane,
boat and train.

In a pamphlet recording the conference I wrote, 'Picasso,
whose pictures in the Tate and other galleries are admired

by thousands, was one of the few foreign delegates to satisfy the scrutiny of the immigration people.'

I added a crack that perhaps they wanted to know if he could earn a living when he got here! Picasso came but he refused a later invitation to visit a special exhibition of his works, as a protest against the treatment of his fellow delegates.

I wrote that Joliot-Curie, 'whom the British people remember and admire, and who smuggled material for atomic research out of France during the occupation and when the war ended, refused to use his genius for anything other than peaceful purposes, was actually banned from coming to Britain.' He was turned back when he arrived at a British port. I also mentioned that the Russian composer Shostakovich was invited by the BBC to give a performance of his music during his stay in Britain, but was denied a visa. Nenni, from Italy, who was wildly applauded at the Labour Party Conference a few years earlier, was told in Rome that he would be regarded as an undesirable if he presented himself at our shores. And Paul Robeson, who was idolised by millions of Britons, was denied a passport by the American government.

In the introduction to my pamphlet I said, 'The Peace Movement in Britain, despite bans and persecutions, is already deep-rooted in the minds and hearts of tens of thousands of sincere, devoted men and women. A people which gave birth to the Tolpuddle Martyrs, the Chartists and other pioneers cannot be intimidated. Men and Women who created the great trade union, cooperative and Labour movements cannot be indefinitely duped by a propaganda which is steadily forced to declare as its allies the reactionary sections of the United States, the German fascists, the Japanese militarists and the bloodstained rulers of Franco's Spain.'

The resolutions adopted by the Congress certainly were not communist propaganda, as the media tried to maintain, but were modest demands, particularly to end the war in Korea.

In the light of history I should put on record the address

by the conference to the United Nations: 'If the United Nations is to realise the hopes that the peoples still repose in it, it must return to the path marked out for it by the peoples since the days of its foundation, and as a first step in this direction, must call a meeting of the five great powers, the Chinese People's Republic, France, Great Britain, the United States of America, and the USSR, to discuss and resolve peacefully these current difficulties.

'Voicing the demands of the peoples weighed down by the burdens of war budgets, and firmly resolved to secure for humanity a firm stable peace, we present for the consideration of the United Nations, of all parliaments and all peoples the following proposals; the unconditional prohibition of all atomic weapons and all bacteriological, chemical, radioactive, and other devices of mass destruction and a declaration that any government that henceforth employs any such weapons shall be considered guilty of a criminal act.'

Looking back on that declaration in the years since then, the weapons cited in that declaration have multiplied a hundred times. They have become more dangerous and more threatening than ever. The Soviet Union at that time had no possibility of making war, but the failure to take the proposed step of disarmament meant that it utilised its resources to make weapons instead of building the peace for which its people had suffered during the terrible years of war.

I recall that during my visit to the Soviet Union, one of the ambassador's colleagues told me at the British embassy that, 'The great mistake the Russians are making is that they are concentrating on capital goods instead of making the consumer goods for which the people are longing, and those shortages will continue for many years.' That prophecy was right, but it was the arms programme imposed on the Soviet Union which played a major part in the continuation of poverty and eventually the breakdown of the regime.

Professor Joliot-Curie talked at the conference about the danger of German rearmament. I wrote in my pamphlet, 'He recalled the pledges of Yalta and Potsdam; destruction of German military forces and war potential, punishment of war criminals, de-nazification, and de-militarisation of Germany. He said, "Ought we not to dread the development of new [German] legions calling for the freeing of Prague from Czech tutelage and Alsace from French oppression. It is better to arrive at an agreement to maintain Germany unarmed, than to fight again to wrest from her the arms which we will have given to her."'

Joliot-Curie went on to say: 'The veto of the five powers, that is more exactly, the rule of unanimity of the five great powers, was introduced into the Charter on the demand of President Roosevelt to safeguard the right of minorities. Without it, the organisation of the United Nations will become purely and simply a new holy alliance with the aim of preserving the world in its present form and halting all social progress.'

That was very prophetic. With the disappearance of the Soviet Union as a great power, the veto is no longer effective on the Security Council. It was exemplified by a report in the press on how a Russian delegate was asked why he was rubber-stamping every American demand. He threw up his hands and said, 'What can we do?' The fact is, as Joliot-Curie forecast, the United Nations today has become little more than a replica of the old holy alliance with America in the driving seat.

There were equally prophetic words from Professor J D Bernal. The most important part of his analysis of the world situation was his reference to the way in which the Western powers were still holding on to their colonial exploitation. He said,

> The basic assumption that underlies the policy of the Atlantic powers is that the governments of the world must not be allowed to pass any further out of the hands that now control it. They consider it right and natural that more than half the people of the world be ruled by less than a tenth. They consider that those born to rule should determine the way in which the resources of the whole world should be developed and used. To those

in their own countries who are beginning to doubt the justice of this system, they offer the promises of the development of backward countries under the celebrated fourth point of President Truman. What weight they give to these promises is shown by the fact that for every million dollars voted for the Truman plan, 4,000 million are voted for armaments. This is the system they accept as the permanent and right state of the world. Any criticism of it in colonial countries is called subversive; any actual uprising against it is called aggression.

That quotation throws light on the subsequent events. It is true many African countries gained independence though not economic independence. It is also true that the attempt by America to maintain its power in Angola, Mozambique, Grenada, and above all in Vietnam, was the attempt to maintain a world division between the rich countries and the poor to which Bernal referred, and it meant that the expenditure on armaments has continued, a burden on the world economy. Professor Bernal stressed there was a new awakening of the peace movement in Britain. He said, 'We have had in the past to face the most elaborate and effective means of suppressing discussion on peace. The press has first ignored then vilified our movement. The official Labour party has imposed and reimposed a ban on any of its members or organisations taking part in it, if they could they would prevent any serious discussion on peace. Now, after Warsaw, it is becoming impossible to maintain this position much longer. The great and representative delegation of the British people of all classes and professions that is here at this congress bears witness to it. The whole tradition of the peoples of Britain is against the policy that their government is more and more reluctantly forced to follow under the leadership of United States' big business.'

The speech that inspired me most in that conference was by Ilya Ehrenburg, the Russian author. He started by saying,

Upon us rests the responsibility of every child, fair or black, for the children of Moscow, London, Paris, and

182

Peking. For the child that plays in the New York sky-scraper, and the child that wanders amid the ruins of Korea. Upon us rests the responsibility of all the lovers, for all the world's books, for the cities and their gardens. People in dread ask one another "war, war, again? Is there really going to be another war?" Can people endure to live in such uncertainty? Can parents bring up children not knowing but that one day a bomb may fall on them? Can the thinkers reflect, the artists create, humanity advance civilisation, darkened by the shadow of war? War is not a typhoon, not an earthquake, war is man-made, and man can prevent it.

We must avoid war. That is the longing of every man and every woman no matter where he or she may dwell. War is not a contest of ideas, it is not an argument in philosophy, war is a terrible calamity that affects all peoples and every embodiment of their culture. If there are Americans who do not particularly like Soviet ideas and Soviet books, then let them try to fight ideas with ideas and discredit books with books. In this realm, bombs can achieve nothing. Those in America who desire to preserve their economic system, their ideology, their way of life are not being particularly sensible in counting upon war. The events of the last forty years have shown that war speeds social change, but war cannot save the capitalist world from the influence of social ideas, neither is it the road to socialism.

As a writer I know the power of words. I say this with pride but with some bitterness. Words can make a man a hero, prompt him to noble deeds, kindle love in his heart, but words can also degrade a man, dope him, blast his conscience. When Hitler led his armies against the peaceful countries, people marvelled. How did it come about that decent middle-class individuals, honest workers could follow such bandits, such assassins? In the course of the trials of nazi criminals some people were puzzled. Whence came these cynical butchers? Whence these murderers who lit the furnaces of Auschwitz? Whence came Ilse Koch who made lampshades from human skins? People remembered Weimar, Heidelberg, they recalled the modesty and the

183

sentiment of the German strolling beneath his ancient Linden trees. They brought to mind the innocent games of skittles that the grandfathers of the SS men played, the sewing and embroidery that delighted the grandmothers of the Kochs. This savagery did not fall from heaven, the cult of force did not lie hidden in the ordinary German's blood. Contempt for those of other races was not a mysterious latent quality in the folk of Weimar and Heidelberg, the spirit of rapine, the racial and nationalist swagger, the brutality and lack of morals, they were inculcated in the Germans by the nazi demagogues, the nazi press, and the nazi schools.

Ehrenberg went on to give quotations from the American press, and again they are worth reading because it is difficult now to realise the hatred and bitterness that had been propagated by the year 1950. Ehrenberg quoted the *Washington Times Herald*,

'We shall send aeroplanes that fly at 40,000 feet. We shall load them with atom, incendiary, and disease-bearing bombs, with TNT, we shall slay the infants in their cradles, the old at their prayers, the workers at their toil.' [Having quoted that, Ehrenberg said,] I shall never say that products of such a kind would emanate from decent Americans, but I'm sad that in a city that bears the name of a great and noble man persons can live, function, and openly incite to murder, who plan the slaughter of children, the butchery of whole peoples. It may be replied that newspapers are produced by irresponsible people, very well I shall allow myself to quote from observations made by people who are alas sufficiently responsible members of the US Congress. Mr John Walsh, a Congressman from Indiana said, "The time is approaching when Americans will flood Russia with atom bombs, not one will be dropped, it will be a flood. We have at least 230 bombs and hundreds of ways of getting to Russia." Senator Stennis from Mississippi said, "We have 440 atom bombs, perhaps more, this is enough to drop 50 bombs on every large industrial city

184

in Russia." Senator Johnson of South Carolina said, "The USA will no longer wage war in the remote corners of the world, but will carry it to the very heart of communist Russia." Congressman Canon from Missouri said, "We must be able to strike at Moscow and any other city in Russia within three weeks after the outbreak of the next war. In the first three weeks we must reduce to rubble all the military centres of the Soviet Union."

Ehrenberg went on to say, The calls for a war of aggression come not only from congressman, they are sounded also from the official representatives of the United States. Two months back Mr Mathews, US Secretary to the Navy, recommended this recipe to his compatriots for preserving peace, "We should be ready to declare war to force the others to cooperate with us in building peace. This would be a new departure for a true democracy for we would appear to be the initiators of a war of aggression." Then the Assistant Secretary for War, Mr Griffiths, acknowledged that he had already recommended to Mr Truman in 1947 that the atom bomb be dropped on the Soviet Union. "Were the Soviet Navy Minister to express the opinion that war should be declared on the United States in order to oblige that country to cooperate, he would be prosecuted. If the Soviet Defence Minister had suggested that a bomb should be dropped on America he would no doubt have been locked up in a lunatic asylum."

Speeches at the conference went on day after day (at that time there was no simultaneous translations), sometimes right through the night, with only a handful of delegates left in the hall. But they were determined, come hell or high water, to put their speeches on record.

The British delegation issued a statement, 'We British were sad and indignant that the Congress was prevented from being held in Sheffield. But the Polish welcome has made us happy. We British have been injured in our patriotism and pride. Our ancient tradition of freedom has been damaged.

'Sheffield gave an impetus to the British peace movement of a magnitude of which we could scarcely have hoped. Out of the experience of Sheffield and the inspiration of Warsaw, members of the British delegation will help the British people to understand the struggle for peace and build a mighty peace movement worthy of their country.'

I gave my own conclusions. I wrote: 'We speak proudly for Britain. We proclaim that once peace is assured, science and nature have already provided the possibilities for illimitable progress in raising the material and cultural level of every nation of the world. That is the challenge which the Warsaw Congress has put before the British people, and Britain, whose land is already committed in advance as a base for atomic war has a terrible responsibility.'

The year 1950 was in many ways the watershed. The Warsaw Congress was not a communist dominated conference but it did express the fear of impending war of millions of people. It did take sides in the sense that it saw the danger of war as coming from the United States, and not from the Soviet Union. The McCarthy witch-hunt, remembered with shame by many Americans, was a ghastly tyranny. Artists, actors and actresses lost their jobs if they failed to denounce their colleagues. Anyone who had marched in May Day processions or who had supported the republicans in the Spanish War, even some who fought in or supported the last war were penalised; sometimes, if they failed to denounce their compatriots, they were imprisoned.

In Britain anti-Russian propaganda took a rather different form. But it did mean that in the Labour party the right wing was triumphant and, as always, once that disunity – already shown by the revolt of the three ministers – was seen by the rank and file as party weakness, the electoral battle was lost.

I had the feeling that Clem Attlee was a haunted man. His hysterical denunciation of the Sheffield and Warsaw congresses was not in keeping. After all he gave his name to the British contingent of the International Brigade that fought Franco in Spain. His writings on the need for a socialist foreign policy were there for all to see. I could only feel that the weakness of the Labour government in following America had destroyed his confidence.

186

While Warsaw gave the peace movement new enthusiasm and hope my worries about the way things were developing in the Soviet Union were real. For example, some brides of British diplomats were not allowed out of the country. There were nonsensical allegations that Jewish doctors had attempted to poison Maxim Gorky or Stalin. I told meetings that 'hysteria in the West has bred hysteria in the East.'

Then there were the terrible trials in the countries which had come under communist control. In Czechoslovakia I knew some victims of one of the trials – Slansky and Sling. They had told me how the communists were collaborating in countries where they had gained power, and how they agreed policies at a party level and then passed them on to the governments. They told me that in this way they were getting joint action to meet the very great difficulties of the time.

Those people were suddenly put on trial. I knew that they were innocent. Later I talked to a member of the Czech government and he told me, 'The trouble was we were very innocent as far as security measures were concerned. False information was fed into one service – mainly the Hungarian – passed on to the other countries' parties and accepted as reality.'

One of the few people released – the others were often only declared innocent in their graves – explained how under torture he alleged Konni Zilliacus was a spy. After his release he said, 'It was so utterly nonsensical I thought that nobody outside these madmen who were torturing me would believe it.' Sadly, Zilli, one of the best fighters for peace of the generation, was ostracised by some on the left. On the other hand he was expelled from the Labour party because he stood so firmly for collective security through the United Nations. I treasure his unfailing friendship.

There was also the trial of Gomulka, communist leader of Poland. I was worried about how far this alliance of socialists was disintegrating, and how far the dictatorship of the proletariat in communist ideology had become the dictatorship of an elite. I was not starry-eyed. But then I looked at the other side of the picture. The view that there was no danger of America going to war was not borne out by American literature. James Forrestal was Secretary of State for Defence; in his memoirs he set out a war policy based on the atom bomb. He wrote, 'The years in which we have the monopoly of the bomb are our years of opportunity. My only fear is lest the American people are not resolute in the use of the bomb.'

Foster Dulles, Foreign Secretary, wrote, 'The American people would crucify me if I did not use the bomb.' There was a definite appeal at the time of the Berlin blockade to send an armoured column through the Soviet zone which would have meant war. That was only called off because, while the Americans could bomb Moscow, the Red army could not be defeated in Europe.

James Forrestal jumped out of the window to his death apparently convinced the Russians had invaded Missouri. I commented, in my review of his diary in the Indian daily *Patriot*, that his publication was not censored by the Official Secrets Act as it might have been in Britain. He had written in his diary, 'The US policy from the end of the war was to attack the Soviet Union economically and diplomatically, backed by the threat of nuclear war.' I said, 'Forrestal records his conviction that there was "unanimous agreement by the American public that the bomb should be used against the Soviet Union" and he quotes Foster Dulles for the remark "the American people would execute you if you did not use the bomb." He alleges that Clement Attlee, Labour Prime Minister, told him in November 1948 "There is no division in the British public mind about the use of the atom bomb. They are for its use. Even the Church in recent days has publicly taken this position."'

Forrestal told in his diary how in 1948 General Clay, American Commander-in-Chief in Berlin, sent a personal telegram to Truman saying 'He had a feeling war was imminent.' On the basis of that warning Truman alerted America. There were detailed discussions on which of the armed forces should deliver the bomb.

Forrestal told how the American Ambassador in London was asked to enquire whether the British had considered the implication of the decision to accept the B29 bombers. The Forrestal diary adds the comment, 'The British bases would bring the atomic bombers within striking distance of Moscow.' Forrestal wrote at the time, 'We have the opportunity *now* of sending these planes – once sent they will become something of an accepted fixture.'

I commented how all the evidence made it clear that the first atomic bombs were dropped on Hiroshima and Nagasaki when the Japanese were suing for peace. I said these bombs were intended to tell the Soviet Union we're the masters now and to throw over the anti-nazi agreements of Potsdam.

Senator Vandenburg wrote that Roosevelt and Churchill had agreed that not only would they not use the bomb against each other, but they would not use it against any other country unless both Britain and America agreed. In other words, a British veto on the American use of the bomb. In January 1948, however, agreement was reached with Britain and Canada in Washington to remove the restriction on the use of the bomb. Vandenburg wrote, 'As a result the final decision for use of the bomb was left in the hands of the President as specified by American control legislation.' Vandenburg and Senator Hickenlooper had threatened to vote against Marshal Aid if the British veto was not removed.

23

Memories – Robeson, Nkrumah

Cedric Belfrage was an old Fleet Street friend. He gave up his job on the *Daily Express* because he was not allowed to write what he wanted: he became a radical figure on the north Korean side in the Korean War, and in the Vietnam War on the side of the Vietnamese people. He was persecuted in Australia but gained the respect of progressive people all over the world. I met Cedric after World War II when he worked for the Control Commission in Germany, organising the German newspapers in accordance with the Potsdam decision and the renunciation of their fascist past. He asked me if I would like to join him, but I refused. I had a suspicion, soon confirmed, that the Potsdam decision as far as West Germany was concerned would soon be abandoned.

After leaving that post, Cedric founded the progressive weekly *National Guardian* in New York. I became a regular contributor, and the paper played a very important part in its time until destroyed by Trotskyist infiltration, as well as by external pressures.

The *National Guardian* published the story of the Trenton Six. They were six black Americans who were picked up in Trenton, New Jersey, after a white woman was alleged to have been raped. They were accused even though there was no evidence: the prevailing atmosphere meant they could be sentenced to death without any protest.

But after the *National Guardian* published the story, I picked it up and gave it a splash in *Reynolds*. Once it became internationally known the barrier was broken, and when Paul Robeson came to Britain on his first post-war visit in the spring of 1949, on the basis of my piece, I at once got to see him. He said, 'I'm very proud that *Reynolds* not only gave the news of the Trenton Six but broke through the press boycott of the case in the United States.'

I ghosted three articles for Paul. He talked and I put his views into shape for the paper; I am proud that he autographed my book of poems by American negro writers which was published in the German Democratic Republic, both in English and in German translation. He wrote, 'Thanks for the opportunity and privilege of talking things over. And deep thanks for your fine creative approach to the material.' That was signed by Paul in May 1949, and I treasure it.

We organised a meeting in Manchester to support the case of the Trenton Six and their demand for freedom. Paul and I had lunch in a Manchester hotel and he gave instructions that he was not to be disturbed during the afternoon. It was a fascinating experience. He told me how, when he first came to Britain before the war, he was taken up by the aristocrats. 'I heard one day,' he said, 'one of the aristocrats talking to his chauffeur in the same way that he would speak to his dog. I said to myself, "Paul, that's how a southerner in the United States would speak to you." That's how I realised that the fight of my negro people in America and the fight of oppressed workers everywhere was the same struggle.'

He went on to tell me about his life in Trenton, New Jersey, which he said was a northern town with all the racist hatred of the south. His father was a freed slave. After his release he became a Methodist minister for many years, but when he grew old, in true capitalist style, they threw him out, and he made his living with a dog-cart. He would convey students from the train to the university. On one occasion, the cart was being driven by Paul's brother, and the student threw the money on the ground and said, 'Dance for it, you bloody nigger, dance!'

That night Paul's brother went out with a sand bag, located the student and hit him over the head with it. Paul said, 'I

191

didn't really suffer from persecution, because I made my way as a baseball player.' He went on: 'Once we had a successful season and I was invited to a celebration dinner, and said I couldn't attend unless my brother came too.' And that was impossible.

At the end of the afternoon Paul said, 'We now have an appointment to keep.' He called a taxi and took me to the outskirts where the boxer, Len Johnson, had established a club, mainly for American residents. In that small room Paul sang his entire repertoire planned for a concert that night. As that beautiful voice came through the open windows on that warm afternoon, people gathered in the streets to listen. A wonderful human being.

Later, Paul was present at many meetings of the World Peace Council, but I must mention two other episodes. His passport was taken away during the communist witch-hunt in America, so we organised a concert over the transatlantic telephone. We had a meeting in London and that beautiful voice came over the air waves, and there was Paul promising that he would come very soon. And in the end he did. When he was due to arrive the communist party, the Labour party, religious ministers, and the theatrical world all gathered to welcome him. A bossy police sergeant kept on moving us around because we were blocking the entrance. When Paul arrived, he was taken into a side room where the press were waiting to interview him. After about 20 minutes he emerged, and the little sergeant had his arm around him, and was saying, 'This way Paul.' I have never seen a man conquered like that policeman!

During the period of the Labour government, I interviewed another black visitor, Kwame Nkrumah, the leader of the people of Ghana (then known as the Gold Coast). Nkrumah had been leading the struggle for liberation and, like many others, was imprisoned. His party, the People's Party, won the election, and he had to be released on becoming Prime Minister.

He had been out of jail for four months and he thanked the British Labour movement for the way they had struggled for the rights of the colonial people; he said that his present position was only a step forward to the full freedom for which he had fought, and he said quite frankly, 'We assert our right to govern or even misgovern ourselves. No country could hope to remedy her economic and social evils unless she is in charge of her own destiny. No people, however poor or illiterate, want to be ruled by others. Freedom for the Gold Coast is a test case for Africa and for the African races all over the world.'

He told me how detailed plans were already finalised for building a dam on the Volta river, thus creating a new source of hydro-electric power. Some years later I visited Ghana and saw that dam operating, supplying electricity not only to the country, but to neighbouring countries as well. And I discovered that the plan for the dam was put forward by the British Commissioner in the Gold Coast in 1912, and nothing was done until liberation. That is a typical story of British colonialism. Nkrumah explained that the electricity would be used to extract aluminium from the bauxite deposits, that cement industries would be created, and that gold, diamond, and manganese mines would be developed. He said that his plan was to improve the varieties and the condition of the cocoa crop, another of Ghana's assets.

I thanked him and asked, 'Mr Prime Minister, can I use everything you've told me?', 'Certainly,' he said. There was a colonial official with me, and after we'd said goodbye to the Prime Minister, he said, 'Let's go and have a drink.' I went to the bar with him. He bought drinks, and then said, 'I just wanted to warn you the fellow's a wild romantic, don't take him too seriously.' The voice of British colonialism!

Later Nkrumah was manoeuvred out of power, clearly by America and went into exile. There he wrote his experiences, and he told how his plans for building the cocoa crop were realised. At the end he produced double the quantity of cocoa, but because of the international cartel, the revenue received was no greater. Aluminium was developed, but dominated by the American aluminium cartel. Nkrumah died in exile, but his memory was restored, and his body brought back to his native country with honour.

I remember my visit to Ceylon (now Sri Lanka) where the Tamils were protesting and demanding independence, which later led to a blood-bath. There was not the hatred which happened later. The same was true in other countries. There was tension in Cyprus when we had a meeting of the World Peace Council, but the two communities, the Turks and the Cypriots, were living side-by-side. There was a possibility of reconciliation, but it deteriorated, and finally the Turks invaded. The Turks, a member of NATO, were allowed to enjoy the fruits of their aggression, rather strange compared with the reaction of the United Nations after the invasion of Kuwait by Iraq!

I visited a number of countries in Latin America and Africa on behalf of the World Peace Council, and it was quite clear that they welcomed us as friends for peace, and allies in their struggles for independence. No one suggested that we were emissaries of Russian communism or anything of the sort; in fact Russian communism as an ideology was not included in their outlook. But what we did find was that where countries were striving for their freedom, they had to face American intervention. That was true in Nicaragua where we talked to Daniel Ortega, who told us how the people were still recovering from the effects of an earthquake during the period of the former regime. We saw how they were trying to modernise the country, and how they were having to face guerrilla attacks which were clearly financed by America. We saw the same thing in Mozambique. I talked to a school teacher who was smuggled across the line at intervals. In Mozambique, the Americans were financing a counter-revolution which drained the country. In Angola, too, the Americans tried to resist the onward march of people's liberation.

In many of these countries the situation of the common people was very often no better off than in the days of colonialism, but as Nkrumah told me, 'You've got to give people their chance. You cannot keep them in colonial subjection.'

In Malawi – formerly Nyasaland – Nkrumah told me how they picked Hastings Banda out of his practice as a doctor in Hampstead, and made him the country's ruler. He turned out to be one of the worst dictators in Africa.

In Nigeria, you were swindled all the time. I was warned at the airport, 'Don't take a taxi unless you agree a price beforehand.' And when my colleagues on our delegation who had foolishly kept a lot of native currency tried to change it at the airport, they were told that it could be changed but they must go to the other end of the airport. Since our flight was nearly due and we had to fight even to get seats on the plane, it was not worth it.

In Senegal, which still has very much a French atmosphere, our delegation was shown the relics of the slave trade, how the kidnapped natives were loaded onto ships, many to perish on the voyage to America. The memories of that martyrdom of the African people is still very much in the consciousness of the peoples struggling for liberation. We were accompanied by an official from the Foreign Office. He looked after our delegation and he would have been equally at home in the Quay d'Orsay or in Whitehall, but not quite. When I thanked him for his kindness I said that it was very kind of him to give up his Sunday. 'I hope your wife will forgive us,' I said. 'That's all right,' he replied, 'they're both busy at home.' 'You've got two?' I said. 'Yes,' he replied, 'I could have four, but two's enough.'

I was not starry-eyed about the situation. I noticed in ex-French colonies that the French influence was still very strong despite the fact they were nominally free. The struggle of these countries for emancipation and economic progress will go on despite the failure of the rich countries to face up to the reality of poverty and starvation in the poor countries.

24

Reynolds *Dies*

Within months of the victory of the Labour government it became clear that the dream that *Reynolds* would add a daily paper to its service, or even that it would become an important factor in the post-war struggle, had faded.

Bill Richardson took over at a time when the policy was absolutely clear. During the war we were ready to criticise but loyally supported the coalition government in the struggle against fascism, and we were, in my view, one of the major factors in the Labour election victory of 1945.

But Bill (and I never lost my affection for him) was not a good editor. He had an incredible ability to fall for phonies. Two of the main people he recruited were Raymond Blackburn and Woodrow Wyatt, both of them elected as Labour MPs in 1945. Blackburn announced his ardent admiration for Winston Churchill and went out of politics. Woodrow Wyatt, we know where he ended – as the most vicious opponent of the Labour party. These men were adopted by Bill as two of the great assets of the paper.

On one occasion Raymond claimed he had got an exclusive about the way demobilisation was to proceed. When I read his story I said, 'You know Bill, this is untrue.' The industrial correspondents group, of which I was a member, were meeting the civil servant responsible for the demobilisation plans and he was giving us every detail; sometimes in confidence, and sometimes for publication. So I knew.

Raymond Blackburn asserted that he had got his version

from Ernest Bevin. It went in the paper and we had one hell of a job answering the letters from disappointed parents who had been assured by us that their boys were coming home, when in fact they had to stay away a term longer.

On one occasion, after my visit to Germany, Bill was on holiday and I was in charge. A dog-eared manuscript came in. It purported to be an investigation, by a freelance journalist, into whether Hitler was really dead. I glanced through it. Clearly it was phoney because it began by telling the story of how the journalist had burned a pig on the site of the Reichstag to see whether there would be anything left of the bones, and by implication those of Hitler and Eva Braun on cremation. I knew that anyone who had dared burn a pig and waste that pork in the starving conditions of Germany at that time would have been lynched. So, on the Friday, I said to the secretary, 'Send that rubbish back.' She left it until Monday but Bill came in and said, 'That's just what we want.' He paid the author a sum near to my yearly salary! I discovered afterwards that this manuscript had been hawked all round Fleet Street and rejected.

Then we went in for serial stories. The first, *Tiger Bay*, was by David Martin, who was with the International Brigade and a poet of some note. It was not a bad story, but it just did not fit in with the needs of a progressive Sunday paper or with the tradition of *Reynolds*. Then we had much worse pornographic stories. I used to say, 'The recipe for a Sunday serial now is that you have to have the girl in bed every Sunday, but she must be in a different bed!'

The decline was matched by a deterioration in the political coverage. Bill was under pressure, I realise that. He used to say, 'As long as we keep a good leader page, that will keep the movement happy.' It was not true. We had all sorts of people coming in with all sorts of stories, some of which were phoney, some not, but they were out of tune with the policy which *Reynolds* had built up as a power in the land in the earlier years.

I often wonder if Sydney Elliot had stayed as editor, and Alf Barnes had remained chairman of the Cooperative Press

197

Board, whether *Reynolds* could have fought back against the circulation people who had convinced the Board that only by following the sensational policies of the other Sundays could *Reynolds* compete in the post-war world. The policy created the paper in its own image. This showed itself in several ways. We had to recruit sub-editors from the other papers for the Saturday night work, and when I was in charge I used to throw back headlines and say, 'That's OK for the *Daily Mail*, but it's not a *Reynolds* head.' It was the way in which the tradition of *Reynolds* was being eroded which was worrying.

It showed itself in other forms. There grew up in Britain, during those post-war years, a sort of venom against anything considered communist, which showed itself to a much greater degree in American McCarthyism. Of all people, one of the protagonists was Richard Acland whom I mentioned earlier. I wrote a story about Michurin, a Soviet scientist, who was breeding new varieties of fruit, vegetables and other products. This story was published in a book which I reviewed. It described how he had to fight the priests who said that 'hybrid plants were illegitimate, and turning God's garden into a brothel.' The sub gave it a very good head, 'Red man with green fingers'. It was a straight report. It was not a theoretical book backing Lysenko, who later became the centre of controversy and advocated theories which were repudiated by our own experts including J B S Haldane. But Richard Acland wrote in saying Schaffer was putting across Soviet propaganda!

One Saturday night an agency reported that the Soviets had used atomic power to blast their way through a mountain. I seized on this and made enquiries and we had a scoop: The Russians had atomic power. It was obvious; if the Russians could do this in an industrial way, they could make a bomb. In my view it was done to warn the West that they had that power. But there was another letter from Acland saying that this was more communist propaganda from this fellow Schaffer.

The most virulent attack came from A V Alexander. His

indictment was that *Reynolds* was pursuing a communist line. He made no particular effort to produce evidence, but made the point that the general tenor of the paper 'was that way'. As usual I was under attack. He said that I was assisting communist propaganda, and he cited an article in which I asked, 'Is this fair shares for all?' I said the White Paper on personal incomes issued by the Labour government was criticised by the TUC, that they were willing to accept a freeze on wages, but they wanted a much more drastic attack on profits and prices. Then I was attacked for an article headed, 'World unions need not split'. Again it was a purely objective picture of what a good many people in the trade union movement were saying. It was rather interesting that he could not really find any example of my work which justified his attack.

Another article he cited was by Jon Kimche. He wrote that an anti-British wave was sweeping the Middle East, and suggested that Britain's position out there had been undermined by the army in Palestine. It was a fair reflection by an eminent journalist.

Another attack was on a leading article by Bill Richardson, championing the authors of a telegram of support to Nenni, the Socialist leader in Italy. But because the left wing of the Labour party sent that telegram, and because *Reynolds* endorsed it, this was a sign to Alexander that we were under the influence of the communists. It was sheer nonsense, but criticism was building up all the time.

Sadly it was accompanied by the policy of minimising the political content of the paper and emulating, as far as it could, the sex and crime policies of the rest of the Sunday press. That was the battle in which I was involved. I argued that *Reynolds* was not in the market for that sort of material, that if we tried to do it we could not compete with the *News of the World*, or *The People*, and that gradually we were going to lose our readers. This is what began to happen.

As I said earlier, Alfred Barnes's conception of a cooperative newspaper was that it should be able to finance itself out of the profits of the movement, just as the capitalists

199

did, and the levy on sales by all the cooperative enterprises achieved that objective, but as the quality of the paper deteriorated so the support from the cooperative organisations declined. The letters of complaint began to come in, and worse still, from the point of view of the paper, various societies were opting out of the collective advertising scheme. The Cooperative Press Board did not want to fight. Alf Dann, Secretary of the Agricultural Workers Union, offered me a quarter of an hour slot in all his county conferences to advocate *Reynolds*.

But that offer was never considered by the Board. It became obvious that the paper's political fervour had drained away. At editorial conferences I was in a minority. On one occasion, shortly after the Gold Coast had become independent, and before Macmillan's 'wind of change' speech about Africa, I said, 'This is the most important event since the end of the war – if one African country can gain its freedom; freedom for a majority African government, then this is going to spread all over the continent.' I suggested a series on 'the liberation of Africa'. They gave me a wan smile – 'another of Gordon's silly ideas' – and started discussing an article on the spread of prostitution in Manchester.

I recently came across a series of memoranda which I wrote to Bill showing how the political content was being massacred. In one I said a very important speech by Nye Bevan had been taken out of the last edition in order to make way for some sex police court case. That was the sort of atmosphere that was developing.

With a heavy heart I played my part in the elections of 1950 and 1951. After the Tories came back I hoped we could resume our position as the spearpoint of opposition against Tory rule, but my hopes were disappointed. Matters came to a head at the Labour party conference in 1952. The conference took decisions, both on foreign and home policy, which were far in advance of the leadership. This caused the leader Hugh Gaitskell to take the view that 'half the conference were either communists or fellow travellers'. He made a vicious attack on all the left-wing papers, the *New Statesman*,

Tribune, and *Reynolds*. Tragically Nye Bevan died young or the story might have been different.

Both the *New Statesman* and *Tribune* told Gaitskell, in other words, to go to hell. But *Reynolds* – and I knew this was a sign of defeat – allowed him to state his case which broadly had been that *Reynolds* was a Bevanite paper. This gives some idea of the bitterness. Gaitskell wrote the article and sent in his manuscript. On the Wednesday before publication the Parliamentary Labour party had one of its fierce debates and decided that MPs should not attack each other in public. Gaitskell had listed in his article a number of MPs whom he condemned as taking part in this 'pro-communist' movement within the Labour party. Since all the MPs were now bound by this decision not to attack each other in public, Gaitskell had to take out all the names except mine, because I was not an MP.

The attack on me continued; I offered to disassociate myself or resign from any of the proscribed organisations, but nobody took much notice of that – I was a member of the Executive of the Labour Research Department (which later became very respectable), and of some of the friendship organisations. My local party supported and refused to expel me.

By March 1953 matters had come to a head. That Saturday evening after I had been in charge of the paper, Bill came back from a Board meeting. He called me in and, very obviously embarrassed, said the board had great respect for my services, but in view of the circumstances they would ask me to consider seeking other employment, or alternatively, discuss terms of resignation. I said, 'Supposing I do neither.' He said, 'You can stay as long as you like, but of course we shan't publish anything you write.'

That is what happened to Frank Allaun. He had exactly the same dilemma put to him on the northern edition of the *Daily Herald* – a so-called Labour paper, but he decided to stay on. Little he wrote went in the paper, but he organised a service of articles for trade union papers, and he secured a nomination for a seat, and eventually went on to be an MP and chairman of the Labour party.

I told Bill that I would not discuss this matter until I had an absolute assurance in writing that there was no complaint about the quality of my work, or my professional capacity, or my integrity during my years of service at *Reynolds*, and that there would also be an assurance that any differences of viewpoint between myself and the paper had not influenced in any way my presentation of objective news. Bill Richardson gave all those assurances.

I wrote a letter confirming these guarantees and added, 'Since 1939 *Reynolds*'s policy had been broadly on the left of the movement; the Board's decision places me in an extremely difficult position. A journalist who is employed to write hard-hitting articles for a left-wing paper (and I have been described, publicly, in *Reynolds* as fearless) has burned his boats professionally.' That was true. I had lots of sympathy from my colleagues in Fleet Street, but no job offers. I insisted that before any further discussions took place, I should have, in writing, the letter saying that there was no complaint about my work, or my professional integrity.

That letter duly arrived, and it read like this: 'This letter is to put on record the appreciation of the directors of *Reynolds* of the efficiency with which you have carried out your duties during the time you have been associated with the paper. Your intimate knowledge of trade union organisational affairs, your familiarity with economic and social problems, and your political knowledge have been reflected in enterprising service to the paper during the 16 years you acted first as industrial correspondent, and later as assistant editor in addition to your industrial and political work. The directors wish me to express their high regard for your integrity, loyalty and zeal.'

Having secured the assurance of my competence I formally submitted my resignation. In his letter of acceptance, Bill Richardson wrote, 'The Board have a high regard for your character as an individual, and your experience as a journalist, but they have been reluctantly forced to the conclusion that in recent times your views on international questions and some of your political activities outside the movement have increasingly placed you out of sympathy with the policies to which *Reynolds* owes loyalty.' I wrote in reply, 'I believe the Board's decision is mistaken and unjust. The last thing I would wish to do would be to harm *Reynolds* by a public controversy because I am convinced that the democratic ownership of a newspaper by the cooperative movement is the most important method yet devised for the establishment of a working class press.'

When the news of my sacking reached the printers, the Imperial Father (the Father of all the Chapels) came to me and said, 'Although some of us don't always agree with your policies, we believe that you are one of the people who is keeping the paper alive, and if you want us to strike, we'll strike.'

It was very flattering, but at that time (it does not happen now), if one paper came out, they all came out. So I could have stopped Fleet Street. But what good would that have done either for the movement or for myself. My letter went on to say, 'I would point out that the Board wishes to dispense with my services after 16 years during which no complaint has ever been made about my work. The reason was my refusal to join in anti-Soviet propaganda which is a source of embarrassment in the board's relations with certain leaders. While this may be true in regard to certain leaders, it is not true of the majority, and certainly does not apply to the rank and file.

'I have letters from readers following the attack on me by Mr Gaitskell, and without exception they supported me. It may be true, though I doubt it, that my dismissal will secure more assistance from a restricted official section in a campaign to attain readers for *Reynolds*, but it will not win readers.'

Then I went on to say that support from readers could only be achieved by an appeal to the progressive ideals for which *Reynolds* had always stood in the past. I added, 'I would say, in all sincerity, that my dismissal will harm rather

203

than assist this objective.' In my letter I pointed out that the salary I had received was far below comparable standards on any other national newspaper, and that I had turned down far more lucrative offers from three national newspapers and the BBC. I stated, 'In 1945, you pressed on me the view that I should not consider the offer of nomination for several safe seats in the House of Commons because of the greater importance of my work on *Reynolds*. Today the situation is changed, the capitalist press is virtually closed to journalists with known left views. When I came to *Reynolds* I had not made a detailed study of the working-class movement, and I relied entirely on professional qualifications. I was offered an increase in salary as assistant night editor of the Press Association as an inducement to remain. It is a serious position when a left-wing newspaper employs journalists to advocate its policies (in my case, certainly with my complete sympathy), and then throws them out because in the light of changing circumstances, the paper changes its views.'

Reynolds Chapel (this consisted of all the journalists on the paper) passed a resolution, saying that they had heard with anger and astonishment the action of the Cooperative Press Board in virtually requesting the resignation of Gordon Schaffer on political grounds. It went on,

> We, as fellow Sunday newspaper journalists, recognise the remarkable way Mr Schaffer has overcome the difficulties of his job. We know that Mr Schaffer's political views have never coloured his work as a reporter, or in the presentation of political, industrial, or diplomatic news. Some of us know that on several occasions he has pressed for publication of speeches and items of information representing views different from his own on the grounds that a news service must be balanced on the presentation of controversial issues. His reports on such conferences as the Cooperative party have shown a capacity to give a fair balance between opposing viewpoints, and this fact has been widely recognised as a tribute to him as a journalist. Mr Schaffer has writ-

ten leaders on various occasions during the last 16 years, and never has it been alleged that he failed to follow the agreed policy of the paper and the movement. We note that he has done a whole number of duties in addition to his job as assistant editor for a salary only 20 per cent higher than the minimum paid in Fleet Street to a junior reporter.

A few days after the notice of my dismissal had appeared, I was invited to meet Allen Hutt, Johnny Campbell, and Harry Pollitt, and they put to me an offer to join the *Daily Worker*. I refused. I said, 'My job is in the Labour movement, and if I were to go over to the *Daily Worker* now, even though I might say it was my only chance of a job in Fleet Street, they would have said "of course the criticisms were right; he was a communist all the time."'

I pointed out that I had never joined the communist party, and that I still remained a member of the Labour party and believed that Labour was the only hope for a future progressive government. I was rather sad when Harry Pollitt turned on me and said, 'You'll be forgotten in a year!' It showed, once again, how the communist party put the party before everything else. And that was my view of the reason for Allen Hutt being instructed to join the *Daily Worker* from *Reynolds*, when *Reynolds* was politically far more valuable.

From the many hundreds of letter which I received, some of them sent with copies to *Reynolds*, I must quote this one:

> Schaffer is the most recent victim in the general degeneration of the press. Wilfred Burchett, of the *Express*, Tom Hopkinson of *Picture Post*, and John Peet of Reuters, Reg Thompson of the *Sunday Times* and *Daily Telegraph*, Archie Johnson of *British Ally*, and Peter First of Reuter who was dismissed with the classic instruction that what his employers wanted was 'someone who would report objectively on foreign affairs from the Western viewpoint.'
> All have tried to do a proper job of reporting and have lost their employment for reporting what they saw. But

Schaffer's offence goes deeper than that. A few weeks ago *Reynolds* came into my house so full of that kind of sugared filth that seems to pass for Sunday journalism that I had to destroy it in case my children should read it. That there should be occasional lapses in the best of papers is admitted, but that our own cooperative newspaper founded in such high tradition has succumbed. Schaffer's offence was to protest against this deterioration in a cooperative newspaper.

The sad fact was that after my dismissal, the readership of *Reynolds* went on declining and the number of cooperative societies supporting the Cooperative Press also declined. There was a desperate attempt made to ease the situation by changing the name of the paper from *Reynolds* to *The Sunday Citizen*. It gained slightly at the beginning because some of the media were persuaded that this was a new paper and it got a good deal of publicity. But that could not stop the trend, and it went on losing readers, and more important losing influence. The *Sunday Citizen* was doomed from the start because it just did not capture the imagination of the movement which *Reynolds* had done from the time it had been taken over by the Cooperative Press until this sad decline. The *Sunday Citizen* died in June 1967 and its final message by Bill Richardson was, 'Speak out, fight on.'

It was a rather curious edition. It talked about *Reynolds Weekly* being formed in May 1850, when Britain 'was a land of goodwill to all men, but evil performance to most men'. It talked about Victorian sentimentalists weeping over Oliver Twist in Fagin's den, and how people went to work in their factories to fight in the iron war of wages against the concession of 6d a week to the income of an underfed family, or how they petitioned their MPs against legislation that would soften the savages of industries in which steam power devoured human life as surely as it increased the output of goods. It described how George Reynolds, the founder of the paper, was one of those who rebelled against this system and founded *Reynolds* to support the People's Charter which included the demand for manhood suffrage, secret ballots, and the payment of MPs; 'rights so elementary that we take them for granted today.'

This farewell issue of the *Sunday Citizen* even went back to the Civil War against Charles I and quoted Colonel Rainborough, one of the Captains of the Commonwealth army, who argued for manhood rather than property on the grounds that 'the poorest he, that is in England, hath the life to live, as the greatest he'. It said 'Rainborough knew what he was about; the Chartists knew what they were about. They knew that in the last resort political power is the one source of power that dominates all others, the final power that must be held by those who want to introduce great changes and great reforms. That was the philosophy that George William MacArthur Reynolds stamped on this newspaper.'

By this time Harold Wilson had won the election and was Prime Minister and this final voice of the *Sunday Citizen* said, 'To Harold Wilson we say this to you: you compromise too much and it is hard to detect distinctively socialist principles in many of your policies even after making the most generous allowance for the compromises that life imposes on any government.'

The leader in this farewell issue continued,

> You ask for sacrifices and they have been made because you are our government and we will strain loyalty to the uttermost limit to help you, but we want to glimpse the New Jerusalem as well as contemplate the import/export figures. We are inspired by Harold Wilson's vision of a great new humane, efficient, self-confident, high technological society. Where is it? These are harsh criticisms and they are intended to be. We elected this government not only to be better than the Tories, that is not difficult, but to be different, different in philosophy, attitude, and policy. We make this other criticism: more could have been done by the government to help the independent press of Britain, not just the *Sunday Citizen*, but others of the fast diminishing number of indepen-

207

dent voices that speak out in print whatever the point
of view they advocate.

We add this warning; unless the government does
act, and acts soon, the press will become a monopoly
of a few faceless men, men wielding great power without social accountability. That will be a bad day for
Britain.

It was an inspiring piece of history, but rather curiously
there was no mention of Sydney Elliot, the first editor of
Reynolds under the Cooperative Press, and no mention of
Alfred Barnes who inspired the development of the method
of cooperative newspaper ownership. I hardly expected that
I would be mentioned, although curiously enough, the front
pages of issues of *Reynolds* and the *Sunday Citizen* were produced in a double-page splash and in one of them, concerning the story of the measures to be adopted by the first
post-war Labour government, they could not conceal my
by-line!

It was a sad ending, and looking back I wonder whether
it could have been avoided. Certainly after the war we could
have had one of the best teams of journalists in Fleet Street.
Reynolds had been the inspiration of the war against fascism.
Some of the journalists who had come back from the forces
wanted to play a part in winning the fruits of victory. James
Cameron, for example, one of the most brilliant journalists
of the century, pleaded with me saying, 'Can't you get me
a job on *Reynolds*? I don't care how much reduction in salary
I would have to take.' I had to say that it was no good. The
new policy of the Board, pandering to reports of sex and crime
like the worst of the other papers, would break his heart.

It was rather amusing that in that final leader Willy
Richardson said more to criticise the establishment and the
right wing that I had done in my period on *Reynolds*. Richardson was not happy with the changes which eventually killed
the paper. I was due to see him just before his death. I was
too late.

I did fight to preserve my position because I still hoped that something could be saved, but being honest with myself, I did not want to stay at *Reynolds*. I was humiliated by the way in which all the ideas I had put forward which suited the old paper were being rejected, and the way in which new people were coming in who had no faith whatever in the mission of the paper. Although the compensation I got, in terms of Fleet Street standards, was poor, it meant we would not be on the poverty line.

My wife, Rosie, who could never understand why I had not taken the opportunity to go into the House of Commons in 1945, could never forgive the Coop for the way they had thrown me out of *Reynolds*. I tried to explain to her that it was a political struggle, that it was no use boiling it down to condemnation of the organisation, but she would not have it. It was rather amusing because we used to share the shopping, and when I shopped I went to the Coop, and when she went, she would not go near the Coop. What we did have from the Coop were two beautiful cats, their mother having kittens on the premises!

25

London Co-op – A Sad Story

After I left *Reynolds* I was determined not to sever my connection with the cooperative movement. At that time, the London Cooperative Society (LCS), which was very prosperous, was controlled by a body called the London Coop Members' Organisation (LCMO). It had complete control of all the Committees: Management, Political, and Education.

But some of the things they did on the Management Committee were ridiculous. For example, they sent a member to America, at considerable expense, to study funeral furnishings.

I stood unsuccessfully for the Management Committee and got a fair vote. Then David Ainley told me he was anxious to form a committee to contest the seats on the various London cooperative organisations. The idea was to form a broad committee which would consist of communists, Labour party members and other supporters of the movement. I said, 'Does that mean complete equality? Because I will have nothing to do with an organisation in which the communist party has its cells and dictates policy from behind the scenes.' He assured me that would not be the case. And I must say, in my long association with him and with the 1960 committee, I saw no evidence that the communists were not acting in a purely democratic way.

So we contested the seats and I won a seat on the political Committee under their auspices. Ted Bedford, a very fine organiser with ideals similar to mine, was Secretary.

Together, we fought battles at the Cooperative party conference for a progressive peace policy.

I missed one year on the Committee; at home in Kingston I received a call from King Cross police station to say that Mr Bedford was under arrest and had asked for me to provide bail. I went and signed the necessary forms. Ted had control of a private fund belonging to the Political Committee and had been drawing on it for his own purposes. Incidentally, he also borrowed £100 from me telling me that he had spent the money on a delegation but had not kept the proper receipts. He knew that when he surrendered bail he would be found guilty and would go to jail. So on the night before his trial I took him out to dinner. I told him, 'Ted, your friends won't forget you.' He pleaded guilty and got three years. If you get a long term and are a first offender you do much better than on a short term.

Ted took advantage of his time in prison to study printing, typography and associated subjects and was allowed out to attend his classes. Ted's wife wrote to me twice because she could not pay the bills and I sent her some money. When Ted came out he got a job through a contact in the Co-op with Pergamon Press.

Ted never wrote to me again after one letter from prison. I never heard anything more of him although he went into *Reynolds* on occasions. He never made contact and never thought of repaying the money he owed me or thanking me. Such is life.

Ted's successor as Secretary of the Political Committee was Frank Beswick, a former pilot. He had won a seat unexpectedly in the general election of 1945, but lost it in the next election. Frank had tried unsuccessfully to secure nomination for a number of seats. He was going to see Harold Wilson, then Prime Minister, on the Isles of Scilly. I said, 'Frank, tell him to make you a Lord.' Wilson did make him a Lord and in the Labour government he became a junior minister.

The Secretary's job was vacant and Alf Lomas, a Labour agent from the Midlands, applied for the job. By then I was

Chairman of the Committee and those I contacted about him were favourable. One said, 'Don't you take our agent away, he's the best in the area.' When it came to the crunch Alf got the job. I saw him to the train after the meeting. I said to him, 'You're not taking on an easy job' – it was at the height of the Cold War.

We had some bitter battles with the old LCMO but Alf got over them. The Political Committee was a power in London. It backed all the progressive causes and made an impact on the London Labour party and through it on the National Executive. At first we had an annual conference which was a replica of the Cooperative party nationally. We had pages of resolutions and always presented a tea-set to the Mayor – but it was divorced from the real struggle. Alf changed it into a broad movement of all the progressive organisations and trade unions, reluctantly excluding the Communist party because of the ban.

I am only sad that all that vision has disappeared. I have to admit that, although the 1960 Committee had won majorities on all the LCS Committees, it did not exert its authority on the Management Committee. The rule was that while policy was laid down by the Committee, the actual job of management lay in the hands of the professionals. I am afraid the professionals let us down. Alf Barnes had pulled together into the LCS all the small societies on the periphery and they were flourishing. One was the Kingston Cooperative where I then lived. Gradually they were closed down. The Oxford Street store and the Ambassadors Hotel – flagships of the Cooperative movement – were sold off by the Management Committee. Just at the time they were capable of expansion.

Later I was living in Kilburn where there was a flourishing Coop store, and that too died. At that time the Management Committee used to give a voucher to anyone who attended the quarterly meeting. It might be a pound of jam or sausages, something of that sort. After the quarterly meeting I would go to the Kilburn store – which had a very good delicatessen department – and while the ladies were making their purchases used to say, 'Are you drawing your present this week?' They would say 'What present?' and I would reply, 'Didn't you go to your quarterly meeting, didn't you get your pound of sausages?' They didn't know anything about it. I said at one of the meetings, 'If Sainsbury's had said we're going to give a pound of sausages to every customer who comes to discuss how we can improve the store the queue would be half-way down the high street.'

During the period when I was chairman of the Political Committee we played a part in the Cooperative party conferences, particularly in opposing nuclear weapons. Frank Beswick, who was on our side, and I met the same kind of hostility I had faced in my period at *Reynolds*, but in the end we secured the vote. It was interesting that one of the counts against me when I left *Reynolds* was that I was opposed to the policy of the Cooperative movement, but in the end the Cooperative party adopted my policy. I was not offered my job back!

The other side of the movement in London was the Labour control of County Hall, headquarters of London government. It was a centre of political and cultural activity. It was open to any organisation, free of charge. Go there on a weekend and you would find activity of every kind. Sometimes there were festivals on the river bank.

The Labour GLC constructed the Thames Barrage which probably prevented the River Thames from flooding. The GLC was abolished by Margaret Thatcher because the Labour party had consistently won the majority on the Council. She used parliamentary power to abolish it. As a result when it came to the Olympic Games London was not even in the running because it had no central authority.

An unhappy incident concerned John Stonehouse, President of the Society and of the London Cooperative Members' Organisation. Jim Mortimer, former secretary of the Labour party and for a time a Management Committee member of the LCS, warned Harold Wilson that Stonehouse was a doubtful character, but Harold took no notice and gave him a job in government. We discovered that he had set up a

213

Purchasing Committee in Sweden which was securing contracts from the Society. The Management Committee could have prosecuted, but it wanted to avoid a scandal. The subsequent story of Stonehouse is well-known. He faked a suicide in America but he was caught.

I attended the International Cooperative Alliance (ICA) conferences on two occasions. One of these was when Greece was under the rule of the fascists. Those who resisted were put in jail. I was determined to raise the issue at the ICA conference. I went through the agenda with the chairman of the British delegation. He said, 'There's no point where you can raise it.'

I said, 'If I get an opportunity will the British delegation agree?' They did. On the standing orders report I managed to get to the rostrum. 'I move that Greece should be included in the agenda.' I obviously had the sympathy of the whole conference when I said that the cooperative movement would never rest until Greece – the mother of democracy – was again free. The cooperative movement, I said, would be failing in its duty and in its inspiration if it did not support resistance in Greece. I told how we kept the memory of Greek freedom alive by laying wreaths on Byron's statue in Hyde Park because Byron died fighting for liberty in Greece. I won the vote.

When the London Society became part of the national body – Cooperative Retail Services – it retained a facade of democracy with a restricted number of quarterly meetings. But shops were closed and in many areas members like myself had no branch within access. It was not the coop I knew during the years I was proud to be the Political Committee chairman. At 65 I had to give up my membership.

It is a sad story because it had such wonderful possibilities. It does represent a section of the economy and of the national life separated from the exploitation and inequalities of capitalism.

I continued my activities with Labour Action for Peace, an organisation within the Labour party which tries to inject a peace policy into the party.

26

Journalists Unite and Divide

Early in the war, I was elected editor of the journal of the
National Union of Journalists. We shared then the determination of the whole trade union movement to carry on in
peace the struggle we had waged during the war. We called
on the newly-elected labour government to set up a Royal
Commission on the press and rather to our surprise, it was
immediately accepted. The NUJ was invited to put in its
own proposals and we had long discussions. Many of our
members were angry then, as now, at the absorption of much
of the press with crime and sex.

I took the view that this was something we should mention
but we shouldn't make it an object of Union policy to seek
to eliminate it. What we should do, I said, was deal with the
real problem, the monopoly control of the press. I cited how,
before the war, there was a longstanding conflict in the provincial press between two of the big newspaper chains, and
how in Bristol there were rival papers, and how they merged
and hoped to become a monopoly.

But the people of Bristol refused to be carved up, and
journalists and public-spirited leaders joined together to
ensure the continuance of a second paper. I wanted to make
this the key to our evidence, that the only solution to the
monopoly of the press was for the people to find a way of
maintaining their own newspapers, answerable to their own
control. I could, of course, have cited my own personal
experience with *Reynolds*. Unfortunately it was a rush job

and Clem Bundock, the General Secretary, agreed to go home and write the evidence and submit it.

His evidence was almost entirely an attack on press sensationalism. It had the inevitable result; our members employed on these papers asked whether it was the duty of their union to launch attacks on them and their livelihood. This was the dilemma, that in a monopoly controlled press, the standards are not determined by the workers, most of whom are union members and proud of their profession. The Royal Commission reported but could do nothing to control monopoly.

Lord Beaverbrook said he had never had any trouble with his editors because they 'were men of like mind to himself'. Lord Rothermere said his staff very soon 'got into the atmosphere of the office', and Lord Camrose said much the same thing. One member of the *Daily Telegraph* staff (Lord Camrose's paper) said to me, 'If at the editorial conference Lord Camrose looks out of the window and says, "It looks like rain", the staff will be put on a weather story.'

Many of us pressed during the war, when we were fighting against fascism, for a genuine International Journalists' Organisation, embracing both East and West. That meant the dissolution of the old organisation, which excluded the Russians, as did the old International Federation of Trade Unions. We looked to the creation of a united movement like the World Federation of Trade Unions. Delegates from all national journalists; organisations agreed to meet in Copenhagen soon after the war ended.

I was on the NUJ delegation and, on the way, at Harwich, one of the members bought a rather moth-eaten sandwich in the waiting room. When we got to the customs one of the officers said, 'You can throw that away, you wait till you get on board that ship.' It was unbelievable, after the years of privation, to see all that food piled up.

We had with us the Crown Prince of Denmark. He joined in the discussions and the fun. When we got to Copenhagen we were received by the King. That was a unique assembly. For the first time delegates from East and West took part. I was chairman of the Drafting Committee which drew up the final resolution for press freedom for submission to the congress. There we were, a Norwegian, Pole, Peruvian, Frenchman, American, Russian, and myself, an Englishman, sorting out our various conceptions but determined to bridge the differences between East and West which had proved an obstacle to other international conferences. It was a long, and sometimes tough discussion. First we asserted that for 'The Press to be free, sources of information and machinery for sending out news must be available to all.' We recognised that responsibility rested with journalists, and newspaper owners, news agencies and broadcasting services. We determined to remove all restrictions on the right to publish news and views, except for fascist and racist propaganda.

On one point the American member of the Drafting Committee disagreed. I said in my draft, 'No journalist shall write what he knows to be untrue.' He asserted that whether a report was true or not was not the job of the journalist but the responsibility of the proprietor. I said, 'We seem to be in agreement except for you. I suggest that we put this resolution forward and you move an amendment expressing your viewpoint.' He did not want to do that and we did not want a division, so we compromised by saying that the New International would support any journalist who refused to write what he knew to be untrue. When I came back from the conference, I was invited to give a talk on the BBC. I said, 'I suppose it was easier for us than for some other international bodies because we journalists do find more opportunities than most to sit with our colleagues from other countries. I think most of us realised the tremendous responsibilities of the newspaper men at the present time. It was in that spirit that we tackled the biggest job, the formulation of the principles of press freedom which is our means of livelihood, and one of the main pillars of your liberty (a radio audience) and that of all the peoples of the world.'

The new International Federation continued for a time, but it was quite impossible, as the Cold War developed, for that unity to be preserved. Some of the members in the socialist countries, ignoring the mote in their own eye (to quote the Bible) looked for the beam in their opponent's eye. They were demanding that the journalists who were making Cold War propaganda in the West should be disciplined. Of course, you could not start expelling your members and the world body split into East and West organisations.

The journalists maintained two organisations. The East-oriented one made very good progress in the developing countries. It was not a lack of ideals on either side, it was one of the inevitable results when the hopes of peace were dissipated in the Cold War.

At home there had always been a conflict between the old established Institute of Journalism and the National Union of Journalism. The former was founded in the reign of Victoria and had a Royal Charter. The journalists were very respectable and wore top hats, but were very poorly paid. Then Northcliffe came on the scene with the mass circulation papers, the *Daily Mail* and the *Evening News* at ½d. To deter competitors, he made newspaper production expensive. He pushed up the wages of the printers and then the journalists, to whom he paid a very good minimum wage. Then he said to the PA, then paying the old rates, that if they did not raise their journalists' rates he would start his own news agency. So that was why when I joined the PA I had a reasonably good salary.

The conflict between the IOJ and the NUJ was weakening our influence, and was a source of gain for the employers because they could play one off against the other. At the central London branch of the NUJ one of our members asked why his trades council was giving press facilities to non-union members. I said, 'Let's put a resolution to the TUC saying that only NUJ journalists should be given press facilities at trade union conferences.' It went on the TUC agenda and was adopted without debate. The General Secretary, Walter Citrine, realised the implications and was furious. I heard him say, 'Ebby, Ebby, what have you done?' (Ebby Edwards was the Chairman of Congress.) The result was that at the next TUC, because this rule was applied, all the national newspapers refused to send their correspondents though most of them were members of the union. Only the PA, *Reynolds* the *Daily Worker*, and the *Daily Herald* were represented.

George Isaacs, the next chairman of the TUC, did not want his conference to be boycotted, so he asked the NUJ National Executive if he could get an agreement with the IOJ, would the union agree that the resolution should not operate? That was agreed. Eventually there was a joint conference to amalgamate the two bodies. The IOJ, which had a Charter from Queen Victoria, had to relinquish the stipulation which prohibited its members from taking part in a trade union. We aimed for a rule book which said that the amalgamated organisation would be a trade union in a real sense. But ultra-left delegates opposed clauses which had no real relevance, and the negotiations broke down. That division between the two bodies, particularly on existing closed shop agreements, was one of the reasons for the widespread attack on the whole trade union movement.

27

Horticultural Interlude

On the Sunday *Reynolds* announced I had left the paper 'because of decisions by the Cooperative Press which made it impossible for me to carry out my duties', I was giving a lecture to a school, organised by the Fire Brigades Union at Wortley Hall, near Sheffield. There, Leo Condon, a former Fleet Street colleague, phoned me. Would I be interested in joining him on a trade paper devoted to commercial horticulture?

I had met him in London some years before the war. He was voluntary editor of *Russia Today*, a journal devoted to Anglo-Soviet friendship. He had been editor of the *Sunday Pictorial*, but was fed up with the Fleet Street rat-race.

He had acquired *The Grower*, a weekly reporting news and developments in commercial horticulture, at a giveaway price, its main asset being a paper quota based on pre-war consumption.

Leo explained that when he took over he knew nothing about commercial horticulture, but he had got together an advisory committee of experts and one of them scrutinised all the proofs. Leo introduced modern production techniques and produced a modern paper.

One or two advertisers actually complained that he was making the editorial pages so attractive that there was a danger readers would ignore the advertisements! That was far-fetched but it is true: trade papers are mainly bought for the advertisements.

Leo was beginning to make progress. He had worked day and night, organising and sub-editing the articles, and canvassing for advertisements. Pictures were paramount. However, he told me that he had a chest complaint and had been warned that he might not have many more years. He offered me the job of assistant editor not much below that on *Reynolds* because we were never near Fleet Street rates. It was an interesting dilemma. The Cold War had changed my whole situation. There was no chance of a post in Fleet Street.

I had to confess to myself that although I fought to keep my job on *Reynolds*, I knew in my heart that it had lost so much support in the movement that it really had no hope of survival. I accepted Condon's offer.

It was a new world, and slowly I began to enjoy it. Growers were served by a chain of research and experimental stations, and an advisory service. I was fascinated by the scientific developments. Some of the scientists had refused to work in war industries or in nuclear research. Condon and I agreed that the art of journalism is to milk people's brains and to know the right brains to milk, and, of course, be able to present the material. He reckoned I had those qualities. I said I would give it a try. That's how I changed my whole profession, and for a number of years I was a journalist occupied with commercial horticulture while my political work with the cooperative movement, and my peace work, became part-time activities. I also managed to get extra income by writing for overseas papers. My first job was to report a dinner organised by a local branch of the National Farmers' Union (NFU). On the train back to town, I said to myself, 'This is square one, back to the *Clapham Observer*.'

Much of it was routine, subbing reports from the areas, mostly by local growers. (Condon's slogan was 'Run by growers, for growers.') I also had to render the language of contributors, some top experts, into accessible English. The rule was that for signed articles changed copy was submitted to the author with an explanation of the reasons. Surprisingly, most agreed. Some even said they were grateful.

221

There were many fascinating stories; for example in the 1950s, photo-periodism was being applied to glasshouse crops (certain crops reacted to long and short days: chrysanthemums, for example, make flower buds in short days and leaf growth in long days). In America they developed year-round chrysanthemums by drawing blinds over the beds to create short days, and putting lights on to make long days.

An American expert gave a press conference at the NFU headquarters. I said, 'People here think of chrysanthemums as autumn flowers. I don't think they will welcome them in other seasons.' He retorted, 'We made them want them, so can you.' He was right.

Another discovery was the growth regulator, which shortened or lengthened the plant. Used on chrysanthemums it made dwarf pot plants possible. Eventually growers would buy cuttings with a tight schedule stipulating both day length and the application of the regulator.

I gave talks to horticultural groups. When talking about chrysanthemums I would begin, 'Tell me the date of your wife's birthday, and I will tell you how you can produce a bloom for her birthday breakfast.' I was beginning to enjoy this new field when Leo died suddenly. We had agreed that I would continue my activities in the peace movement, and that weekend I had prepared everything for the next issue and left for a conference in Stockholm.

I returned at once in time for the funeral. In the office I found Solly Chandler, a friend of Leo's and of his wife, in my chair. Leo had arranged for me to take over and had always told me, 'If Solly turns up, buy him a drink, but don't let him interfere with the paper.'

Leo wanted to include in the constitution of the journal a clause stipulating that the appointment or dismissal of an editor could be done only by the Editorial Board, but he was advised that if he ceased to be editor he would lose all the perks in his income tax return – lunches, and the cost of experiments in his garden, and so on.

When he died, I was not officially editor. Mrs Condon, who inherited, installed Solly in the editorial chair. Solly was a good journalist, but he did not have the meticulous regard for accuracy which a trade paper demanded. However, the new arrangement suited me. I arranged to go round reporting, while Solly produced the paper. If he had not come on the scene, out of loyalty to Leo, I would have stayed on. As it was, after a year or so, Solly brought in one of his pals. I went to the rival weekly, the *Commercial Grower*, which agreed to take articles on a freelance basis at an agreed fee. I taught myself to use an Exacta camera to illustrate my articles. Rosie, my wife, learned to develop and print films, and between us, we made a living.

I found that the scientists at the research and experimental stations were anxious to talk about their work, but were terrified of being misrepresented by the sensational press. I always agreed to submit my reports. I would say, 'If you don't like the way its written, that's my job, but if there are any inaccuracies, please correct them.' It was very much a closed world, different from the political struggle, but the political background remained.

One example was the work at a station in Aberdeen devoted to research on food preservation. The aim was to provide supplies for any climate in which the British army might have to fight. That meant simulating the conditions in the Middle East, the Far East, and so on. A system of vacuum freeze drying which preserved all the food values of the fruit, vegetables and meat was devised.

I was given a few spoonfuls of powder which, with added water, assumed the appearance and flavour of plums. Other foodstuffs reacted in the same way. In a world where millions were starving, this looked like a miracle. A small ship could carry a cargo which previously had required a huge vessel. And there was no danger of deterioration in storage. It was fascinating.

The station was financed by the War Office, and for a time had no lack of funds. But the military experts decided that they did not expect a war for a long time. The technique was offered to the food manufacturers. But firms, both at home and overseas, had installed deep-freeze equipment at thousands of retail outlets. They were not interested.

I tried to interest the cooperative movement, but without success. In the end the technology went to one of the main suppliers and only many years later were some products brought out in the vacuum dried form.

I also reported international horticultural conferences and was inspired by the friendly atmosphere between experts from the West, the East and the Third World.

At one meeting in Nice the programme announced that an Indian professor, with his young female colleague, would describe with illustrations how the musical rhythm of dance stimulated crops. To everybody's disappointment they did not turn up. But I learned later from India that the work was taken seriously. Music had been played to certain crops with some success. There was a later report in England that there were crop improvements when radio sets were played in the greenhouse.

At the Glasshouse Research Station in Sussex, a detailed study was made into tomato flavour. The difficulty was that even if you identified a variety with an improved flavour, tomatoes all looked alike. They found the answer by taking the best flavoured variety and breeding in yellow stripes. They called it 'Tiger Tom' and released it to selected growers, who gave a sample to their salesmen. Customers asked for more. But when it appeared in the shops, people thought the yellow stripes meant it was partially unripe. I suggested a publicity campaign boosting the flavour. There was no response. The last I heard of 'Tiger Tom' was in a list of unusual varieties in a seed catalogue.

Sam McGreedy, the Irish rose breeder who had produced some of our best known varieties, took me for a walk along the rows of his seedlings. Every year he made many thousands of seedlings, each with a pedigree as carefully listed as a racehorse. Out of these thousand he would select perhaps a hundred. They would be given further tests and eventually, one or two would survive. Even then, there was no assurance they would qualify as a new variety. Sam's main regret was that in producing modern rose varieties, particularly the reds, they lost their perfume. He told me he would never release another variety unless it had the perfume of the old fashioned types.

The cost of finding a winner is astronomical. Breeders in America (for example, the producer of the 'Elizabeth Rose') are said to make as much as a star baseball player. I cannot resist the story of a would-be rose millionaire. One of the London evening papers carried an item in the news in brief column that someone had produced a blue rose. To the ordinary reader that would not mean much, but to the rose specialist it was astonishing.

I went to see this miracle man, for all the geneticists agree that a true blue rose is impossible. The nearest, 'Blue Moon', is a weak lilac. His story was convincing. He and a partner had worked on a nursery near Antibes in the south of France where large quantities of roses were grown for the perfume industry. One day his partner on a dawn inspection found a sport (a mutation) which was perfect blue. They guarded their discovery, multiplying it from the buds, and now it was to have its first showing at an exhibition in Hamburg.

He had a fantastic knowledge of rose varieties. He knew the geneticists' view about the impossibility of a true blue variety, but he quoted at length the parentage of the most popular varieties and their record in producing different coloured mutations.

I regarded myself as a hard-bitten reporter, but I was almost convinced. He could not, he explained, show me a specimen bloom, because it was still under wraps. The PA training to double-check every story was always in the back of my mind. I got through to the post office in Antibes. The name of the rose nursery he had given me did not exist. I rang Harry Wheatcroft, one of our best-known rose specialists. 'Gordon,' he said, 'fancy you being taken in.' I had rung *Garden News* telling them to expect a scoop, but it went no further.

I do not suppose that the poor fellow had ever been near Antibes. He lived in a dream world but he had peopled it with all the right scenery. Apart from nearly taking me in, it was a harmless fantasy.

I found that horticultural developments in the German Democratic Republic almost paralleled our own. One East German programme was to produce named varieties of gerbera, a lovely daisy-like flower which formerly grew from seed in an unpredictable range of colours. The work succeeded and the new varieties released. But was it worth the effort of a whole team of scientists?

The East Germans developed a method of utilising sewage and household waste as fertiliser. Sadly I found after unification that because they were using brown coal for industry, huge areas were poisoned and there was widespread ill-health.

On a visit to the Soviet Union I visited a nursery where they were growing cucumbers under glass. They took a beehive into the house to ensure the plants were pollinated. I asked the interpreter to explain that in England we had bred varieties which did not need pollination. One of the young women scientists protested, 'That is impossible. Where can I find the literature?' It turned out the interpreter had translated 'pollination' as fertilisation or manuring. Here was this Englishman saying they grow cucumbers without manure. How easily misunderstandings can occur.

On the border of the Pyrenees I was shown an intricate system of irrigation. I asked who designed them. 'Richelieu in the reign of Louis XIV,' was the reply.

There was a splendid atmosphere of cooperation and friendship between the growers and the scientists at the experimental and research stations. For a time I edited the journal of the Tomato Board which operated within the government scheme, levying a tariff on imported crops which had ripened before the British tomatoes became available. All that disappeared with the EEC.

The National Seed Development Organisation was set up to market at home and abroad varieties bred by the state research stations. It was successful with both agricultural and horticultural varieties. It paid very considerable sums to the treasury but fell victim to the hatred of any form of state enterprise which marked the Thatcher years.

The post-war Labour government introduced the system under which home grown crops were protected against imports from countries which were able to produce earlier crops. Growers were given subsidies to construct glass-houses, but with entry into the EEC this system could not operate.

The result has been that home production of many crops has been unable to compete with imports from countries with more favourable climates. Glasshouses that were formerly subsidised were pulled down. We have closed our mines and shipyards, and we have taken areas of our precious land out of cultivation. There must be some other way to deal with the problem in a world where millions starve.

I would have liked to continue with these sad events, per-haps help awaken public opinion to their lunacy, but the *Commercial Grower* folded. That modest source of income ended, but a new avenue opened. I was invited to act as London correspondent for the Indian daily *Patriot*, of which more later.

28

I Address the United Nations

I have mentioned some of the world leaders who took part in the World Peace Council and anyone knowing Joliot-Curie, J D Bernal, Ilya Ehrenberg, Krishna Menon, and many others, would agree that to suggest they were stooges of the Soviet Union is nonsense. Many were in the same position as the Webbs, who wrote a monumental history of the Soviet Union, which they called *Soviet Communism: A New Civilization*. They were well aware of the difficulties; they stressed the tragedy inflicted on the peasantry, they did not disguise their criticisms of Stalin, but nevertheless they stood by their beliefs that the Soviet system was providing the way forward to utilise the human and material resources of the human race, sharing resources without one class exploiting the other. This was the attitude that I took during the pre-war years.

Noel-Baker, the Nobel Prize winner, and Fenner Brockway, the veteran Labour leader, both told me that Lord Mountbatten was preparing to give public support to the UK branch of the World Disarmament Campaign. He died before that could happen. I wonder if that had something to do with his death. For a Royal to come out in support of the peace movement would have been an epoch making event. I sometimes wish I were 30 years younger so I could investigate his murder and find why so little is known about his death, and the fate of those alleged to be responsible for his assassination, or even details of their trial.

Another important member of the World Peace Council (WPC) was Senator Nino Pasti of Italy, a prominent member of the NATO Council Military Committee, and Deputy Supreme Commander for NATO Nuclear Affairs. He openly left his position and gave his support to the WPC.

He was a member of a delegation, of which I was also a member, which went to America. He told me,

> During all the time I was involved in NATO nuclear affairs I continually pressed for negotiations to reduce and finally remove nuclear weapons from Europe. I have no doubt that the nuclear weapons deployed in Europe represent the worst danger for the peoples of our continent.
>
> The nuclear bomb was making a war more likely . . . the papers which I submitted to NATO analysing the situation and warning of the dangers gained some support, but they were always rejected by the US generals and the Secretary-General. On one occasion they wanted to double the number of nuclear weapons, although they already had 7,000 deployed in Europe, and another 1,000 deployed at sea. I fought against the plan, and it was abandoned. From my personal knowledge of NATO I state that none of their propaganda can be believed – never accept statements from their generals and admirals without checking every detail. Personally, I found it difficult to find one true statement by General Haig, the Supreme Commander. The media propaganda which talks of the enormous Soviet forces capable of occupying Western Europe in 48 hours is completely untrue – and must be countered if we are to secure the support of the NATO nations against the arms race.

Senator Nino Pasti went on to quote General Goodpastor, a former Supreme Commander of NATO, at a congress hearing where he was asked, 'If the decision were taken by the US to use nuclear weapons, but other nations did not concur, how many of the 7,000 nuclear weapons in NATO would be available to you?' he replied: 'All 7,000 would be available.'

229

This is a point that has been repeatedly stressed in the peace movement, that Britain's so called nuclear deterrent is not a British nuclear deterrent at all. It is entirely dependent on the facilities and permission of the Americans.

The WPC had non-governmental status at the UN and in 1973 I attended as a member of the WPC delegation. I had the thrill of addressing, on behalf of the WPC, the political committee of the UN on which all the members had their representatives. This was a special session devoted to apartheid and my speech was circulated by the press office throughout the world. I began by saying that the opportunity to speak to the committee was especially welcome because it came immediately after the World Congress of Peace Forces in Moscow – 'the largest and broadest peace conference in history'.

I said, 'The struggle to destroy the evil of apartheid does not seek only to remove the unequal treatment of black and white citizens. It must remove, for all time, this affront to human dignity and to our common humanity which a race-hating minority seeks to perpetuate. Many honourable delegates are closer to this problem than I can hope to be. Many have suffered. It is a great step forward that movements waging the struggle are accepted and proudly welcomed here.'

I told the meeting that in Britain many were awakening to the evil of apartheid, and that we were challenging the fact that our country was the largest investor in South Africa with a figure estimated at $4 billion, making South Africa one of our largest export markets. I then quoted the *Guardian*, giving detailed evidence that British firms were paying black South African workers below subsistence level wages of $10 a week, against a recognised starvation level of $30.

I quoted the World Council of Churches which had issued a list of 650 British, American, Dutch and Swiss companies directly involved in investment and trade in Southern Africa, and how they had set up a fund to combat racism.

I referred to the voices in the UN which were still refusing to accept the draft convention which had declared apartheid a crime against international law, and who were offering the same opposition to liberation movements in other parts of the world. I continued, 'but, Mr Chairman, these voices have been heard opposing every advance. They declared themselves against the abolition of slavery and the ban on children working in factories and mines. The conscience of mankind cannot be imprisoned or fettered by legal contortions. Your struggle, and that of progressive men and women in every land against the evil of apartheid must be accepted as a right and a duty.'

I concluded with this anecdote, 'Very shortly after Paris was liberated at the end of the last war, I saw displayed a copy of an underground newspaper, published on the morning before the people of Paris rose and liberated their city. Across the front page, in large type, were the words *"Chaque Français et Française son Boche!"* That was the reply of the French men and women to the years of Nazi murder and oppression. The oppressed millions of South Africa have been patient for many years. The South African white minority launched the racial war. They should beware lest they become its victims.' (For a full account of the speech, see Appendix on page 269.)

I am proud to have made that speech but I am more proud that the WPC was in the forefront in that struggle against apartheid. I presented the original of my speech to the London embassy and it is a treasured exhibit in a free South Africa.

At that meeting of the UN, the Soviet delegation put forward proposals for a permanent ban on nuclear weapons, for renunciation of the use of force, for a world disarmament conference, and for a 10 per cent cut in the arms budget of the nuclear powers with part of the saving being devoted to the developing countries. Those were proposals which the progressive members of the assembly could not resist. The leader of the Soviet delegation, Jacob Malik, pointed out that the Soviet proposals had received the widest support from the countries of the Third World as well as the socialist countries. China, at that time, was at loggerheads with the

Soviet Union. But the only argument used by the Chinese, said Malik, was that 'the proposals are a fraud', 'let us check whether it *is* a fraud.' He continued, 'The Americans said that if the Chinese opposed, then they would oppose. France and Britain said they would agree, but since America was their NATO ally they had to go along with them.' Malik stressed the importance of the UN, and emphasised that the Security Council, especially the eight non-aligned members, play a significant part in preventing local conflict in the Middle East from becoming a world conflict.

I was inspired by that meeting. The chances of a resolution of world problems with coexistence replacing armed confrontations seemed marvellous.

Looking back over that period, I reached the conclusion that America, when it had the monopoly of the bomb, when it believed it could destroy Socialism by force of arms, might well have launched war but for the resistance of the peace movement. I am fortified in that belief by the published report of a discussion by a group of American professors under the title *Open Secret*. During the discussion, Henry Kissinger, Foreign Affairs adviser in Nixon's administration, was quoted as having expressed regret in *Nuclear Weapons And Foreign Policy* that America did not take advantage of the period in which it had a nuclear majority to suppress the Soviet Union. He attributed the failure to use that opportunity to the ban the bomb campaign.

I think we should read the lessons of that Kissinger admission. The Soviet Union knew that while America had the monopoly of the bomb they were in desperate peril and so devoted resources to becoming a nuclear power. It meant cutting down on reconstruction, lowering the living standards of the people, and made it difficult to keep the population in line, particularly the younger generation which saw the failures and mistakes made by the communist administration.

I said to Soviet friends many times that the idea of having a one party communist state with the support of what Stalin once called 'non-party Bolsheviks' was plain nonsense. The communist party, if it had the confidence of the people, and I believe that at that time it had, should have held free elections with other parties involved to maintain its position. I reminded them that Lenin did not expect the communist party to have monopoly power; he was prepared to collaborate with the Social Revolutionaries, but when they adopted armed intervention, the communist party was alone. After the war that certainly should have changed, and with failure came the corruption and disillusionment which we saw disastrously in operation later on.

Shortly after Khruschev came to power in the Soviet Union I wrote to him as chairman of the British Peace Committee enclosing an appeal signed by many thousands of people in Britain calling for the governments of Britain, America and Russia to take urgent steps to remove the threat of nuclear war which loomed over the world. To my surprise, a special messenger arrived from the Soviet embassy with a four-page reply signed by Khruschev. He wrote,

> Your call for an end to the threat of a new war cannot and must not remain a voice in the wilderness. This voice calling upon the reason and conscience of mankind will undoubtedly meet with a response and approval of people of all countries, and those governments which in the first place bear the responsibility for the dangerous state of affairs in the world, must harken to it . . .
>
> The path of negotiation which the appeal suggests is in our opinion perfectly correct and essential. This path may not be easy, but in the present situation it is the only way to solve outstanding problems in the interests of conserving and consolidating peace. Unless one entertains thoughts of war there is no escape from negotiation . . .
>
> The Soviet government strives untiringly for an end to the armaments race. This dangerous and costly competition, the production and stockpiling of means of conducting war which creates a state of tension throughout the world. The Soviet side has proposed concrete

measures for the reduction of armed forces and armaments and this has been recorded in a whole series of international documents. The Western powers display no desire to come to agreement on the carrying out of at least some of those measures.

The trouble clearly was that suspicions on both sides prevented progress, but I am convinced that the Soviet Union was sincere in its desire to lift the arms burden by agreeing measures of disarmament. Looking back on that period, and the subsequent collapse of the Soviet Union, I believe that Russia bankrupted itself in the arms race. That collapse was the object of American policy, once the idea of using the bomb was abandoned.

There were a number of influential people in the Soviet Union to whom I spoke who believed that Russia could have taken greater risks in disarmament, and that public opinion would have been strong enough to prevent any weakness being an encouragement to America to make war. One of them was Ilya Ehrenberg whom I mentioned earlier. He told me how disappointed he was with Khruschev. He deplored the dictatorship of the communist party and its idols, as he called them. He referred particularly to the corpse of Lenin in Red Square and said, 'I thought that nonsense had gone out with the Egyptians.' He would not have dared to say that in public at the time. He was a great patriot and desperately anxious to preserve all the achievements of his country.

I left him a very sad man. There he was with a Moscow flat (which I visited) and his country dacha. He was surrounded with pictures sent to him signed by Picasso and other Western artists, and some Soviet ones. I visited his widow after his death and she told me that his treasures would go to the nation. Had they been sold on the Western market, they would have fetched hundreds of millions of dollars.

I was very proud of my friendship with Ehrenberg. He was a sincere patriot. His writings during the patriotic war were an inspiration to millions, but he was also a rebel and he hinted to me that during the very bad period when leading people were being arrested by the Stalin regime he believed it was only because he was so well-known in the West that he escaped. After his death I suggested to the Soviet Peace Committee that we have a special memorial for him. It received a very cold reception.

29

Germs – A Hidden Story

One of the activities of the British Peace Committee was to organise a conference through the J D Bernal Peace Library, which we had helped to set up, about chemical and biological warfare. It was held in London in 1968 and dealt largely with the possibility of new chemical and biological weapons adding to the arsenals of the powers. Lord Richie Calder, the well known science writer, wrote, 'There has been a conspiracy of silence about chemical and biological, especially biological warfare, which are as fraught with ultimate peril as great as nuclear armaments. I know distinguished scientists who can be as forthright as the rest of us in denouncing nuclear weapons but who will avoid the subject of biological weapons. It is a psychological inhibition. They just do not want to believe their fundamental work can be perverted, but I tell you the Doomsday Bug is under wraps.'

Richie added in a later interview, 'Somewhere in the world a germ is being cultured to which we have no natural resistance, and to which there would be no sure defence.' He also told how botulinus toxin was made during the war. He said, 'Supplies existed and might have been used but only if the Germans had used something of the same, a principle affirmed by both Churchill and Roosevelt in relation to chemical and biological warfare. So we contrived to serve notice on the Germans. Certain Canadian servicemen were briefed that if they were taken prisoner they would, in addition to name, rank, and number, reluctantly disclose that they had been vaccinated against botulin – a dicey game of poker. It would have meant, as intended, "Don't do anything rash, chum, or else!", which might have provoked a pre-emptive strike and a chemical and biological war.'

Richie recalled how the scientists made the atom bomb in secret. He said, 'One recalled Attlee's statement as one who had concurred in the dropping of the bomb on Hiroshima. "We knew nothing whatever at that time of the genetic effects of atomic explosions. I knew nothing at all about fall-out and all the rest that emerged about Hiroshima. As far as I know President Truman and Winston Churchill knew nothing about these things either. Nor did Sir John Anderson who coordinated research on our side. Whether the scientists directly concerned knew I do not know, but if they did they did not inform those who had to make the decisions."'

I must challenge that view. Eric Burhop, who helped make the bomb, told me that the British scientists had told their government that if they succeeded they would produce a weapon of unimaginable power. They suggested that such a bomb should be exploded with neutral observers present in an unoccupied area. The enemy powers would be warned that if they did not surrender, the bomb would be used. That pledge was broken.

The conference made a very modest demand. It simply asked that the experiments in England, which were claimed only to be for defence, should be transferred to the Ministry of Health and the details made public. There was no reply to that request and the germ warfare investigations remained under wraps and must be looked at in the light of the allegations subsequently made that the Aids virus did not originate naturally, but was created in the laboratories at Fort Detrick, the centre for the American germ warfare research.

The Japanese are known to have carried out the most horrendous and inhuman experiments on POWs with various biological agents. After the war various Japanese scientists were put on trial in Moscow and given prison sentences, but others were taken to America and given immunity. We can only assume that they went to work at Fort Detrick. There had been an exchange of information between Fort Detrick, the Canadian station at Alberta, and the British station at Porton Down.

The *Guardian* on October 29th, 1981, published a report by Walter C Patterson on the Japanese germ warfare experiments. He wrote,

> The story which follows is ugly and disgusting. It is unsurprising that those involved kept it secret for more than 35 years. But the documentary evidence that has come to light seems incontrovertible. From 1930–1945 Japan carried out germ warfare experiments and actual attacks. In the course of these activities Japanese scientists pursued a programme of research on human subjects including Chinese, Russian, and American prisoners of war. Japanese germ warfare experiments cost the lives of more than 3,000 human victims after prolonged agony. The facts of the case were made known to the American State Department and War Department immediately after World War II, but the American authorities concealed them, and granted the Japanese germ warfare scientists immunity from trial as war criminals in order to gain exclusive American access to the Japanese data and experiments about germ warfare technique and effects.

The report describes how, in 1931, shortly after Japan had occupied China's eastern provinces (including Manchuria), a Japanese army surgeon named Ishii Shiro persuaded his superiors that microbes could become an inexpensive and potentially devastating weapon. He was authorised to set up a biological warfare experimental station a few miles from Harbin.

> It was a large, self-contained installation with sophisticated germ and insect breeding facilities, a prison for the human experimental subjects, testing grounds, an arsenal for making germ bombs, an airfield, his own

238

special planes, and a crematorium for the human victims. Thousands of Chinese, Russian, and American
prisoners died there as a result of massive doses of
bubonic plague, typhus, dysentery, gas gangrene,
typhoid, cholera, anthrax and smallpox. The Japanese
not only used their human guinea-pigs to determine
lethal doses, but also in pursuit of exact scientific information they made certain that the experimentees did
not survive. A disease would be inflicted on a group
and then as the infection developed, individuals would
be killed, autopsies performed and an array of tissues
and other pathological samples assembled for the progress of the research.

This report goes on to assert, 'A restricted American memorandum dated July 1st, 1947, said that "since any war crimes
trial would completely reveal such data to all nations, it is
felt that such publicity must be avoided in the interests of
defence and the national security of the United States." So
General Ashi and his colleagues were spared embarrassment
and many members of the unit lived out their full lives suffering the natural affliction of old age.'
    Other revelations indicated that these Japanese scientists
were taken to Fort Detrick, given immunity and continued
their experiments. The material obtained from the Japanese
represented data which had been obtained by Japanese
scientists at the expenditure of many millions of dollars and
years of work and could not be obtained by US laboratories
because of the scruples attached to human experimentation.
These data cost a mere pittance in comparison with the actual
cost of the studies.
    Our conference aroused considerable interest. But the
suggestion Porton Down should be open to public inspection
was never accepted. We were always assured that any germ
warfare experiments were purely defensive. Incidentally,
one of the scientific workers at Porton Down died of smallpox
(a disease which had been almost eliminated throughout the
world); those germs could only have been kept for experimental purposes.

Nothing about germ warfare came into public discussion until *Patriot*, in July 1983, announced that a 'well-known American scientist and anthropologist had sent a letter to the editor of *Patriot* analysing the history and background to the deadly disease Aids' which started in America and has now spread to Europe. 'The writer, who wants to remain anonymous, has expressed the fear that India may face a danger from this disease in the future.'

At that time I was producing a newsletter for the British Peace Assembly and hesitated whether I should publish this allegation. I decided against, because it was such a terrible accusation that I felt it would be dismissed as communist propaganda. And so I left it in my desk. Then the *Sunday Express* came out with banner headlines, 'Aids Man-Made In Lab Shock' (October 26th, 1986). The front-page story said the virus was created in laboratory experiments in America which went disastrously wrong. It added: 'a massive cover-up has kept the secret from the world.'

The *Sunday Express* quoted a British expert, Dr John Seale, who first reported his conclusion that the virus was man-made the previous August in the Royal Society of Medicine Journal. He said that his report was met with 'a deadly silence' from the medical profession and that made him very suspicious. The editor of the medical journal agreed that it sounded like a conspiracy of silence. The *Sunday Express* said that a Dr Robert Strecker, a specialist from California, stated 'it must have been genetically engineered'.

The third expert quoted by the *Sunday Express* was Professor Seagal, retired director of the Institute of Biology in East Berlin. The paper said, 'Our investigators have revealed that two US embassy officials made a two-hour visit to Prof Seagal at his home two weeks ago questioning him about what he knows, what he thinks, where he got his information and what he intends doing about it. The professor said that one visitor said he was a historian and one a political counsellor, but he was positive they were from the CIA and they were very concerned that the cover-up about the origin of Aids was going to be exposed. He told them he had known that in the mid-1970s experiments were being carried out at Fort Detrick where the US Army Medical Research Command had its headquarters, and the experiments were on volunteers promised their freedom after the tests. Almost certainly the scientists were unaware of the extent of their terrible creation, the Aids virus.'

The denials were not long in coming. The story was dismissed by statements from American embassies all over the world as Russian propaganda. In fact the Russians were not concerned at all, and their scientists were prepared to accept the official American explanation that the virus had developed in some natural way.

I was included in the American denunciation, although I had simply been a reporter. The sources I quoted were authentic, and I added a number of other statements which indicated that research into germ warfare was going on, and that it carried the most terrible consequences should it ever get loose. The London *Observer* on June 30th, 1968, quoted from an article in the *Journal of General Microbiology* by W D Lowton of Fort Detrick and R C Burrows of Portland which said, 'By engineering the genetics of individual strains, microbiologists aim to produce a single strain containing the most deadly combination of properties.' The article said that Porton Down was, according to the government, only concerned with defensive applications of research, but Fort Detrick was also committed to developing microbiological weapons for offence. The *Daily Telegraph*, which was one of the papers denouncing the stories that the Aids virus had been created in the laboratory, reported on September 24th, 1986, from Washington that, 'Enough of a debilitating virus to infect the whole world disappeared from an American germ warfare laboratory five years ago and has never been traced, an environmental group claimed in a Washington court action, aimed at halting biological weapons research.'

On a visit to America I met the Women's League For Peace and Freedom (WILPF) in Boston where they had compiled a dossier of various diseases which were being developed in laboratories. They cited a book by Brigadier General

241

Rothschild describing in over 45 pages the principal diseases of biological warfare,including bubonic plague and anthrax. He said that in 1965 a New England firm was given a contract with the Department of Defence to facilitate the airborne spread of bubonic plague in Vietnam.

I reported in the British Peace Assembly's newsletter at the beginning of 1989 how Women's Strike for Peace (WISP) – an American organisation with a long record of activity – had published in their newsletter that the American government was building a germ warfare laboratory in the Utah desert at a cost of $5.4m, and that more than 500 scientists had refused to have any part in this scheme. It said, 'The typical biological weapon is a highly infectious disease against which there is no natural immunity. It is easy enough to produce, yet hardy enough to survive and reproduce itself outside the laboratory, and could accidentally escape or be stolen.' It added that, 'Funding for biological and chemical weapons has been increased by more than 500 per cent in that ten year period. A Pentagon spokesman is quoted as saying, "It is believed that the Soviets have a chemical and biological potential. We certainly want to be prepared to negate them should these weapons be used against us."'

After the collapse of the Soviet Union no evidence was found that they had reached this stage of biological and chemical warfare. I commented in the BPA newsletter, 'It's a horrifying thought that with the world threatened with the Aids virus, research should still continue on infectious diseases against which there is no immunity.' I added, 'If the United States was sincere in its support for an international ban on chemical and biological weapons the world has a right to know whether it is still experimenting with deadly viruses, and why it is still manufacturing binary chemical weapons.'

As the story spread throughout the world, together with the spread of Aids, the authorities took every step to prevent discussion.

In April 1967 the *New Scientist* reported that, 'the blow by blow story of how the Aids virus was discovered may never

242

be told. As part of an agreement signed last week between the Pasteur Institute in Paris and the US Dept of Health and Human Services, which disputed each other's claims on the discovery of the Aids virus, there is now a definitive official history of the discovery. Both parties agree to be bound by such a history and further agree they should not make or publish any statement which would or could be construed as contradicting or compromising the integrity of the said history.'

The international scientific establishment has abided by the decision not to investigate the origin of the disease, but the question still reverberates around the world. The drug companies are looking for a cure: and no one disputes the sincerity of that effort, but nevertheless they are well aware that vast profits will be made if they are successful. Some of the drugs that have helped slow down the disease have already run up large profits. The story could not be kept out of the press of how haemophiliacs had been infected with blood from Aids sufferers. It turned out that in America the down-and-outs had been selling their blood, and that sterilisation did not come in until later.

In March 1987 the *Guardian* ran a story that the Research Establishment at Porton Down was once more looking at the possibilities of biological warfare, an area of research virtually abandoned in 1972 when Britain signed the convention banning production of germ weapons. Porton Down laboratories were turned over to civilian research and it became the Chemical Defence Establishment, mainly devoted to the development of protective equipment for gas warfare. But rapid advances in genetic engineering had prompted renewed fears shared by the American military that biological weapons would once more pose a real threat. Porton Down, said the *Guardian*, had accordingly begun to recruit additional scientists in this field. Dr Steven Rose recalled in an article in *New Scientist* in March 1987 how the Japanese carried out direct experiments on Chinese and American prisoners during the war, and that after 1945 America and Britain concentrated on biological weapons. These were disabling or lethal agents made up of living organisms and their toxic products. Agents could therefore be bacteria or viruses which cause diseases, such as smallpox, cholera or the plague, or the poisonous products of such living organisms as bacteria, fungi, plants, snakes and fish.

There were many scientific conferences discussing ways of meeting the mounting Aids epidemic, but every time the question of the origin of the disease was kept under wraps – no mention in the official reports. Then, unexpectedly, at the end of 1989, Channel 4 broadcast a detailed report denying the possibility that Aids developed naturally.

I commented in my report in *Patriot* on the courage of Channel 4 in defying the attempts by the authorities to prevent such a discussion. I talked to the producer afterwards and told her I had a lot more information if they returned to the subject. I also asked if they were having any difficulty with the authorities; she replied tersely, 'You've said it.'

The programme had not drawn on much of the material presented in earlier discussions, but it gave particular attention to what it called the 'myth that the disease originated in Africa'. The programme said that the evidence that the virus was of artificial origin, and that it was a recombination produced from a brain disease of sheep and goats and human leukaemia is pretty convincing, and added, 'Even scientists who reject this thesis must be alarmed at the description of how the deadly viruses are the subject of experiments, not only in America, but in laboratories overseas including Britain and Germany.' And the comment was made that 'in America the Freedom of Information Act gives some right to know what is going on, and so it may well be policy to contract out the work to countries where no such freedom exists.'

This is what Jeremy Rifkin of the Foundation for Economic Trends said on the programme: 'All the well-known pathogens on this planet have been worked on by the department of defence. It increased its work five-fold in the last five years of the Reagan administration. It has contracts with 120 universities, corporations and military laboratories in

America and overseas. They are working on every dangerous pathogen known to humanity from the plague to yellow fever, botulism to anthrax and cobra venom.' The programme recorded how a quantity of a virus sufficient to destroy vast numbers of people went missing. It is still missing, said the report. A year ago cobra virus, sent by post, never arrived. The military referred enquiries to the post office; it might, they said, be in the lost letter office!

The programme described how, while the scientific establishment rejected the Aids artificial creation theory, by 1984 a number of scientists had begun to ask whether the Aids virus might be an accident which occurred in the early stage of some new technique, when dozens of viruses were being experimented with, and human cultures injected experimentally. The programme told how British scientists discovered that animals, having been subjected to all sorts of infections, had been shunted to and fro between university laboratories and military institutions and that the recombination of viruses could well have happened.

Much of the Channel 4 programme was concerned with the attempt to place the origin of the disease in Africa. At one time it said there were more researchers than victims of the disease. The various theories, according to the programme, were disposed of because they failed to give any evidence that the virus could have occurred naturally. One theory was that it began in a small African village, infected humans and later spread; another was that it was a jump over from green monkeys, that it spread because Africans drank monkey blood to improve potency and children played with dead monkeys; yet another that it originated with the pygmies. These theories have been discredited. Nigeria and Kenya repudiated the suggestion that it began in their countries, they asserted that it was more likely to have been brought by French soldiers because it appeared in Paris before Africa. The programme recalled that there was also a battle for the million dollar market which would open up for the pharmaceutical industry if a cure were found and that a dispute between the French and the American

245

drug companies was settled behind closed doors by President Reagan and Prime Minister Chirac.

So far, the scientific establishment has, in the words of one commentator 'refused to think the unthinkable'.

30

Lost in the Pentagon

Since the conference in Warsaw in 1950, my life has been dominated by the belief that mankind must either win the struggle for peace or perish. Although we do not hear so much today about the menace of the bomb, the situation is even more dangerous than when we had the precarious balance of power on the Security Council of the UN.

In December 1969 I attended a meeting of the World Peace Council in the Sudan. There, together with Cheddi Jagan of Guyana and William Gollan of Australia, we interviewed the leader of the Sudan, General Mohammed Nimeiri.

The General told us frankly the army was the only source from which the revolution could be carried forward. He added, 'Democracy in the Western concept has failed ignominiously to offer the Sudan the leadership and the machinery to move forward. The army was the only organised and powerful force able to stage a revolution for the people.' Then he said, 'All the forces of the nation are called upon to participate in this task. The workers, farmers, national bourgeoisie and intellectuals.'

Nimeiri told us,

> Sudan is a vast country and under populated. Illiteracy is as high as 85 per cent among men and 95 per cent among women. The ethnic situation is creating difficulties and my job is to secure the wise and full support of the masses. The whole educational system is being

revised in order to link education with the pattern of life in the country. In the agricultural areas schools will teach technical skills as well as general education. In the industrial areas we shall train cadres for the factories and the same procedure will be carried out in the cattle raising areas. We shall ensure that no one capable of proceeding to higher education will be denied a place. At the same time there will be a campaign locally and nationally to deal with illiteracy.

Our five-year plan is designed to exploit our resources, which are very great, with the application of modern technology. We are planning the economy but let me elaborate on the question of control. We expect the public sector to play a leading role. This is true of all developing countries where private capital is meagre and fears of foreign capital have not been entirely removed.

My report continued, 'The President went on to speak of his government's policy of cooperation with Russia and the other socialist countries. This, he said, is in the interests of our people. The Sudan, when it first gained independence, maintained its traditional links with the Western countries and has held these links so tenaciously that it has been deprived of the help which the socialist countries could offer.

'The policy of the government since he took over had been to encourage all who offer assistance or enter into transactions free of strings. The Soviet Union and other socialist countries have offered us assistance on very favourable terms in areas where the Western countries refuse to assist. Our relations with the socialist countries will grow stronger in other fields as well as trade. Opposition to this policy came from reactionary forces and some who serve certain foreign interests.'

It is a sad commentary on the failure of these hopes that the whole policy of the Sudan has changed, with Moslem irridentism taking a leading part.

There was a delegation to America in 1981. It consisted of people from a number of countries including Mexico and

Guinea; Abe Feinglass, a prominent US trade union leader, Romesh Chandra, President of the WPC, Ellen Hammerskjold from Vienna, Carlton Goodlett and other leaders who joined us on the way. We went right across America. We found far more support than any of us expected. The way in which we were allowed to get onto radio and television was quite surprising. Nothing like it is possible in Britain.

I made a half-hour television appearance in Denver and was able to tell my story on tape with complete freedom and at the end of it I said, 'You'll never get that across.' The interviewer said, 'Boy, if I put that in the can it goes out!' and it did, over three states. All the members of the delegation had radio interviews. The idea that we were some sort of pro-Soviet, pro-communist delegation was plain nonsense.

The only time the Soviet Union was mentioned was by a representative from Guinea. She said when the French withdrew and Guinea ceased to be part of the French union, they withdrew all help. The West gave nothing, but the Soviet Union generously came to their assistance. Apart from that the Russian card was not being played anywhere. We found a very strong pro-peace movement. As in Britain it only came to the fore when it could break through the press boycott.

We started our visit across America in Washington. We had meetings with many organisations and again it was very clear there was considerable support for the peace movement. In fact there had been some massive peace demonstrations. There was one personal incident in Washington. We went to the Congress building where we were due to meet a number of Congressmen. In one room they were discussing the so-called subversive activities of the World Peace Council, and in the other room we were meeting a number of Senators who had expressed considerable sympathy with our work.

After we left, we had to go along a very long corridor to get a lift down to the waiting cars for our flight to Boston. I went into the men's room and, when I came out, turned the wrong way. I took the wrong lift and ended up in the bowels of the building. I wandered around the corridors; there were rooms open with papers lying about. No one seemed to mind me. I found an armed guard. I said, 'I'm looking for the way out.' He said, 'Where do you come from?' I said, 'I'm with a delegation and there's an Indian on it.' 'That doesn't help much, does it? Go along there and take that lift.' So I managed to get to the exit.

I often thought that if they had run me in – with all those documents lying about – God knows how long they might have kept me. I knew I could not find the car with the delegates, so I asked a policeman, 'How do I get to the airport?' He said, 'Which one?' I showed him my ticket. He said, 'You will never get there by taxi at this time of night. Go down there and find the subway.' I ran to the subway and when I got to the entrance everything was automatic. How the hell was I to get a ticket to Boston airport? A lovely woman came and asked if she could help me. She showed me how to get the ticket and directed me to the platform. I got on the train – it seemed to go on forever – all through the Pentagon buildings. When I got to the airport, the woman at the ticket office said that flight was just leaving. I just caught it on time.

When we arrived in Boston we found that there was a strike in progress. It was against the cuts in the budget of the city administration. As a result a number of fire and police stations were closed. We watched a demonstration with policemen and firemen in uniform closing the streets. On TV that night it carried a report that the strike had been successful, and the dismissed policemen and firemen re-employed.

Our visit to the school board in Boston showed a picture similar to Britain. The Reagan administration had forced a cut in the budget, and from the following September 27 schools in the city would be closed. Classes would have 40 children or more. The schools would not be able to provide

250

services for education which were laid down by federal law, and could be fined.

Boston was a centre for peace activity. The Quakers are very active as was the International Physicians for the Prevention of Nuclear War (IPPNW) and Physicians for Social Responsibility (PSR). We were told how they organised symposiums which sought to draw the attention of the public to the danger of war, particularly nuclear war. These symposiums were particularly popular. Tickets were in great demand. In Seattle, for example, tickets were sold for the symposium on the black market at $100 each!

Our next stop was Detroit where the city council handed Romesh a testimonial resolution signed by each one of the nine members. It said, 'The council is honoured to have this delegation of world citizens in our city and commends their effort on behalf of world peace.' The Secretary, told us, 'All our problems are related to the massive arms build-up in our country. We have to fight back; someone has declared war on our human rights.' She told us the resolution had become part of the official records of the city council.

In Pittsburgh, a town devoted to arms manufacture, we found that it had the highest record for youth unemployment in America with 75 per cent of black youth unemployed. The black population constitutes about 20 per cent of the population of Pittsburgh.

At San Francisco we were officially welcomed at City Hall, the very same place where, 20 years before, the McCarthy Committee had conducted an inquisition and the protesters on the stairs were flushed away by firemen with their hoses. Harry Bridges, the leader of the Seamans Union for the Pacific Coast, had been under arrest during the McCarthy visit, but was with us as an honoured guest. We were also given an official welcome by the City Council of Los Angeles, and the university.

An evening was spent by the delegation at the home of Carlton Goodlett. He was one of the most active members of the World Peace Council. He was also the owner of a black newspaper. He and other black editors had periodic

251

meetings with Kennedy. He told me how President Kennedy had said, 'When I come back from Dallas we must get down to this question of Vietnam because we are way out on a limb.' That hope was never fulfilled.

We flew back across America to New York. Ellen Hammerskjold and I were taken out to dinner by a good friend. She said we were going to the best restaurant in New York. And it was a wonderful restaurant. However, just as we were finishing the sweet, suddenly our hostess said, 'Look, cockroaches!' There were two cockroaches on the back of our seats. She called the waitress. The waitress said, 'How many?' She replied, 'Call the manager!' The manager came and said, 'Madam, what can I do, how can I apologise, of course there will be no bill.' As we were going out some people at the next table called out, 'Any cockroaches?'

Abe Feinglass was due to meet the leaders of the Catholic University in New York. They told him that General Haig, Commander-in-Chief, had telephoned them and said, 'You must support our policy because we are fighting communism and Soviet subversion.' The Catholic leaders replied, 'Don't tell us that, who killed Archbishop Romero in El Salvador, who raped and killed the nuns and murdered tens of thousands? Your friends of the right-wing.' They went on with the meeting with Abe.

I visited Cuba with a British delegation on the fourth anniversary of the revolution on January 2nd. There, we were told something of the obstacles which Cuba was overcoming, obstacles placed by America in banning all trade and supplies. I noted that British firms had secured a number of valuable contracts with the Cubans and wrote, 'Here is an opportunity for Britain if we decide our policy in Whitehall, instead of allowing it to be dictated in Washington.' Of Fidel Castro, I said, 'his army has brought social change with it as it fought its way through the mountains, and when victory was achieved, the people took over. This was not a communist revolution in the sense of a trained communist elite taking control; the Marxist basis grew out of the experience of revolution, but Castro took drastic measures against any efforts to reserve key positions for communist party members. There is an intimacy between the people and their leaders which must be unique in history.' That is interesting because it was the failure of the communist elite to maintain and nourish contact with the people which led to their isolation and the tragedy of the socialist states of Europe.

I wrote, 'Out of the revolution has grown a creative movement of ordinary people which overcomes every obstacle. More than a quarter of the adult population could not read or write when the revolution took over. In the villages the figure was as high as 50 per cent. Illiteracy has been wiped out, with the help of hundreds and thousands of young people; students, teachers, factory workers, professional men and women who made it their task to go out in the evenings and weekends to play their part. The same volunteer effort was used to bring in the sugar cane harvest. Thousands of volunteers helped the skilled building workers put up the houses and flats which are steadily replacing the ghastly slums, and to construct hospitals, schools, and other social buildings.' During that visit I talked to one woman who had come illegally from Guatemala for the anniversary celebrations, and she told how she was one of the trade union leaders organising workers employed by the United States United Food Company in her country. The United States intervened to destroy the progressive government in Guatemala, and 81 of her fellow trade unionists were murdered. She escaped and was hidden by friends. She told me how the police fired on crowds who demonstrated some months earlier in favour of Cuba.

Reporting on a visit to Chile, I wrote, not long before President Allende was murdered by the fascist reactionaries, 'There is no doubt that the government of unity has brought a springtime of hope. They understand the meaning of the measures taken by the government to return the resources of the land to the people. They know how the American countries have drained their wealth away. They have enjoyed substantial improvements in educational standards and living conditions.'

253

I met a well dressed man who was one of the lucky jews to get away from Germany in 1939, and he said, 'Churchill was a good man.' I said, 'Yes, and his finest hour was when he welcomed the alliance with the Soviet Union which defeated Hitler.' He replied, 'No, the best thing he did was at Fulton when he warned us about Russia and the communists.' He launched into propaganda, about how the country was in chaos and heading for economic disaster, and the trade unions were terrorising the country.

You soon found out that the class war, in this small, poor country that had defied the economic power of the United States and was beginning courageously to lay the foundations of Socialism, was fought with vicious bitterness and why it was taken over by dictatorship.

I reported: 'When you meet the workers, students, many technicians, and cultural leaders who support this great adventure, you find plenty of evidence that despite still desperate poverty and privations affecting everyone, the poor are better off. The position of the lower paid workers has definitely improved and the children are a priority. The rich and a good proportion of the middle class join in the clamour of the opposition, but the real position was put to me by a doctor who said, "Before the present government took over I knew what the children needed but I did not dare tell the parents to give them milk and other essentials because I knew that they could not afford them, but now I can tell them."'

The story of the children being given milk was reinforced when we met President Allende. He told us that the government had taken the decision, despite the dangerous shortage of foreign exchange, to provide milk for the children as a first priority. 'Knowing that the future lies with the children,' he said, 'we buy the milk which we are not producing ourselves, to give half a litre a day to every child in Chile. Now the price of powdered milk has increased from $500 a ton to $960. That means that with extraordinary efforts to allocate $50 million from our slender budget we can only buy a percentage of what we planned.' I commented, 'As the President spoke, the recollection flashed through my mind that in the West European Common Market they were paying subsidies to farmers to slaughter their dairy cows to reduce the production of milk.'

I explained in a report of this visit that, 'Chile is the first country setting out to build socialism through the democratic processes of a bourgeois society with an elected Parliament, and most of the instruments of power still in the hands of the enemies of socialism. Allende had no alternative but to operate strictly within the legal and constitutional framework, and several decisions of the constitutional court are contrary to decisions taken in favour of previous governments and are designed to curtail his authority.

'The so-called freedom of the press allows the newspapers and many of the radio stations, of which there are more than 20, to maintain a ceaseless stream of abuse and lying propaganda. Despite it all, the Chilean revolution has gone further than any similar attempt. When, as a British observer, I recall the failure of British Labour governments to make any significant inroads into the power of the capitalists even though they have overwhelming majorities, I'm filled with admiration for the courage of President Allende and his colleagues. His action in defying the United States and declaring support for Vietnamese patriots when a British Labour government supinely backed the Americans shines like a beacon.'

It was a very different picture when I was a member of the WPC delegation to Japan. The peace movement there was divided. The Japanese Peace Committee split between a pro-Chinese faction, which was bitterly anti-Soviet, and the other faction which was more or less in line with our British Peace Committee and the World Peace Council. The WPC was invited, and replied that it would only come with the understanding that it was invited by both factions.

When we got to Tokyo there was no one to meet us. We made our way to the conference venue which was some way out of the city, and had to make our own accommodation arrangements.

The procedure was that international delegates would hold a discussion prior to the main conference. The first conference was dominated by the pro-Chinese faction. They told us that we were observers and therefore could not take part in any of the committees. So we changed our status and said we would be there as full delegates. But that did not have much effect. The bitter battle went on between the two sides. When the full conference met, the hatred in the meeting was unbelievable – something I thought could never exist in the peace movement. Carlton Goodlett, the American delegate, left. He said he could not take the atmosphere. I stayed and put my name down to speak because I was frightened, but I had to persuade myself I was not.

One of the pro-Chinese delegates, who had only arrived that morning, was called to speak, while the delegate to speak from our side was barred because he had not submitted his manuscript. Obviously the recent arrival had not either. We decided we could not take this nonsense any longer and walked out. We met on the roof of a nearby hotel and after a long discussion I drafted a letter which explained how we had come there to talk peace, about coexistence and so on, and how we had been prevented from doing so. That was where I met Romesh Chandra for the first time, a young delegate from India. Hirano, who was a Japanese delegate we had known for a long time, was obviously broken hearted by what had happened. I wrote him a personal letter because I was there as a representative of J D Bernal, President of the WPC. I said I believed that in the end we would solve the difficulties and become one again. I did that on my own initiative and was very glad because in the end the breach was more or less healed.

We went on to the second conference which was called by the Japanese Socialist party at which I spoke, and which was very successful.

31

Shattered Dreams

Three meetings towards the end of my life set out some of
the ideas and failures which I have recorded. The first was
when I was invited, on behalf of Labour Action For Peace, to
take part in a cruise organised by the Soviet Peace Committee
going from Kiev to Odessa. There were mostly Americans
taking part, but we also had two leading experts from the
Soviet Union. We discussed the problems of the world
during the day, and visited various organisations in the
evenings.

I shall put on record one of the debates when I intervened
on these terms: I said that we had had a very interesting
discussion in which our friends in the Soviet Union told
how they were trying to make good the mistakes which had
become evident in the last years – how they proposed to
restore democratic institutions and so on – but I said that
there were some points on which they had not made themselves clear.

One was the right of the constituent Republics to secede.
I said when, in the 1930s, the Soviet constitution was
reexamined, and all over the country people were asked to
submit their ideas, and tens of thousands of ideas were submitted, Stalin – of all people – went through the main ideas.
Many demanded the cancellation of the right of the constituent Soviet Republics to secede. Stalin said, 'No, we should let
them retain that right,' and went on to justify that position. I
said:

'You may say that if one of them had tried to secede in those days when repression was pretty bad it would have met with resistance and punishment, but nevertheless that principle was still in the Soviet constitution.' I asked my friends, 'Is that still the position? Because if so, you have to face the reality that some of them might still want to secede.'

The second point I made was that in the very early days of Soviet power, Lenin never intended that the Bolshevik party would have a sole monopoly. He hoped for an alliance with the social revolutionaries but, in the desperate days of the War of Intervention, they deserted and the Bolshevik party was left on its own.

In the Stalin days they talked of party and non-party Bolsheviks which was nonsense, and I said, 'In the present circumstances, you cannot go on with one party holding a monopoly. However much you try to extend responsibility in other fields, the fact that party monopoly has not been abolished is going to impede the development of these changes that are now taking place.' When one of the Soviet speakers answered, he made complimentary references to my long friendship with the Soviet Union and my Lenin Peace Prize, but he did not answer my two points. Those two points emerged, as we all know, as basic problems before the break-up of the Soviet Union.

Also during the discussions, I mentioned how when we met the students at some of the colleges and the workers from the factories, I discovered they had very little knowledge of the struggles which their fathers had waged, and that they failed to understand how the Soviet Union had played a major part in saving Europe from nazi domination. I said, 'I don't know how their educational system, with all its emphasis on Marxism and all the other "isms", could fail to mobilise the enthusiasm which showed itself in the early days of reconstruction after the Revolution and in the Great Patriotic War, as they proudly call it.'

I recalled how recently I had visited the Exhibition of the Siege of Stalingrad – marvellously conceived – which showed the entire course of that battle which changed history. I asked how any Soviet youngsters seeing that, or the writings of the soldiers on the cliff walls, could fail to be enthused. It was a sad picture of one of my last visits to the Soviet Union.

In India I realised the terrible gulf between rich and poor. We were driving through the streets of Delhi and were held up in one of those inevitable traffic jams. The children threaded their way through the cars and traffic and held out their hands. I gave what coins I had and when I had nothing left, a tiny little child held out her poor little hand. Her little face was so poignant and I did not have anything to give her. To me that symbolised the picture of India. We comfortable people had been discussing the world situation, and here on our doorstep was this ghastly poverty, a poverty which affects a very great proportion of the human race. It is a poverty which affronts our common humanity.

Another visit to India was in July 1989 when I was invited by my paper, the *Patriot*, to discuss my work for the paper and attend a conference. While there I was given accommodation in a beautiful house outside Delhi which was used as the centre for our conference. We discussed the problems in that part of Asia.

I did not have time to prepare, but I had been at the discussion for about a day when the chairwoman, who came from Australia, called on me to speak. I had no manuscript but said,

> Friends, I've been listening to your discussions, and I wonder whether you are facing up to the fundamental problems which must be solved in this part of the world. When you think of Japan with a population of 100 million, and New Zealand hardly approaching two million, and areas not very different – is that balance going to continue? When I think of Australia, 14 million, I know there are lots of desert which it is not possible to cultivate, but I can't believe that if the Japanese had the opportunity, they would not find ways of making use of that vast territory. Somehow or other these problems are going to come to the fore in the coming years, and I don't really think we're facing up to them. There are

259

other countries in the area, Singapore, Malaysia, Indonesia, South and North Korea, all going forward with technology, alongside Japan, and China now nearing two billion people. The picture of this vast population taking on modern technology is one which is going to change the face of our world.

I described to this conference a meeting I had in Europe when China was still a member of the World Peace Council. We were having a discussion on European affairs. We talked all day as we always did, and the following morning I was in the chair. I said that we had had a fairly full discussion, and suggested I prepare a draft resolution. I put the resolution to the meeting. We had a long discussion and out of 43 countries represented, only three: China, one section of Japan (there were two Japanese delegations), and Indonesia would not agree. The Chinese delegate said that the resolution was 'too statesman-like', and that what was wanted was a 'burning condemnation of American imperialism'. I said if we put that sort of resolution to our members in Europe it would be thrown out as pure propaganda. What we wanted was a resolution which put across the problems of the continent and a plea for peaceful coexistence. She would not have it, and at 4 pm – we had been talking all day – I said that as they would not discuss the details of my proposed draft, I would put it to the meeting. There were 43 votes in favour and 3 (or really 2½) against, because the Japanese delegation was divided. So I declared the meeting closed. Afterwards the Chinese delegate came up to me. She said, 'I'm ashamed of you! I thought you were a fair chairman.' I said that I'd tried my best, but there is a point at which you must take a democratic decision. She said, 'Democratic decision! We represent one quarter of the human race!' There is a warning there, that the world will have to heed in the coming years.

My intervention in which I drew attention to the problems of the vast populations in China and Japan, and the small populations in New Zealand and Australia, was perhaps a cat among the pigeons. But I would not like to give the impression that this was not a very constructive conference. It did show the course the world would have to take if we were to have a constructive and progressive development. As the final document pointed out, 'non-alignment, both as a foreign policy perspective of most new states of Asia, Africa and Latin America, and as an international movement, is a crucial factor in contemporary international relations in favour of peace and development.'

The document said, 'The non-aligned movement had to seek realisation of its ideals for indestructible world peace and a new international economic and political order on sure foundations of universal humanism, social, economic, moral, cultural and political, to create new guarantees for full growth of human personality in every land. Science and technology has made it a realisable objective to unite all human beings.'

An indication that we have made some progress from that time was that the statement called for the 'immediate unconditional release of Nelson Mandela and other political prisoners in South Africa'. At the same time it condemned the operation of Unita in Angola.

The declaration called for the immediate withdrawal of all Turkish occupation forces and settlers from Cyprus as an essential basis for the solution of the Cyprus problem. On the question of Israel it said, 'The participants feel it is a matter of significant concern that Israeli occupation of Palestine, the Syrian Golan Heights and southern Lebanon continues unashamedly, in spite of positive reconciliatory steps undertaken by the PLO. We reaffirm that the question of Palestine is the core of the Middle East crisis and the root of the Arab–Israeli conflict. We therefore call upon the non-aligned movement to vigorously work for Israel's total and unconditional withdrawal from all Palestinian and other occupied territories.'

The statement called for the peaceful settlement in Kampuchea (Cambodia) and demanded guarantees for preventing the Pol Pot forces, responsible for unprecedented genocide,

261

from participating in the country's future government. (Pol Pot is still being supported by America and other powers, and is actually still preventing a settlement in that part of the country.)

That, I suppose, was my swan song as far as my international activities are concerned, and I have quoted these demands by the conference because, looking back, it seems to me that there is the real hope of a world in which peaceful progress can be secured for all races and peoples. It is in marked contrast to the situation in Europe following the collapse of the Soviet Union and the other socialist countries. America is the supreme military power in the world and is determined to dictate policy. The resistance to that domination must be in the hands of the countries in the continents which the non-aligned movement covers – the future lies in their hands.

Nehru and others when they founded the non-aligned movement invited all struggling and emerging countries of the world to join hands in order to retain freedom of judgement and a right to promote the processes of complete independence in Asia, Africa and Latin America.

32

US Takes All

In the spring of 1992 I attended the Annual Conference of
the British United Nations Association in Bath as a delegate
for Labour Action For Peace, and I moved a resolution on
behalf of my organisation. It welcomed the role of the United
Nations in ending the war in El Salvador and its efforts to
bring peace to Yugoslavia. Then the resolution went on to
say that these contrasted to the UN attitude to the Gulf crisis
when Security Council resolution 678 was used to give UN
backing for war. My resolution stated, 'Council agrees that
the Charter is clear, that the United Nations' main aim is to
end the "scourge of war". Council believes that the United
Nations' most effective role is in relation to conflicts within
and between member states in peace-making and peace-
keeping, allied to conciliation and active diplomacy.'

It went on to condemn the UN's attitude in the Gulf crisis.
There was an amendment by the establishment to delete this
last point and the debate hinged on that particular sentence.
There were two opposed viewpoints. I made the point – and
I think that history will show it was correct – that it was not
a UN war, but an American one. I said, 'We know that
American officers disclosed their intention to use modern
weapons to destroy the Iraqi war machine before the UN
sanction was obtained, and far from being a conflict, it was
a massacre. The retreating Iraqi soldiers were mowed into
the desert sand. It was designed as an experiment in the
use of modern weapons rather than manpower in order to

achieve victory.' I also pointed out that when Iraq was fighting Iran, American policy was to arm Iraq, and that the regime in Kuwait, which the war was designed to protect, was one of the most dictatorial in the world, and for that these sacrifices were made.

I and other supporters got a lot of applause, but when it came to the vote the chairwoman declared that the amendment was carried. If there had been a count I am not sure that it had a majority. However, it did demonstrate the problem which the future will have to face: America's domination of the UN. I pointed out that the UN was now an American-dominated organisation. I said that the veto – the unanimity rule – had been introduced on the recommendation of Roosevelt because he recognised that if the great powers could not agree they would fight, and there would be no sanction within the UN which could alter that. Therefore the idea that five great powers had to agree, with any one of those powers having the right to veto, was to safeguard the UN. I pointed out that the whole system had collapsed. 'With the collapse of the Soviet Union there is only one power able to dominate the world, and that is the United States of America.'

That is another problem, I said, which the future has to face. I told the story of two episodes reported in the press. One was when Yemen, which was originally divided between the socialist south and capitalist north and was now united, dared vote against an American-inspired resolution in the Security Council. The American delegate said, 'That's the most expensive vote you've ever cast.' Any support for Yemen from America was withdrawn. The other story was of a Soviet delegate being questioned by a well-wisher, 'How is it that you're always going along with American policy?', and he replied, 'What can we do – we are on the floor.'

The democratic forces throughout the world have got to face up to this change – its a new problem, very different from the one that faced the powers immediately after the war.

In the 1992 election the Labour leadership refused to promise to cancel building four Trident submarines costing billions of pounds, each capable of destroying vast areas of our planet, so repudiating a previous decision to cancel them. They did so, not because they believed there was any enemy in sight, but because they had not the courage to tell the workers that arms manufacture was not economically sensible, and they failed to pledge training for new industries, or to support those workers displaced. The Tories won in my view because of this failure of the Labour leadership.

This dilemma recalls how in the 1960s the shop stewards of Lucas Aerospace, one of our big manufacturers, formed a combined committee representing 14,000 manual and technical staff at 17 factories, embracing a number of trade unions. Its task was to make a detailed study of the design, development, and production capabilities of each plant, and they aimed to involve the whole workforce in discussing what socially useful products could be manufactured as an alternative to their present arms programme. The detailed projects that emerged, many of them making use of advanced technology, provided an inspiring illustration of the creative abilities and skills waiting to be unleashed in a world dedicated to peaceful progress. The plan was submitted to the management of the factory and also to the government, and put forward as an alternative to the threatened redundancies.

The document said, 'Our combined committee resulted, in the first instance, from fear of unemployment, and the idea of proposing alternative projects was put forward in 1970 when we resisted the closure of a factory in London. Tony Benn, then Industry Minister, warned that there would be cutbacks in military projects and that the committee would be well advised to consider alternatives.'

When I reported on this project at peace meetings I commented that Tony Benn was removed from his post after a concerted campaign against him, and no other minister showed interest. The merchants of death were still active.

Mike Cooney, who was chairman of the committee drawing up the plan said,

The committee anticipates that Lucas Aerospace will attempt a rationalisation programme with its associated companies in Europe facing all the workers with the same problem of creating new generations of war machines or switching to projects of peace . . . 'The desire to work on socially useful projects is now widespread in large sectors of industry. The aerospace industry is a particularly glaring example of what technology is capable of providing and what it actually does provide to meet the wide range of problems we see about us. There is something seriously wrong about a society which can design and build Concorde but cannot provide enough simple urban heating systems to protect the pensioners who are dying each winter of hypothermia. We believe that scientists, engineers, and workers have a profound responsibility to challenge the underlying assumptions of large scale industry, and to assert their right to use their skill and ability in the interests of the community.'

I did not understand then, and I still do not, why the Labour and trade union movement did not welcome and endorse the plan.

That was said in 1970 and we still have economies based on the production of armaments. The production of useless armaments goes on because our leaders have not the courage to face the problem of transferring from war to peace production, or to admit that capitalism cannot solve the problem.

33

Epilogue

I near the end of the journey and ask myself whether my experiences, my hopes and despairs accurately mirror a century in which changes more portentous than in any other period of recorded history have taken place. Perhaps they may provide some lessons for a perilous future. Empires have disappeared. The domination of the white races has ended. Most of the countries freed from colonial exploitation have still to gain economic independence. The wealth of the planet and its productive resources are still divided between the few rich nations and the many poor. Public opinion is slowly being alerted to the grim reality that the environment is being undermined, and that we tamper with the balance of nature at our peril.

Before the middle of the 21st century world resources may well have to cope with the needs of a population explosion on a scale never before contemplated. Millions of young people, unless there is a change in the whole economic system, will be without work with all its perilous implications. In 1992 the Pope and a British archbishop argued for and against contraception. Perhaps as they looked out from the Vatican onto Rome they had a vision of Nero fiddling while Rome burned.

As I look back, I wonder on the might-have-beens. The nations that stumbled into World War I after the slaughter of millions, really believed that it had been a war to end war. The arms kings and the merchants of death thought otherwise.

Under the leadership of Lenin the Russians set out to end the tyranny of the Tsars, to create a society based on the principles of socialism. The great experiment was possible only because of the defeat of the Tsarist armies, and the exhaustion of the allies after the collapse of the Kaiser's Germany. There were excesses in the Russian Revolution as there are in all revolutions, but the revolution was backed by what Lenin called 'the creative genius of the awakened masses'. The various republics which formerly created the Soviet Union have now broken away. It is as well to remember that they were colonies of the old Tsarist regime. Some were brought to nationhood only under the Soviet system. Some even had their languages written for the first time. Under Soviet power they built universities and created modern societies, but behind it all was still failure. It was not a failure of socialism but of socialists.

Another might-have-been – had Lenin lived instead of being cut off when he had many years ahead, would the development of the Soviet Revolution have been different? Nevertheless, the creative genius which fuelled the revolution was still sufficient to win victory in what they proudly called the Great Patriotic War. And in so doing they saved us all from evil fascism. My story tells how near we were to defeat at the hands of Hitler. Today there are voices in the British Conservative party which declare that it would have been better for Britain if she had given in to Hitler in 1940.

The UN, on which so many great hopes have been set, is now the instrument of America and her reluctant allies. The new nations like India will demand their place on the Security Council, and Germany and Japan will certainly not remain junior partners while Britain and France retain their veto powers. The Non-Proliferation Treaty, which preserves the position of the nuclear powers and relegates the rest, cannot continue to endorse this division of the world.

The changes since the collapse of the Soviet Union, and the other socialist countries, have not brought a better world.

They have not brought peace, they have brought war; war in the former Yugoslavia, which under Tito maintained a unity and a measure of prosperity. Today that country has broken up into warring factions similar to those that precipitated World War I.

There is war between some of the constituent republics of the former Soviet Union and there is a revival of religious wars. Afghanistan which in alliance with the Soviet Union was a reasonably peaceful and progressive country is now torn between rival factions in which Islam plays a part. We saw in Algeria Islam trying to take over the democratic machinery and being frustrated by a coup on a part of the government. No one denies the sincerity of Christians, Muslims or any other religious community, but Marx's warning that religion can be the opium of the people is seen to be true in many parts of the world.

It is clear now that the Western powers used the arms race to maintain their precarious economies and had no real fear that Russia was going to launch a war.

If there is one lesson to be learned from the period I have tried to portray, it is that fascism is a method by which reactionary power destroys democracy in order to take over on behalf of power and privilege. Bertolt Brecht's warning of fascism has never been truer today than when he said, 'the womb is still fertile'.

The struggle for socialism goes on. It is the only way in which we can end the tragedy of a world divided between the few who are rich and the many who are poor. It is the only way to ensure that the resources of the world are used for the benefit of the people. Socialism is beginning to reemerge from the collapse of the communist countries and it is a vital force in the Third World. In the coming years it will develop as the hope of the peoples.

As far as Britain is concerned the Labour party will need to remember that it won the great election of 1945 under the slogan, 'We are socialists and proud of it.' A return to that faith is the formula for its return to its mission: to provide a more equitable society and a better life for millions of our people.

This is the picture at the heart of the story I have tried to tell. In our own country and throughout the world the task is to use the resources of nature, the discoveries of science and the skill of human hands to build a world of peace. An impossible dream? Maybe, but the alternative is continuous poverty and the threat of annihilating war. We cannot abandon hope or we abandon life.

APPENDIX

STATEMENT BY GORDON SCHAFFER
Member of the World Peace Council Presidential
Committee (Britain)

At the Session of the Special Political Committee of the General Assembly United Nations, New York, November 15th, 1973

Mr Chairman
Distinguished Delegates,
It is a great privilege as a member of the delegation of the World Peace Council to offer congratulations and support for your struggle against apartheid, one of the most evil aspects of the international scene today. This opportunity to speak to you is especially welcome because it comes immediately after the World Congress of Peace Forces in Moscow, the largest and broadest peace conference in history, a conference which was greeted by the UN Secretary General and in which organisations of the United Nations took an active part. One theme ran like a thread through all the debates, that the struggle for national liberation is an essential part in the struggle for peace. No nation can be half slave and half free; no continent can be half slave and half free; the world cannot be half slave and half free.

The struggle to destroy the evil of apartheid does not seek only to remove the unequal treatment of black and white citizens. It must remove, for all time, this affront to human dignity and to our common humanity, which a race-hating

271

minority seek to perpetuate. Many honourable delegates are closer to this problem than I can hope to be. Many have suffered. It is a great step forward that movements waging the struggle are accepted and proudly welcomed here.

What I would like to do is to give some encouraging evidence that the consciences of increasing numbers of people in my country, Britain, are awakening to this and to their responsibility. Britain is the largest investor in South Africa, with a figure estimated at $4 million and South Africa is her fourth largest export market. For many years various movements sought to mobilise public opinion in support of the struggle against apartheid but with very little impact. Typical, perhaps, of our people, it was a movement to prevent racialist South African rugby football and cricket teams from playing in our country, which brought an understanding of what racial persecution means to the notice of a wider section of our people. Then, a few months ago, the London newspaper, the *Guardian*, published a series of articles giving detailed evidence showing that British firms are paying black South African workers below subsidence level. It gave cases of wages of $10 a week against a recognised starvation level of $30.

Members of Parliament reacted quickly and an official parliamentary enquiry was set up. There have been, and there will be attempts to whitewash the firms concerned, but the salient facts cannot be denied. The Church of England which has been silent in the past, although individual priests have voiced their protest, also took action. Its Board for Social Responsibility sent a memorandum to 45 large companies describing conditions of the South African workers and adding the warning: 'British industry cannot afford to neglect the interests of the black employees in South Africa, even on the ground of self interest. They cannot hide behind South Africa's apartheid laws.'

The World Council of Churches has issued a list of 650 British, American, Dutch and Swiss companies directly involved in investment and trade in Southern Africa and has set up a fund to combat racialism.

The massacre by the South African police of the gold miners at Carltonville horrified the British people in the same way as did Sharpeville, and this tragic event, coupled with the revelations in the *Guardian*, resulted in an official visit by members of the British TUC to South Africa. Knowing the trade union leaders who took part, I can express the conviction that they were not taken in by South African government propaganda. They came back convinced that there is no freedom for trade union organisation for black or coloured South Africans, and they will continue to press the demand for a declaration of intent by the South African government to recognise race equality in industry.

The Labour party conference, last October, took a much more decisive stand for a complete arms embargo against South Africa, for trade sanctions and for support for African freedom fighters.

There is an English expression that 'fine words butter no parsnips', and I know how tragically little these steps are in the light of the seriousness of the situation – the daily persecution of opponents of the racialist regime, both black and white, compared with the long drawn-out agony of Mandela, Fisher, and all the other patriots enduring imprisonment. But we know the movement grows in strength, and all we can do is to mobilise support for the African people who will assuredly win their freedom. Today, there are already strikes by African workers, despite the vicious measures of oppression.

There are still powerful voices in my country defending apartheid or at least advocating no action against it, as for example, a Conservative MP who spoke recently in the House of Commons about what he called 'the hysterical preoccupation of the left with conditions in South Africa'.

He asked, 'Will the government resist strongly the temptation to assume some sort of broad moral responsibility for economic and social conditions for a part of the world we ceased to have any responsibility for 63 years ago?'

There were also voices here, in the UN, opposing the Human Rights Commission draft convention declaring apartheid a crime against international law. There was some opposition to the participation in UN deliberations of the national liberation movements but, Mr Chairman, these voices have been heard opposing every advance. They declared themselves against the abolition of slavery and the ban on children working in factories and mines. The conscience of mankind cannot be imprisoned or fettered by legal contortions. Your struggle, and that of progressive men and women in every land against the evil of apartheid, must be accepted as a right and a duty.

The Christian Science Monitor wrote on September 9th, 1973, 'A new situation has crystallised over the last six months in South Africa. Warning lights are flashing one message; if white South Africans do not move swiftly to change laws and customs that are obstructing and humiliating black South Africans, there will be strife, possibly on a large and bloody scale.' The question today is whether that warning will be heeded in time.

Very shortly after Paris was liberated at the end of the last war, I saw displayed a copy of an underground newspaper, published on the morning before the people of Paris rose and liberated their city. Across the front page, in large type, were the words '*Chaque Français et Française son Boche!*'

That was the reply of the French men and women to the years of nazi murder and oppression. The oppressed millions of South Africa have been patient for many years. The South African white minority launched the racial war. They should beware lest they become its victim.

INDEX

275

279